First World War
and Army of Occupation
War Diary
France, Belgium and Germany

49 DIVISION
Divisional Troops
Royal Army Service Corps
Divisional Train (463-464-465 & 466 Companies A.S.C.)
12 April 1915 - 31 May 1919

WO95/2791/2

The Naval & Military Press Ltd
www.nmarchive.com
Published in association with The National Archives

Published by

The Naval & Military Press Ltd

Unit 10 Ridgewood Industrial Park,

Uckfield, East Sussex,

TN22 5QE England

Tel: +44 (0) 1825 749494

www.naval-military-press.com

www.nmarchive.com

This diary has been reprinted in facsimile from the original. Any imperfections are inevitably reproduced and the quality may fall short of modern type and cartographic standards.

© Crown Copyright
Images reproduced by permission of The National Archives, London, England, 2015.

Contents

Document type	Place/Title	Date From	Date To
Heading	WO95/2791/2		
Heading	49th Division W.R. Divl Train ASC Apr 1915-May 1919		
Heading	West Riding Divl Train Vol I 12-30.4.15		
Heading	War Diary of Lieut Col. J.C. Chambers (Commanding West Riding Divisional Train). From April 12th/1915 To April 30th/1915 (Volume I)		
War Diary		12/04/1915	30/04/1915
Heading	49th Divisional Train Vol II May 1915		
Heading	War Diary of O.C. 49th (W.R.) Divisional Train From May 1st 15. To May, 31st. 15 (Volume		
War Diary		01/05/1915	31/05/1915
Heading	War Diary of Lieut. Colonel J.C. Chambers Commanding 49th (W.R.) Divl Train From June 1st 1915 To June 30th 1915. Volume 3		
War Diary		01/06/1915	30/06/1915
Heading	49th. Division. 49th Divl. Train Vol IV July 1915		
Heading	War Diary of O.C. 49th (W.R.) Divl Train. From 1-7-15 To 31-7-15. (Volume 4)		
War Diary		01/07/1915	31/07/1915
Heading	49th Division War Diary of J.C. Chambers Lieut. Colonel, Commanding 49th (W.R.) Divl. Train. August, 1915 From 1-31.8.15 Volume V		
War Diary		01/08/1915	31/08/1915
Heading	49th Division 49th Divisional Train Vol VI September 15.		
Heading	War Diary of Lt. Col. J.C. Chambers O.C. 49th (W.R.) Divl Train. From Sept 1st. 15 to Sept 30. 15 (Volume. VI.)		
War Diary		01/09/1915	30/09/1915
Heading	49th Division 49th Divisional Train Vol VII Oct 15		
Heading	War Diary of Lt Col J.C. Chambers. Commdg. 49th (W.R.) Divl Train. From Oct 1st 1915 to Oct 31st. 1915 (Volume 7)		
War Diary		01/10/1915	31/10/1915
Heading	49th Division War Diary of Lieut. Col J.C. Chambers Commdg. 49th (W.R.) Divl Train Vol VIII From Nov 1st 15 to Nov 30.15. (Volume 8)		
War Diary		01/11/1915	18/11/1915
Heading	49th Divl Train. Dec 1915 Vol. IX		
War Diary		01/12/1915	31/12/1915
Heading	49 Div Train Jan 1916 Vol X		
War Diary		01/01/1916	31/01/1916
Heading	War Diary of Lieut Col J.C. Chambers. C.B.V.D. Commdg. 49th (WR) Divl Train From. Feb. 1st. 1916 to Feb. 29.1916 (Volume XI)		
War Diary		01/02/1916	29/02/1916
Heading	War Diary of Lieut Col J.C. Chambers. Commdg. 49th. Divl Train. From. 1-3-16 to 31-3-16 (Volume 12)		
War Diary		01/03/1916	31/03/1916

Heading	WR Div Train Vol XIII		
War Diary		01/04/1916	30/04/1916
Heading	War Diary of Lieut Col J.C. Chambers & Major B. Haigh Commanding. 49th (WR) Divl Train. From 1-5-16 to 31.5.16. (Volume 14)		
War Diary		01/05/1916	31/05/1916
Heading	War Diary of Lieut Col B Haigh. Commanding 49th (WR) Divl Train From June 1st. 1916 to June 30th. 1916 (Volume 15)		
War Diary		01/06/1916	30/06/1916
Miscellaneous	D.A.G. G.H.Q. 3rd Echelon	31/07/1916	31/07/1916
Heading	War Diary of Lt Col B Haigh Commanding 49th (WR) Divl Train. From July 1st. 1916. to July 31st. 1916. (Volume 16)		
War Diary		01/07/1916	31/07/1916
Heading	War Diary of Lieut Col B. Haigh Commanding 49th (WR) Divl Train. 49 Div Train Vol 17 From. aug. 1st. 1916 to August 31st 1916 (Volume 17.)		
War Diary		01/08/1916	31/08/1916
Miscellaneous	D.A.G., G.H.Q., 3rd Echelon	30/09/1916	30/09/1916
Heading	War Diary of Lieut Col. B. Haigh. From September 1st, 1916 To September 30th-1916 (Volume 18.)		
War Diary		01/09/1916	30/09/1916
Miscellaneous	Headquarters 49th Division	01/11/1916	01/11/1916
Heading	War Diary of Lieut Col B Haigh Commdg. 49th. (WR) Divl Train. From 1.10.16 to 31.10.16 (Volume 19)		
War Diary		01/10/1916	31/10/1916
Heading	War Diary of Lieut Col B. Haigh Commdg. 49th (WR) Divl Train From 1.11.16 to 30.11.16 (Volume 20)		
War Diary		01/11/1916	30/11/1916
Heading	War Diary Of 49th (W.R.) Divisional Train For December 1916. Vol 21		
Heading	War Diary Of Lieut Col B. Haigh. Commanding. 49th (WR) Divl Train From 1-12-16 to 31-12-16 (Volume 21)		
War Diary		01/12/1916	31/12/1916
Heading	War Diary Of 49th (W.R.) Divisional Train For January 1917. Vol 22		
Heading	War Diary of Lieut Col B. Haigh Commanding 49th (WR) Divl Train From 1-1-17 to 31-1-17 (Volume 21)		
War Diary		01/01/1917	12/01/1917
War Diary	Visited 465 & 466	12/01/1917	12/01/1917
War Diary	Pack Train Late	13/01/1917	15/01/1917
War Diary	Train H.Q.	16/01/1917	16/01/1917
War Diary	Pack Train	17/01/1917	19/01/1917
War Diary		20/01/1917	31/01/1917
Heading	War Diary Of For 1917		
Heading	War Diary. Of 49th (W.R.) Divl Train For February 1917 Vol 23		
Heading	War Diary Of Lieut Col. B. Haigh. Commanding 49th (WR) Divl Train. From Feb. 1.1917 to Feb. 28.1917. (Volume 23)		
War Diary		01/02/1917	28/02/1917
Heading	War Diary. Of 49th (WR) Divisional Train For March. 1917. Vol. 24		

War Diary	War Diary of Lieut Col B. Haigh. Commanding. 49th. (WR) Divl Train. From 1-3-17 to 31-3-17 (Volume 24)		
War Diary Heading	War Diary. Of 49th (WR) Divl Train For April 1917. Vol 25	01/03/1917	31/03/1917
Heading	War Diary Of Lieut. Col. B. Haigh. Commanding. 49th Divisional Train. From. 1.4.17 To. 30.4.17. (Volume 25)		
War Diary Heading	War Diary Of Lieut. Col. B. Haigh. Commanding. 49th Divisional Train. From. 1.5.17. To 31.5.17. (Volume 26)	01/04/1917	30/04/1917
War Diary Heading	In The Field War Diary. Of 49th (WR) Divl. Train For June 1917. Vol 27	01/05/1917	31/05/1917
Heading	War Diary of Lieut Col. B. Haigh. Commanding 49th W.R. Divisional Train from June 1st, 1917 to June 30th, 1917. Volume 27		
War Diary Heading	War Diary of 49th (WR) Divl Train for July 1917 Vol 28	01/06/1917	30/06/1917
War Diary		01/07/1917	02/07/1917
War Diary	2 Lt Tom Mallinson Joined From the Base posted to No 2 Coy.	03/07/1917	31/07/1917
Heading	War Diary of Lieut Colonel B. Haigh. Commanding 49th W.R. Divisional Train. from August 1st to 31st, 1917. Volume 29		
War Diary Heading	War Diary of Lt. Col. B. Haigh. Commanding 49th W.R. Divisional Train. From 1st to 30th September 1917. (Volume 30)	01/08/1917	31/08/1917
War Diary Heading	War Diary. Of 49 Divisional Train For 1st to 31st October 1917 Vol 31	01/09/1917	30/09/1917
Heading War Diary	Headquarters 49th Division War Diary of Lieut Colonel B Haigh. Commanding 49th W.R. Divisional Train From October 1st to October 31st, 1917. (Volume 31)	01/11/1917	01/11/1917
War Diary Heading	War Diary of Lt. Col. Bernard Haigh Commanding 49th W.R. Divisional Train From November 1st 1917 to November 30th, 1917 (Volume 32.)	01/10/1917	31/10/1917
War Diary Heading	War Diary of Lt. Colonel B. Haigh. Commanding 49th W.R. Divisional Train. From 1.12.17. to 31.12.17. (Volume 33).	01/11/1917	30/11/1917
War Diary		01/12/1917	15/12/1917
War Diary	2/Lt. W.T. Annett Joined from B.H.T.D. Posted No 1 Coy	16/12/1917	31/12/1917
Heading	War Diary of Lt. Colonel B. Haigh. DSO. Commanding 49th W.R. Divisional Train. from January 1st to January 31st, 1918 (Volume No. 34.)		
War Diary		01/01/1918	16/01/1918
War Diary	2/Lt. Maudlen Joined from Base Posted No 1 Coy	17/01/1918	31/01/1918

Heading	War Diary Of Lt Colonel B. Haigh. DSO. Commanding 49th W.R. Divisional Train From February 1st 1918 to February 28th, 1918 (Volume 35)		
War Diary		01/02/1918	28/02/1918
Heading	War Diary of Lt. Colonel R.G.J.J. Berry Commanding 49th W.R. Divisional Train From March 1st 1918 to March 31st, 1918. (Volume 36)		
War Diary		01/03/1918	31/03/1918
Heading	War Diary of Lt. Colonel R.G.J.J. Berry. Commanding 49th W.R. Divisional Train From April 1st to April 30th 1918. (Volume 37.)		
War Diary		01/04/1918	30/04/1918
Operation(al) Order(s)	49th Divisional Train O.O. No. 35	09/04/1918	09/04/1918
Heading	War Diary of Lieut Colonel R.G.J.J. Berry Commanding 49th (West Riding) Divisional Train from May 1st 1918 to May 31st 1918 (Volume 38)		
War Diary		01/05/1918	31/05/1918
Heading	War Diary of Lt Colonel. R.G.J.J. Berry Commanding 49th W.R. Divisional Train from June 1st to June 30th 1918 (Volume 39)		
War Diary		01/06/1918	30/06/1918
Heading	War Diary of Lt Colonel R.G.J.J. Berry Commanding 49th W.R. Divisional Train from July 1st to 31st 1918 (Volume 40.)		
War Diary		01/07/1918	31/07/1918
Heading	War Diary of Lieut Colonel R.G.J.J. Berry Commanding 49th (West Riding) Divisional Train from August 1st to August 31st, 1918 (Volume 41.)		
War Diary		01/08/1918	31/08/1918
Operation(al) Order(s)	49th (W.R.) Divisional Train O.O. 40	18/08/1918	18/08/1918
Operation(al) Order(s)	49th Divisional Train O.O. 41	19/08/1918	19/08/1918
Miscellaneous	Railhead-18th Midnight-19/20 Consumption 20th		
War Diary	Railhead-21st Midnight-21/22 Consumption 22nd.		
Miscellaneous	Railhead-23rd Midnight-23/24 Consumption 24th		
Heading	War Diary of Lt. Colonel R.G.J.J. Berry Commanding 49th W.R. Divisional Train. from Sept 1st, 1918. to Sept 30th 1918. (Volume 42.)		
War Diary		01/09/1918	30/09/1918
Miscellaneous	Amendment To 49th (W.R.) Divisional Train O.O. No. 42.	12/09/1918	12/09/1918
Operation(al) Order(s)	49th Divisional Train O.O. No. 42	11/09/1918	11/09/1918
Operation(al) Order(s)	49th Divisional Train O.O. No. 43	21/09/1918	21/09/1918
Heading	War Diary of 49th. (WR) Divisional Train October. 1918 Vol 43		
Miscellaneous	Cover for Documents. Nature of Enclosures.		
War Diary		01/10/1918	31/10/1918
Operation(al) Order(s)	49th Divisional Train O.O. 44	06/10/1918	06/10/1918
Miscellaneous	March Table to accompany 49th Divisional Train O.O. No. 44.		
Heading	War Diary of Lieut-Colonel D. Hamilton T.D. Commanding, 49th (W.R.) Divisional Train. From November 1st to November 30th. 1918. (Volume 44)		
War Diary		01/11/1918	30/11/1918
Miscellaneous	49th (W.R.) Divisional Train O.O. 45.	03/11/1918	03/11/1918
Miscellaneous	Headquarters, 49th (W.R.) Division "A"	31/12/1918	31/12/1918

Heading	War Diary of Lieut-Colonel D. Hamilton T.D., Commanding, 49th (W.R.) Divisional Train, From Dec. 1st 1918. To Dec. 31st 1918. (Volume 45.)		
War Diary		01/12/1918	31/12/1918
Heading	War Diary of Lieut-Colonel D. Hamilton T.D. Commanding, 49th (W.R.) Divisional Train. Volume 46. January 1st/1919 to January, 31st/1919		
War Diary		01/01/1919	31/01/1919
Heading	War Diary of Lieut-Colonel D. Hamilton T.D., Commanding, 49th (W.R.) Divisional Train. From Feb. 1st 1919. To Feb. 28th 1919. (Volume 47.)		
War Diary	In The Field	01/02/1919	28/02/1919
War Diary	H.Q. 49th Division "A"	01/02/1919	01/02/1919
War Diary	Douai	01/03/1919	31/03/1919
Miscellaneous	H.Q. 49th Div. "A"	30/04/1919	30/04/1919
War Diary	Douai	01/04/1919	31/05/1919

No 95/2291/2

49TH DIVISION

W.R. DIVL TRAIN ASC

APR 1915 - MAY 1919

121/5/61

West Riding Dis C Train

Vol I 12 — 30.4.15

Original

CONFIDENTIAL

War Diary of

Lieut. Col. J. C. Chambers
(Commanding West Riding Divisional Train).

From April 12th/1915 To April 30th/1915

(Volume 1)

WAR DIARY
or
INTELLIGENCE SUMMARY.
(Erase heading not required.)

Army Form C. 2118.

Instructions regarding War Diaries and Intelligence Summaries are contained in F. S. Regs., Part II. and the Staff Manual respectively. Title pages will be prepared in manuscript.

Hour, Date, Place	Summary of Events and Information	Remarks and references to Appendices
April 12th	Left Doncaster 3-45 A.M.	
13th	Arrived Southampton 3-30 P.M. Left for Havre 8-45 P.M. All correct no casualties. Had on board HQ 8th Bde. Div Transport, HQ 2nd Coys & HQ 4 Coys Transport, also transport details of 5th Y & L and 5th K.O.Y.L.I.	
14th	Arrived Havre 9-45 A.M. – no casualties – disembarkation complete by 3-0 P.M. Troops left by rail for Hazebrouck from 6-30 & 10-0 P.M. – All arrived Hazebrouck during day of 15th.	
16th		
17th	Details proceeding to Rollets – No 3 Coy arrived and billeted in East Hazen [?]. No 2 Coy arrived from Doigette by road at 7-30 P.M. and proceeded to Rollets in neighbourhood of Le SART. – Refilling point for Nos 2, 3 & 4 Coys fixed in main street of Hauf Berguin – Transport today was at 2.30 P.M. Refilling point for H.Q. Coy fixed at Le SART.	
18th	Arranged for 1st Brigade to draw supplies at Le Sart refilling point.	

Army Form C. 2118.

WAR DIARY
or
INTELLIGENCE SUMMARY.
(Erase heading not required.)

Instructions regarding War Diaries and Intelligence Summaries are contained in F.S. Regs., Part II. and the Staff Manual respectively. Title pages will be prepared in manuscript.

Hour, Date, Place	Summary of Events and Information	Remarks and references to Appendices
18th (cont)	Waited of at Huy Bergin. Supply Column arrived early this morning from Havre.	
19th	Received Telegram from Lord Dunboyne, expressing good wishes for Corps, which is published in Orders. &c Leaving arranged for 2.30 P.M. but Column did not arrive till 4.30. 4.7c. Advised that the W.R. C.S. will bring our supplies to-morrow instead of the Col. which has been working.	
20th	New refilling point going to-day. All went smoothly and supplies were issued in 1½ hours. 22 Wagons were taken over by order of D.D. S+T and allotted as follows W.2 C.S. G; W.2 C.S. 4; W.3 C.S. 5, W.4 C.S. 5.	
21st	Routine.	
22	Visited to dist refilling point — Col. Long expected but did not come.	
23	" Huy Bergin refilling point and arranged position for all dumps — saw Brit. Gen. Douglas Haig in Huy Bergin — told him all was working satisfactorily.	
24	L. dist refilling point removed to Huy Bergin — Councirated to	

(9 29 6) W 2794 100,000 5/14 H W V Forms/C. 2118/13

WAR DIARY
or
INTELLIGENCE SUMMARY.
(Erase heading not required.)

Army Form C. 2118.

Instructions regarding War Diaries and Intelligence Summaries are contained in F. S. Regs., Part II. and the Staff Manual respectively. Title pages will be prepared in manuscript.

Hour, Date, Place	Summary of Events and Information	Remarks and references to Appendices
24. (Cont.)	Movement of troops will necessitate alteration in supply points. Orders received down to Estaires on Monday 26th – visited Estaires and arranged to take over lines now occupied by 2nd Brig. H.Qs. Completed inspection of all transport with 1st & 2nd line. First line transport has mules chiefly – the war horses issued just before leaving England is unfit for big horses, and the mules very badly – they will be able to work but I anticipate trouble with galls. The breeding particularly is very bad, and can never be altered satisfactorily. All units have been advised that greasing of wheels is much needed. Only a few of the mules are shod on the hind feet, but this work is being pushed on. Deficiencies in equipment such as nose bags, wagon covers, buckets etc. are fairly plentiful, but this is being rectified.	
25th	Sunday – Actus Divin. Divine Service Noon.	
26th	Decided to move H.Qrs. to Rue St. Maur – A.S.C. Hqrs. to Estaires. Took over billets recently occupied by 2nd Inf. Brig. Hqrs.	

WAR DIARY

OR
~~INTELLIGENCE SUMMARY~~

(Erase heading not required.)

Army Form C. 2118.

Instructions regarding War Diaries and Intelligence Summaries are contained in F.S. Regs., Part II. and the Staff Manual respectively. Title pages will be prepared in manuscript.

Hour, Date, Place	Summary of Events and Information	Remarks and references to Appendices
26th (cont.)	Refilling point moved nearer to Estaires except for Sig^l Troops. Truck towards at North end of Neuf Berquin. /A/	
27th	Tried to get billets in Neuf Berquin & Estaires for H.Q. 2 Coy & No. 2 Coy, but none available - where some of troops already there could be removed. No two Companies will have to remain in present billets in Merville. Visited near Brig. H.Q. at Rue St. Maur also Inf. Brig. H.Q^{rs} at Forbeiq. /A/	
28th	Our Hd.Qrs. removed to Estaires - H.Q. Coy managed to billet in Neuf Berquin. Removed them from Merville in evening. No 2 Coy still in Merville. Unable to get billet in Neuf Berquin or Estaires owing to as many troops being quartered there. /A/	
29th	Sig.l Coy moved up to Neuf Berquin and H.Q. 0.5 ~~Estaires~~ Re-arranged with D.A.Q.M.G. new position for Train - loading our 6 Cork's Carts - Difficulty in getting coal - S.S.O. advised /A/	
30th	No billets could be found for No 2 Coy in Neuf Berquin nor Estaires - decided to rest till Monday 2nd Prox. when 1st ~~Corps~~ Inf. Div. Brig. leave - /A/	

121/5444

49th Divisional Train

May 1915

Vol II.

Confidential

War Diary
of
O.C. 49th (WR) Divisional Train

From May 1st. 15.   To May. 31st. 15.

(Volume   )

Army Form C. 2118.

WAR DIARY
or
INTELLIGENCE SUMMARY.
(Erase heading not required.)

Instructions regarding War Diaries and Intelligence Summaries are contained in F.S. Regs., Part II. and the Staff Manual respectively. Title pages will be prepared in manuscript.

Hour, Date, Place	Summary of Events and Information	Remarks and references to Appendices
May 1st	German aeroplanes over Estaires this morning and damage done in town by shells which had been fired at them — aeroplanes dropped notices for the inhabitants warning them to leave the town as the Germans intended bombarding same early tomorrow morning. It is indicated the Maire has left.	
2nd	No. 2 Coy moved from Fleurbaix to Estaires and occupied billets vacated in moment by 5th W.Y. Regt. 1st West Brigade left Estaires for Rue St Pers. Heavy artillery firing during afternoon in direction of Ypres.	
3rd	Troops passing through Estaires during early morning.	
4th	5th W. Yorks. Battn arrived during night from Rue St Pers to relieve Lancs — Several Battns arrived in Estaires during day and up to 12-0 P.M.	
5th	A quiet day — all routine work carried out — the day being so cold up at Fleurbaix in the morning of each day makes it late before the arrival at billeting front and consequently morning is spent as to late each day.	

Army Form C. 2118.

WAR DIARY
or
INTELLIGENCE SUMMARY.
(Erase heading not required.)

Instructions regarding War Diaries and Intelligence Summaries are contained in F.S. Regs., Part II. and the Staff Manual respectively. Title pages will be prepared in manuscript.

Hour, Date, Place	Summary of Events and Information	Remarks and references to Appendices
May 6th	Ordinary Routine work. Instructions received to be prepared to billet all No 2 A.S.C. companies in smaller space, owing to arrival of troops in district.	
May 7th	Issue at refilling point ordered for 7.30 A.M. instead of 9.30 A.M. and trains to return to billets towards evening. Battalions required to proceed to billets after 7.0 P.M. Ordinary instructions received from H.Q. Dn. to carry out at 6-30 P.M. Instructions received from H.Q. Dn. to carry out orders given and to move supplies as usual.	
May 8th	Orders re convoy of supplies yesterday repeated to-day - made arrangements for all trains to fill and return to billets towards relief. At 3 P.M. fresh orders given for trains to proceed to transfer point as follows :- No 2 Coy to carry on as usual; No 4 Coy train to be at Pas St Maur canal bridge at 11-30 A.M.; No 3 Coy at new point at 12-30 P.M. and No 1 Coy train at new point at 1-30 P.M. All arrangements made with Officers concerned.	

WAR DIARY
or
INTELLIGENCE SUMMARY.
(Erase heading not required.)

Army Form C. 2118.

Hour, Date, Place	Summary of Events and Information	Remarks and references to Appendices
May 9th 1915	All trains filled up by 9.30 A.M. and proceeded as arranged yesterday - carried out as arranged except that 20th Coy and H.Q. 9th Coy transferred tp carts out on Main Road opposite H.Q. 3rd Inf Bde. at BAC ST MAUR. The road was very busy with ambulance wagons bringing in wounded but there was no block. Ordered all train wagons to carry a supply of straw in case they should be required to convey wounded cases - they were not required however. Several units G.O. with their cookers carts, and some (chiefly artillery) past over at all, and their supplies waited on road for arrival.	
10h.	Heavy firing from 5.0 A.M. continued all day in direction of LAVENTIE fr. Issue of supplies as yesterday - worked much better - much more prompt in sending carts carts to transfer point. nothing unusual to-day. fr.	
11h	Issue of food supplies satisfactory - hay did not arrive at	

WAR DIARY
or
INTELLIGENCE SUMMARY.
(Erase heading not required.)

Army Form C. 2118.

Instructions regarding War Diaries and Intelligence Summaries are contained in F. S. Regs., Part II. and the Staff Manual respectively. Title pages will be prepared in manuscript.

Hour, Date, Place	Summary of Events and Information	Remarks and references to Appendices
Mar 11th (Cont)	at Refilling point till 7.0 P.M - Train to R to units and returned to Billets at 12-30 A.M. 12nd JM	
12	Entrained transport with IV Corps the remainder of Refilling at 9-30 A.M. arrived at 7.30 - they arrived at 11.0 A.M and went to trucks of Units by 1.30 P.M. JM	
13th	Refilling about 6 to 9.0 A.M as before 15th - then was delivered by Column direct to Bde. & Maur JM	
14th	Rain during night so made roads bad - Lorries hardly any sight at refill arranged for inspection & hour after return from issuing - Inspection satisfactory JM	
15th	Inspected 1st line transport of 1st Brigade - Everything very good except a few minor details which the Brigade Transport Officer will attend to. Most of the mules are fully shod - about three horses are unfit and may have to cast for a time owing to their being worn down. JM	

WAR DIARY
or
INTELLIGENCE SUMMARY.
(Erase heading not required.)

Army Form C. 2118.

Hour, Date, Place	Summary of Events and Information	Remarks and references to Appendices
May 16th	39 horses arrived from remount dept – draughts horses very good – riding horses exchanges fair – 6 L.D. horses for artillery good until the exception of one which is thin and properly useless.	
17th	Hempstein – roads bad, but all supply & transport duties carried out without hitch.	
18th	Iowa supplies. Hay wagons transferred to 1st F.A. by order of H.Q. to be used in connection with baths. Road No 1 BAC ST MAUR via CROIX DE BAC stopped for convoys which are to go & return by main road from ESTAIRES. Road must congested thereby. Serious complaint will arise hereby – it does not seem clearly understood that receipts should be opening used, and Convoy Officer are instructed to ensure units all they possibly can – to its use.	
19th–20th–21st	Routine work.	

WAR DIARY or INTELLIGENCE SUMMARY

Army Form C. 2118

Place	Date	Hour	Summary of Events and Information	Remarks and references to Appendices
	May 22nd		Accident in No 3 Coys lines – man cleaning his rifle with cartridge left in, with usual result, the trigger pulled and bullet passed through thighs of two men inflicting flesh wounds, the burried itself in flank of a H.D. horse. JW.	
	23		Aeroplane passing over ~~Headquarters~~ NEUF BERQUIN this morning about 9-30 fell near No 3 Coys lines – two occupants, both killed, and plane smashed to pieces.	
			Visited Headquarters and confirmed that changes take place in units drawing supplies, and no notification sent to me, hunting in transport coming up of which I know nothing, and blocking of road ensues. Also arranged to write supporting changing transfer point of 3rd Brigade CoSc and Divisional Troops. JW.	
	24		Accident to supply train caused delay in delivering hay, which only left refilling point at 5. P.M. – Horses from returned to billets at 11. P.M.	
			7 hay wagons transferred to-day to Lahore Divn north of LESTREM. JW.	
	25		Routine work – nothing special to-day. JW.	
	26		Heavy issue of supplies – 106 wagons in the fwd train convoys – Great heat to-day, but horses all right, although some of them marched 22 miles in worst part of day. JW.	

WAR DIARY
or
INTELLIGENCE SUMMARY
(Erase heading not required.)

Army Form C. 2118

Place	Date	Hour	Summary of Events and Information	Remarks and references to Appendices
May	27		Refill altered 1/2 hour earlier than hitherto - slight block on road caused by one of Glennon Lorries sticking in soft ground - country vehicles coming in to market emphasised the block, but all cleared in 20 minutes. Attended Board of inquiry re Capt. Foster. A.V.C.	
	28		Nil	
	29		—	
	30		Drew attention to long journey made by No 4 Coys Convoy from refilling point to Units and suggested that Units should meet the convoy at some transfer point. S.A.P.M.G. promised to hasten. 49 remounts received at 5.30 P.M. and taken to H.Q. 21 Corps lines for the night.	
	31		Refilling very satisfactory - Three Units late on ground, and ordered away clear of main road, and not to return till 10.15. Remounts distributed.	

49th Division

Confidential

WAR DIARY

of

Lieut. Colonel J. C. Chambers
Commanding 49th (W.R.) Divl. Train

From June 1st 1915
To June 30th 1915

Volume 3

WAR DIARY or INTELLIGENCE SUMMARY

Army Form C. 2118

Place	Date	Hour	Summary of Events and Information	Remarks and references to Appendices
1915 June	1		Visited Indian Corps # 2 with Major Brigham and suggested moving refilling point from Pet[?] NEUF BERQUIN road to BAC St MAUR and that Column carried supplies direct there, units drawing direct — leaving Officers & personnel each morning with the Column. — Corps H.Q. agreed, subject to approval of S.O.O. It was also pointed out that the train at present is billetted too far behind French line, but that no room exists nearer the front. This was agreed, and the VIII th Divn will be approached with the view of getting a small part of their area N of SAILLY or BAC St MAUR billeted for.	
	2		Refilling points at BAC St MAUR approved by Corps H.Q. and actual points fixed. Arranged with Column as to dumping. Visited proposed new area for billeting train, and found it hopeless. Suggested to H.Q. that as refilling point is now moved forward, the trains will be more convenient if they remain billetted as at present, no going to the refilling point empty, remove the objection of having to go so far loaded. ⟨init⟩	
	3		New refill worked satisfactorily. Units drew supplies direct from Column, and train trans rested. Arranged some slight alterations in refilling points. ⟨init⟩	

Army Form C. 2118

WAR DIARY
or
INTELLIGENCE SUMMARY
(Erase heading not required.)

Place	Date	Hour	Summary of Events and Information	Remarks and references to Appendices
June	4		G.O.C. inspected Companies & have been & Col. Lipp accompanied him. Had new area allotted for billeting &c.	
	5		Visited new billeting area, which is small, and will accommodate the train with difficulty — made tent arrangements possible for men to-morrow &c.	
	6		Moved in to new area — Companies somewhat scattered, and each with very poor accommodation — no room for Mess who are bivouacing. New re-fit for Divisional troops in Extensive spread — satisfactory &c.	
	7		Made all arrangements for trains to proceed delivering supplies to transfer points to-morrow &c.	
	8		Delivery of supplies by trains very satisfactory, and with no hitch. Saw Col. Lipp and Major Bingham at H.Q. D.S. re one or two details concerning the return of trains after transferring &c.	
	9		Routine work carried on — Visited roads where trains were transferring to Cook's Carts — all quite in order two blocking of routes &c.	
	10		Altered Transfer point of No 4 Coy, which shortened the train route from 12 miles	

1875 Wt. W593/826 1,000,000 4/15 J.B.C. & A. A.D.S.S./Forms/C. 2118.

WAR DIARY or INTELLIGENCE SUMMARY

Army Form C. 2118

(Erase heading not required.)

Place	Date	Hour	Summary of Events and Information	Remarks and references to Appendices
[Front]	10 (Cont.)		miles to 9 miles. Heavy rain during night made roads heavy; two wagons stuck in mud & had to be d.g. loaded before getting out, otherwise all went right.	
	11		The 3rd Brigade started to new transfer point, and road arrangements were made which were satisfactory to all concerned.	
	12		All transport work satisfactory — Rode out to three Transfer points and saw trains leave for home — no interference with traffic at any point.	
	13		Train returned home from Transfer points earlier than previous days. This is gratifying remembering that Sunday has a special issue of extra supplies.	
	14		Visited all refilling Transfer points — Shells were dropped over No. 3 C.S. Transfer point just during time of transfer, but no casualties.	
	15		Enemy shelled all district near transfer points, but during time of transfer, but no casualties.	
	16		Routine work — Got instructions to prepare to move all Companies from present billets to new area. Arranged to get our billets to-morrow.	
	17		Proceeded new billets and arranged for removal to-morrow. All supply work carried out — no hitch. Visited H. Quarters in new billets.	

WAR DIARY or INTELLIGENCE SUMMARY

Army Form C. 2118

(Erase heading not required.)

Instructions regarding War Diaries and Intelligence Summaries are contained in F.S. Regs., Part II. and the Staff Manual respectively. Title Pages will be prepared in manuscript.

Place	Date	Hour	Summary of Events and Information	Remarks and references to Appendices
France	18		All companies removed to new billets and old billets evacuated by 2.0 P.M. JR	
	19		Visited refilling — afterwards inspected all companies' billets and arranged various alterations with Coy Commanders. Went with A.D.V.S. to secure a new billet for the Mobile Vet'y Section, which is required to move from its present position. JR	
	20		Inspected the various water supplies in billeting area — each farm has a well with pump, and in each case the quality is doubtful, & quantity various. Various streams and ponds exist for watering animals, but there is very little flow, the water however is fairly good & plentiful. JR	
	21		Received instructions for all blanket wagons to be returned — all units ordered by N.2 to hand over their blanket wagons as complete turnout, to draw to-morrow. Arranged to park them in N.º 3 Coy's lines for examination before being sent away. JR	
	22		Spent the day in mustering, examining and completing the blanket wagons sent in by units — all fairly complete. JR	
	23		Received instructions to send hay wagons to units, to assist them in lieu of the blanket wagons withdrawn — this was carried out — 9 a.c. sent to wagons with arrival teams to augment the service. JR	
	24		Brief advance instructions re coming move — getting together certain details information preparatory to the move. Details to details respecting which will come later. JR	

WAR DIARY
or
INTELLIGENCE SUMMARY
(Erase heading not required.)

Army Form C. 2118

Instructions regarding War Diaries and Intelligence Summaries are contained in F.S. Regs., Part II. and the Staff Manual respectively. Title Pages will be prepared in manuscript.

Place	Date	Hour	Summary of Events and Information	Remarks and references to Appendices
June	25		Discussed with Col. Lugg the details of the moving of the Division, and fixed up various details – Also went to new area with S.S.O. and fixed on new refilling points in readiness for troops arriving in new area.	
	26		All arrangements for removing suspended, and all units to stand by in readiness for removing at short notice – as troops have moved to temporary rest camp a new refilling point arranged to-day to start on 28th.	
	27		Received orders to move units on 29th. – Visited refilling point for 28th and made all necessary arrangements with train companies as to approaching departure [?] – Spending detail arrangements for removing – No 2 Coy with 146" Brig left at F.P.M.[?].	
	28th		Train H.Q. moved to HOUTKERQUE – inspected billets prepared for all companies.	
	29th		Reported to Brig. H.Q. at PROVEN – visited refilling points – fixed up train Post Office –	
	30th		visited all Battns. in 146th Brig: to look into ration[?] in lieu of Kitchens [?].	

July 1915

18/6214

49th Division.

49th Divl: Train

Vol IV

CONFIDENTIAL.

War Diary
of
O.C. 49th (W.R.) Divl Train.

From. 1-7-15.   To. 31-7-15.

(Volume 4.)

Army Form C. 2118

WAR DIARY
or
INTELLIGENCE SUMMARY

(Erase heading not required.)

Instructions regarding War Diaries and Intelligence Summaries are contained in F.S. Regs., Part II. and the Staff Manual respectively. Title Pages will be prepared in manuscript.

Place	Date	Hour	Summary of Events and Information	Remarks and references to Appendices
July	1		Interview of Checking differences in Transport - Most Units show uncertainties to declare any surplus - H.Q. 2 & H.Q. 2 Coy moved into their billets. Water is scarcer, and may become a serious question. Local inhabitants are by no means friendly, and prefer peace at any price.	
	2		Completed return of transport differences. Templates and horses sent to H.Q. — Visited refilling points and discussed road control with Transport Officers. No 3 & 4 Coys moved in to their billets and the whole train settled down.	traffic
	3 & 4		Routine work.	
	5		Prospect of move forward in few days - visited new area N.E. of POPERINGHE, and arranged approximately the refilling points.	
	6		No. 2 Coy. preparing to move - supply wagons refill to-morrow, and march full to Units who move on night 6-7, and remain. Remainder of Coy march during day to temporary billets.	
	7		No. 2 & 3 Companies marched to new billets.	
	8		No. 4 Company marched to new billets. travelled at new front. Visited refilling point, and arranged several details with officers as to road traffic.	

1875   Wt. W593/826   1,000,000   4/15   J.B.C. & A.   A.D.S.S./Forms/C.2118.

WAR DIARY or INTELLIGENCE SUMMARY

Army Form C. 2118

Place	Date	Hour	Summary of Events and Information	Remarks and references to Appendices
S⁰ (Cont)			Traffic from refill to Units. Also re-arranged direction of dumps, and advised O.C. Column. /u.	
	9		H.Q. marched from Lillers. Spent from 9-6 hours to CASSEL to draw Vidauge east to POPERINGE. SSO and his staff moved their quarters from Lillers east to POPERINGE.)	
	10		Received 15 remounts from CASSEL station and to [struck through] at Hoogstade. Own Headquarters removed and established new office NORTH of POPERINGE. /u.	
	11		Received 65 remounts from 6th D.A.C. 10 Belgian Interpreters reported for distribution. Orders received for front movements. /u.	
	12		Visited new area and arranged billets. /u.	
	13		Visited all Coy's and gave instructions as to move to-morrow. Owing to constant changes in the position of Units, small parties are frequently arriving in for supplies at short notice - considerable work caused in supply office, but all carried through without confusion. /u.	
	14		All routine work carried through - still engaged with constant changes for supplies. All train companies moved to new area. /u.	
	15.6.18		Ordinary routine work — Inspection of transport &c. /u.	

WAR DIARY
or
INTELLIGENCE SUMMARY
(Erase heading not required.)

Army Form C. 2118

Place	Date	Hour	Summary of Events and Information	Remarks and references to Appendices
July	19		Took over 14 horses from remount depôt near HAZEBROUCK - a very poor form lot indeed.	
	20		Distributed the 14 horses taken over yesterday - visited H.Q. re personal matters. Two S.S. Wagons (G.T.) arrived & taken over from 12th Divn. Pte Kerr PLATE onto & the probable arrival of what we were notified on the last, were delivered this morning, and issued to Units - the quality was very inferior, mostly dirty & unfit for issue. H.Q. advised.	
	21		No repetition of PLATE onto supply. Received intimation that 1000 men of Labour Corps would be joining Division and to be detained from the 24th inst.	
	22		Visited refilling point, and allotted position of No 2 dump arriving & unloading of same. Got notice of 19 remounts to be taken over in morning at ARNEKE station. Also that advance parts of French Labour Corps would arrive tomorrow a.m.	
	23		Took over 19 remounts - very good lot - best by far of 3rd previous lots. Advance parts of Labour Corps with transport arrived.	
	24		Visited railhead - everything satisfactory. Distributed the 19 remounts which arrived yesterday. Front 1070 of Labour Corps arrived, with transport consisting of 4 G.S. limbered wagons and 10 water carts - form of latter sent to 2nd Army Signal Coy, South of CASSEL.	

WAR DIARY
or
INTELLIGENCE SUMMARY

Army Form C. 2118

Place	Date	Hour	Summary of Events and Information	Remarks and references to Appendices
July	25		Routine Work ƒ/c	
	26		Sent 2 S.S. wagons to YPRES to collect 2000 bricks, also iron rods and 1 barrel cement from R.E.s for Trenching Battalion ƒ/c	
	27		Second Battalion of Entrenching Bat. arrived – no supplies – had to draw from Supply Column direct for to-morrow's consumption ƒ/c. The two entrenching Batts have only 25th	
	28		4. S.S. arrived wagons between them for Supplies, baggage &c. – totally inadequate. Informed H.Q. that we cannot possibly carry on without more transport. Drew supplies again to-day for from Column direct, for to-morrow's consumption. ƒ/c	
	29		More bricks & cement conveyed from YPRES for entrenching Bat. a "taube" machine flew over our lines and was shelled by an Anti aircraft Gun – prevented [?] the shells fell in our lines, but no damage done. ƒ/c	
	30 & 31		Enemy's aircraft very busy over our R.O.1 refilling Garage which is in any exposed position, and 20 bombs have been dropped in immediate neighbourhood, some suggesting a removal of H.Q. & removal of the dump. ƒ/c	

CONFIDENTIAL

49th Division

WAR DIARY

of

August, 1915

J.C. CHAMBERS Lieut. Colonel,
Commanding 49th (W.R.) Divl. Train.

From 1 - 31. 8. 15

Volume V

WAR DIARY or INTELLIGENCE SUMMARY

Army Form C. 2118

Place	Date	Hour	Summary of Events and Information	Remarks and references to Appendices
Aug	1st		Received instructions to take over 4. S.S. Sections wagons at THEROUANNE on the 4th inst for two Infantry Battalions - also 1 Maltese cart for the 16th Div't. - made arrangements accordingly. JW	
	2		Redistribution of horses ordered by D.A.Q.-M.G. came in from reserve units, and 34 FF issued. JW	
	3rd & 4th		Routine work - Arranged alteration to refill hour, owing to late arrival of meat & bread train at railhead. From 5th including the 6th refill time will be 10 A.M. JW	
	5		12 riding horses handed over to us by the Mobile Vet: section - instructions sought from H.Q. as to disposal. Received instructions to send party to take over 20 waggons at THEROUANNE on 6th inst. - One days preserved rations required for 148th Brigade to-morrow, received order at 6.0 P.M. - At 10 P.M. received orders to send for 31 remounts at GODIWAERSVELDE - made necessary arrangements. At 11.45 P.M. received urgent request for 200 preserved rations for Cyclists section. JW	
	6		Column drew the rations for 148th Brigade, followed at refill point at 7. A.M. - had difficulty in getting them owing to short notice, but succeeded by working all night in getting them in time. The 31 remounts brought in and distributed to various units - The transport taken over at THEROUANNE on 4th inst, arrived after two days march. JW	

Army Form C. 2118

WAR DIARY
or
INTELLIGENCE SUMMARY
(Erase heading not required.)

Instructions regarding War Diaries and Intelligence Summaries are contained in F. S. Regs., Part II. and the Staff Manual respectively. Title Pages will be prepared in manuscript.

Place	Date	Hour	Summary of Events and Information	Remarks and references to Appendices
Aug	7		Order from H.Q. to Major Hays S.S.O. Poperinghe in England for duty until new arrivals — POPERINGHE heavily shelled in afternoon.	
	8		Transport convoy from THEROUANNE arrived all well.	
	9		Major Hays left for England — Transport to which arrived yesterday distributed to units, to new additional machine guns — Attended conference of S.S.Os with DDQST at CASSELL — Heavy bombardment by our troops in	
	10		neighbourhood of YPRES during early morning. POPERINGHE again heavily shelled during the day, by shells of very large calibre. Arranging removal of S.S.O.'s office to my H.Qrs, and old S.S.O's billet given up. Quiet day Generally.	
	11		Visited HOUTKERQUE & investigate complaints from inhabitants who have billeted troops and not received payment. Reported same to H.Q. — Certificates have been duly sent in, but delay appears to be due to time between the visits of the French Prefects, who make the payments — were received at 9.30 P.M. to take over 14 remounts for Artillery Units, at GODNAERSVELDE to-morrow morning at 7 o'c.	
	12		Drew the 14 Remounts and distributed same to units as per instructions from H.Q. — At 9.0. P.M. a fire broke out in the farm buildings in x̶o̶f Corps Lines, the adjoining farm had	

1875 Wt. W593/826 1,000,000 4/15 J.B.C. & A. A.D.S.S./Forms/C. 2118.

WAR DIARY
or
INTELLIGENCE SUMMARY

(Erase heading not required.)

Army Form C. 2118

Place	Date	Hour	Summary of Events and Information	Remarks and references to Appendices
	Aug 12 (cont'd)		a narrow escape from being involved, but was saved by our men getting on the roof and by a constant string of buckets from a pond was able to save it. There male occupants of the farm trust were placed under arrest together with a man whose movements were suspicious. By 11.0 P.M. the fires was well in hand; all men were then returned to their lines, and civil police arrived. I handed all prisoners over to the Police, together with charge of all property recover from the buildings. Left 20 men on duty to assist Police. JHC.	
	13		Routine work – Held enquiry re fire last night – no satisfactory result, and cause not known JHC.	
	14		Instruction received to send an Kitchen body to Canadian Trip near BAILLEUL, also 1 O.S. wagon to Gunnade school at TERDEGHUM, arranged to start them off first thing in morning JHC.	
	15		Visited Windmill dump and arranged for some casks to be handed over to be used for securing rain water from roofs of buildings. General Percival inspected all Companies to-day. JHC.	
	16		Instructions received to send all surplus wagons away details to be forwarded to-morrow. Advise received for a redistribution of the surplus horses in the Division. All horses to be delivered...	

Army Form C. 2118

WAR DIARY
or
INTELLIGENCE SUMMARY
(Erase heading not required.)

Place	Date	Hour	Summary of Events and Information	Remarks and references to Appendices
	16 (Cont.)		Delivered to Train between 2 & 4 J.C. and redistribution to Units between 4 & 6 J.C. Asked A.D.V.S. to undertake redistribution. Three wagons sent to ELVERDINGE to load up bricks, after 1½ loads enemy shelled the place and our wagons ordered out.	
	17		Three wagons sent to ELVERDINGE for bricks, but turned back empty, not allowed in the place owing to enemy shelling. Distribution of horses very unsatisfactory, no second horses due to some in did not arrive, and no explanation sent. Since of staff employed wasted. Units only received one third vegetable rations to-day owing to supply officers motor cars not being available yesterday for purchasing, lorry & to few cars at 2nd H.Q. or in workshops, or doing S.S.O. duties, remaining ones being insufficient.	
	18		Wagons for bricks to ELVERDINGE again returned empty. Capt Milne thrown from his horse & put his shoulder out - taken to No 1 field ambulance.	
	19		Capt Milne evacuated from 1st F.A. to base hospital. Capt Shaw appointed Adjutant temporarily pending decision as to Capt Milne. Had instructions to collect bricks from ELVERDINGE - wagons sent but again unsuccessful. Returned empty. The S.S.O. returned from leave & notice to attend conference with DAT QMG 2nd army tomorrow at ABEELE.	
	20		Attended Conference at ABEELE - output discussed and proposed rearrangement of getting supplies up and delivered, without using the MT Column during the Autumn & Winter months. Notes to hand of my arguments. To be taken on at Mailhead tomorrow.	

1875 Wt. W593/826 1,000,000 4/15 J.B.C. & A. A.D.S.S./Forms/C. 2118.

WAR DIARY or INTELLIGENCE SUMMARY

Army Form C. 2118

Place	Date	Hour	Summary of Events and Information	Remarks and references to Appendices
	21		9 Remounts received from paddock and distributed. Drinking nets for water fp:	
	22		Routine work — instructions received that bricks can be brought from VIAMERTINGE. ordered 3 wagons to bad som to morrow. Enemy's Tanks aeroplane very busy in afternoon — aeroplane passed over billets about 11 P.M. fp:	
	23		Exchanged two horse water carts with one motor w cart — Railhead for to-morrow changed to CAESTRE fp:	
	24		Transfer of Capt. Shaw O.C. No 2 Coy to Royal Flying Corps returned approved. arranged to relieve him to-morrow. Wagon sent to VIAMERTINGE for bricks returned empty, no guide as arranged with DAQMG fp:	
	25		Capt. Shaw cleared up papers Handed duties of Adjt. Orm to Lt. Reynolds. Command of No 2 Coy taken over by Capt. Scott from the O. Coy fp:	
	26		Re-arranged approaches by trains to Refilling points, owing to bad state of roads. Water going out in all billets, carts leading from anywhere it can be got. Rat proofer rolay of men a well drinking fp:	
	27		Canadian railway corps attached for rations, billeted in French area near HOOGSTADE. made necessary arrangements with DA.DMG and S.S.O. Also allotted 1 S.S. Lieut wagon on loan. To take over their supplies from lorry and deliver to details fp:	

Army Form C. 2118.

WAR DIARY
or
INTELLIGENCE SUMMARY
(Erase heading not required.)

Instructions regarding War Diaries and Intelligence Summaries are contained in F.S. Regs., Part II. and the Staff Manual respectively. Title Pages will be prepared in manuscript.

Place	Date	Hour	Summary of Events and Information	Remarks and references to Appendices
	Aug 28		Getting close to end of water supply for horses - urging on work of well sinking, not much encouragement up to present. Railhead removed to GODEWARSVELDE from to-morrow inclusive.	
	29		Rain fell in afternoon and as much as possible was conveyed from roofs of buildings by temporary conduits to storage tubs - well sinking still being pushed on with; no great results yet, but signs fairly hopeful.	
	30		Arrangements made for watering horses at Chateau COUTHOVE - no water in wells yet.	
	31		Late rains having replenished ponds slightly, and with a view of relieving COUTHOVE as far as possible, arranged to send 70 horses only to that place for the present. 12 S.S. Wagons handed in from Brigade A.C.S. - instructions received to hand over 119 horses to VI D.A.C. who refused to take them without men. H.Q. arranged with the B.A.C.s to lend men to VI D.A.C. until reinforcements arrive.	

121/6901

only 56

49th Division

49th Divisional Train

Vol VI

September 15.

CONFIDENTIAL.

War Diary
of
Lt Col J C Chambers. I.C. of L.(UR) Ford Train.

From Sept 1st 15.   To. Sept 30. 15.

(Volume VI.)

WAR DIARY or INTELLIGENCE SUMMARY

Army Form C. 2118

(Erase heading not required.)

Place	Date	Hour	Summary of Events and Information	Remarks and references to Appendices
	Sept. 1		Exchange of horses in Division - surplus horses brought in to H.Q. C.S. and redistributed to Units with deficiencies. Order received for all troops to be confined to billets until further orders.	
	2		Routine work - Heavy rain in afternoon - ponds for watering horses considerably replenished.	
	3		Very heavy rain during night and which continued during greater part of to-day has made roads very difficult for transports; all duties carried out without accident. Received orders to draw a remuneration for the Division from CAESTRE, which was handed over to troops who wished it, at refill point at PESCHOOK.	
	4		Making arrangements for sending 32 wagons + 128 horses to Advanced Transport Base - Cleaning billets, and arranged for H.Q. C.S. to move.	
	5 + 6		Completed arrangements for convoy to Transport Base - Received notice of 24 remounts coming. H.Q. C.S. moved into F.24.A Sheet 27. Arrived at 11.30 P.M. that remounts would be at railhead at 9 A.M. to-morrow.	
	7		Inspected Vet. Officer reports to take over remounts - Ponds to refill altered owing to bad state - remounts distributed at H.Q. P.M.	

WAR DIARY or INTELLIGENCE SUMMARY

Army Form C. 2118

(Erase heading not required.)

Place	Date	Hour	Summary of Events and Information	Remarks and references to Appendices
Sept	8		Convoy of 32 wagons despatched to Base. Road at refill much blocked today by horses exercised - refill operations much hampered. JW	
	9		Wagon convoy arrived at THEOURANNE 5.0 P.M. no party from BASE to take them over - and looking for reserve dump proceeding retrospectively. JW	
	10		Our convoy of parts instructed to take wagon convoy through to ABEELE - 30 tons reserve coal led from station. An English tank fell in field adjoining turnace at 12. noon - no explosion - fired and dug out at 2.0 P.M. marked HALE'S patent. Reported to H.Q. - a party from R.F.C. took charge of it at 7.0 P.M. - evidently dropped from one of our aeroplanes by accident. JW	
	11		Received notice that no more coal will come to POPERINGE station, but will have to be drawn from GODEWARSVELDE. Units will now have to be supplied from reserve dump. JW	
	12		Routine work. JW	
	13		S.O.C. Corps inspected 1st Line transport of the three Inf. Brigades - a few notes were taken re various matters raised by the S.O.C. and necessary instructions given. JW	
14 & 23rd			On leave. JW	

WAR DIARY
or
INTELLIGENCE SUMMARY

(Erase heading not required.)

Army Form C. 2118

Instructions regarding War Diaries and Intelligence Summaries are contained in F.S. Regs, Part II. and the Staff Manual respectively. Title Pages will be prepared in manuscript.

Place	Date	Hour	Summary of Events and Information	Remarks and references to Appendices
Sept.	24		Took over duty during last night. Went through all current papers. Saw D.A.Q.M.G. re arrangements for transport and supply in case of an advance. JW.	
	25		Heavy firing in early morning SOUTH & EAST. Gave out confidential instructions re same. JW.	
	26		Routine work. JW.	
	27		Visited all Companies and discussed plans for winter quarters — accommodation in existing farm buildings very meagre — materials for making shelters very difficult to get — sandbags much needed but Ordnance cannot supply — R.E.s can only supply wood & in small quantities. Outlook far from good. JW.	
	28		Visited railhead — all working smoothly. Visited Company lines and instructed them to proceed with preparations for winter billets, notwithstanding possibility of a move. JW.	
	29		Very wet day — roads difficult for transport — refilling hampered by wet. Issue of rum ordered by S.O.C. Brig. JW.	
	30		A.D.S.S. Forms C. 2118. A reserve rum ration ordered by S.O.C. to be held in readiness. JW.	

121/7341

49th Division

49th Divisional Train

Vol VII

Oct 15

Confidential

War Diary
of
Lt Col J. C. Chambers. Commdg 49th (WR) Sinl Train.

From. Oct 1st. 1915.   To Oct. 31st. 1915.

(Volume 7)

Army Form C. 2118

WAR DIARY
or
INTELLIGENCE SUMMARY
(Erase heading not required.)

Place	Date	Hour	Summary of Events and Information	Remarks and references to Appendices
Oct	1		Very quiet — Visited companies who are preparing winter quarters for 130 men of Labour Battn. attached to us for returning from 3rd endeavour.	
	2			
	3		Visited refilling point, all working satisfactorily — road very bad but is being rapidly repaired. Examined one or two likely places for winter quarters for H.Q. Train.	
	4		76 remounts for the Division taken over at railhead that in H.Q. Coy lines. Instructions received to fetch 5 wagons from HOOGSTADT for the Canadian and convey down to THEROANNE.	
	5		Redistributed the remount which arrived yesterday. Sent to Canadians for 5 wagons which were not ready, all arrangements upset thereby, convoy today at HAZEBROUCK and returning at THEROUANNE cancelled.	
	6		9 wagons, 17 horses, 6 riders, 6 mules received from Canadians — made arrangements for their being conveyed to THEROUANNE tomorrow. Lines & refill changed from 10.0 A.M. to 9.0 A.M. from today. Many complaints in from units re shortage of paraffin oil & candles — the quantities sent up from base are very inadequate, but are distributed as evenly as possible. Received notice to evacuate form at A.19.C.2.9. — this places any unit	

Army Form C. 2118

WAR DIARY
or
INTELLIGENCE SUMMARY
(Erase heading not required.)

Instructions regarding War Diaries and Intelligence Summaries are contained in F. S. Regs., Part II. and the Staff Manual respectively. Title Pages will be prepared in manuscript.

Place	Date	Hour	Summary of Events and Information	Remarks and references to Appendices
Oct.	6th (cont)		Unit is in an unsatisfactory position for winter shelter, as other farms have very bare barns & shed accommodation.	
	7th & 8th		Convoy for THEROUANNE left at 8.0. a.m. under Capt. MANTLE. Coal dust and cinders wanted urgently. Got 2 tons at CAISTRE, and arranged with O.C. Column to load some to dump tomorrow. Routine.	
	9th 10th		To C.R.E. H.Q. Dr. re Creosote and tar purchased fortnight ago in BOULOGNE and not yet to hand — taking matter up with railway authorities. Got supply of felled timber from 6th Corps park.	
	11th		Saw C.R.E. re building rough shelters at refilling point, to protect perishable supplies — arranged for C.R.E. to supply materials and we even will fix. Horse show held to-day — very successful.	
	12th		Quiet day — Made enquiries for purchase of straw — S.S.O. near the D.DqS+T with a view if possible of getting the ration allowance increased, the straw is wanted however to be used for drying men's boots in wet weather. POPERINGHE shelled in afternoon, fr.	
	14		Saw C.R.E. re materials for building shelters at refilling points for bread, meat and grocery issues — arranged to draw the materials and an un antifieres trade the shelters. Arranged transport to draw daily drawing of fuel from various dumps, supplying same from	

WAR DIARY or INTELLIGENCE SUMMARY

Army Form C. 2118

Place	Date	Hour	Summary of Events and Information	Remarks and references to Appendices
A (Cont)	14.		from station, also daily. JW	
	15 & 16		H.Q. Coy who had occupied farm at 19 B.I.E. as allotted to them, had to turn out and hand over to the D.A.C. thereby enhancing the difficulty of providing unit accommodation for men. Sent wagons to ABEELE for corrugated sheets for shelters at refill. JW	
	17		Visited Companies lines and inspected bivouacs and horse shelters — more materials required, but difficult to get. JW	
	18		Arranged with D.A.Q.M.G. for transport of corrugated roofs for dug outs from VI Corps R.E. Park to 148th Inf. Brigade. Divisional Transport generally, and the whole of the Transport of the Division is worked to the utmost — new railway under construction along ELVERDINGE road should relieve the pressure considerably. JW	
	19		Transport of corrugated roofs diverted to wrong place by 148th Inf. Brigade, and roofs brought back to our lines to await further instructions. JW	
	20		Went thoroughly through work done by transport each day in order to find out what transport can be made available for extra work urgently required — arranged to examine wagons in order to allow every possible wagon to be detailed for special work as required — 4 wagons detailed to take corrugated roofs from VI Corps R.E. Park to trenches daily, until completed, probably 4 to 5 days. JW	
	21		[crossed out] 75 memoranda received at railhead and brought to H.Q. Coy Lines. JW	

Army Form C. 2118

WAR DIARY
or
INTELLIGENCE SUMMARY
(Erase heading not required.)

Instructions regarding War Diaries and Intelligence Summaries are contained in F.S. Regs., Part II. and the Staff Manual respectively. Title Pages will be prepared in manuscript.

Place	Date	Hour	Summary of Events and Information	Remarks and references to Appendices
Oct.	22nd		Distributed all remounts received yesterday. Preparing plans for building shelters for supplies at refilling point.	
	23		Saw D.A.Q.M.G. re transport – received letters re sending Senior Officer to England to assist new A.S.C. Units in Training.	
	24		Evacuated 6 H.D. horses out of 14 sent in by 3rd R.F.A. to CAISTRE, together with 7 which were seen by D.D.R. in D.A.C. lines – the remaining 8 out of the 14 not fit for work & therefore sent to Mobile Vet Section.	
	25		Saw D.A. & Q.M.G. VI Corps at new railway platform on POPERINGHE – ELVERDINGE road – prepared to make it new railhead. Schemes for drawing to be prepared and discussed with D.A. & Q.M.G. VI Corps tomorrow. Two officers arrived from England.	
	26		Again met D.A. & Q.M.G. VI Corps re new railhead. Submitted scheme for drawing in detail from dump on platform – supplies to be taken from train, and then arranged in group supplies.	
	27		Received notice of 36 L.D. remounts coming to railhead tomorrow morning – all for 3rd R.F.A. His Majesty the King visited the Division.	
	28		36 remounts received, one injured in train, and sent to Mobile Vet section. Remainder handed over to 3rd R.F.A. A very wet day, and roads in very bad state. Horse & wagon lines very bad, owing to mud.	

WAR DIARY
or
INTELLIGENCE SUMMARY

(Erase heading not required.)

Army Form C. 2118

Place	Date	Hour	Summary of Events and Information	Remarks and references to Appendices
Oct	29		G.O.C. inspected Company lines to-day. Expressed satisfaction, except that the horses of 466 Coy shew signs of overwork. An endeavour will be made to correct this by re-arranging transport work. JS.	
	30		Supply column reports having received orders to load up at station railhead at 7 A.M. — This will entail alteration in refill hour. JS	
	31		Refill hour commencing 1st Nov. fixed at 5 A.M. Transport work difficult owing to very heavy state of roads. JS.	

49th Division

121/7637

Confidential

War Diary
of
Lieut Col J. C. Chambers. Commdg: 49th (WR) Divl Train.

Vol VIII

From Nov: 1: 15.   To Nov: 30: 15:

(Volume 8.)

Army Form 'C. 2118

WAR DIARY
or
INTELLIGENCE SUMMARY
(Erase heading not required.)

Instructions regarding War Diaries and Intelligence Summaries are contained in F. S. Regs., Part II. and the Staff Manual respectively. Title Pages will be prepared in manuscript.

Place	Date	Hour	Summary of Events and Information	Remarks and references to Appendices
Nov.	1		Weather very wet — visited all Companies — Ground in a deplorable condition and partly flooded. JW	
	2		Attended H.Q. and discussed state of ground in train billets — arranged to park wagons at refilling point to save traffic at billets. This to be tried for 2 or 3 nights, report to be made. JW	
	4 & 5		Visited refilling point — found parking of wagons on road to be impracticable — road to be narrow and is completely blocked when column is drawing up. Suspended the proposal arranged for further consideration. JW	
	6		No coal up from mines since Nov. 1st — partly due to a block on railway — mine trucks = 90 tons advised as having left mine on 2nd, but not yet arrived — protein acute — bought 7 tons locally at 66 Frs per ton. Purchased 9 tons locally. JW	
	7		Sent Requisitioning Officers round to buy coal — 3 trucks from mines arrived at HAZEBROUCK — 10 tons from column went to DUNKERQUE to purchase all they can bring if possible — 14th Div. giving us 20 tons. JW	
	8		Supply Column returned from DUNKERK during night with 48 tons coal in 16 lorries. 3 trucks also to hand from mines trains on way. All units drew tanks today. JW	
	9		Four senior Officers left for England this morning to stiffen the 2nd Div, as per instruction from	

WAR DIARY
or
INTELLIGENCE SUMMARY
(Erase heading not required.)

Army Form C. 2118

Place	Date	Hour	Summary of Events and Information	Remarks and references to Appendices
Nov. 9th (Cont'd)			from H.Qrs. 90 remounts brought up from railhead and distributed to Units.	
	10, 11, 12		Chiefly occupied in dealing with coal – a large quantity up by rail, which had to be cleared each day – old dump stood too by VI Divisions. Had to dump on road temporarily. Arranged another temporary dump at A 21 – I.1. Pending completion of railway siding which is promised.	
	13		Visited all Companies. Bivs in a deplorable condition – all horses standing exposed of overwork – nine cases of horses newly shod having shoes torn off in the deep satisfying mud – horses thrown all night at night, except that horses cannot be groomed. Have suggested to A.Q. that horses should have a week's rest, otherwise, if present weather conditions continue we may have a sudden & heavy casualty list among the horses.	
	14		Routine day – many roads impassable for transport.	
	15, 16 + 17		Making various arrangements for reducing wheel traffic in billets, by pacting part of the train on the refilling road and finding other ground for the remainder – also arranged a double refill on the 19th that, to enable supplies to be cut up specially in time for the trenches daily.	
	18		Coal issues very heavy, and railway arrangements still unsatisfactory – no coal up for two	

Agts. Sind Train.
Dec 1915
vol. IX

WAR DIARY
or
INTELLIGENCE SUMMARY
(Erase heading not required.)

Army Form C. 2118

Instructions regarding War Diaries and Intelligence Summaries are contained in F.S. Regs, Part II. and the Staff Manual respectively. Title Pages will be prepared in manuscript.

Place	Date	Hour	Summary of Events and Information	Remarks and references to Appendices
Oct	1		Met D.A. & Q.M.G. VI Corps at new railhead and arranged several details for the first days issue on the 6th inst. - Also saw O.C. Labour Battalion re repairing road from HAM HOEK to POPERINGE - promised to take temporary measures to make it useable - at present it is hopeless.	
	2		Had conference of Transport & Supply Officers re details for supplies on the 6th. - also visited new railhead with J. a. Q. M. G. and found out what it is proposed to do re issuing. 50 tons of coal arrived.	
	3.		Saw D.A.Q.M.G. re scheme for 6th half - A.A. & Q.M.G. having notified certain roads being stopped, necessitates alterations in the scheme. Until definite information came to hand, and a final decision as to roads, the further consideration of first details is postponed.	
	4.		Further conference re issue on 6th inst. as yesterday. Final arrangements made.	
	5.			
	6.		Refill at new railhead - worked satisfactorily considering new method - Little delay in unloading from railway trucks to platform owing to train being at one end whilst	

1875. Wt. W593/826 1,000,000 4/15 J.B.C. & A. A.D.S.S./Forms/C. 2118.

WAR DIARY
or
INTELLIGENCE SUMMARY
(Erase heading not required.)

Army Form C. 2118

Place	Date	Hour	Summary of Events and Information	Remarks and references to Appendices
	6. (cont.)		necessitated supplies being manhandled to the other end – finished unloading at 9-30, when issuing began – all completed by 11-7 p.m.	
	7		Unloading at railhead began at 9-17 and completed by 9 p.m. Issuing began at 8-17 by 14th D. Coy & finished at 9-17 – 147th began 8-25, finished 9-25 – 49 Coy began 8-45, finished 9-50 – 146th began 9-50, finished 9-55 – all clear by 10 p.m. Orders received to exchange open "Sunbeam" car for closed "Wolseley" with 14th D. Division. Arranged to make transfer to-morrow at 8 A.M. p.m.	
	8		New refilling worked smoothly. Capt Simpson ordered to report to D.D.S & T re his application to transfer to Regular forces p.m.	
	9		Conference of Transport Officers re condition of Transport in case of move. All transport badly in need of repairs due to abnormal work and heavy roads. All artificers working long hours but are unable to keep pace with requirements – reported same to H.Q. p.m.	
	10		Visited I.O.M. with D.A.Q.M.G. & try to get some stores send on Colts, iron ran for refusing impro – cannot spare any p.m.	
	11/12		Routine work – Pack train 1 & hours late at railhead on 12th p.m.	

Army Form C. 2118

WAR DIARY
or
INTELLIGENCE SUMMARY
(Erase heading not required.)

Instructions regarding War Diaries and Intelligence Summaries are contained in F. S. Regs., Part II and the Staff Manual respectively. Title Pages will be prepared in manuscript.

Place	Date	Hour	Summary of Events and Information	Remarks and references to Appendices
	13		R.E. 465 Company of train practically isolated owing to state of ground – no wagon with supplies or stores can reach it – urged H.Q. for laying of tram line from main road, about 200 yards. J.B.	
	14		Ground at coal dump broken up, and wagons cannot get in. Applied for labour party to lay platform few days ago – urged same today – necessary sleepers are on the spot. French Tramway Fr 465 Coy. delivered and laid down – relieves the situation, and this Company now able to turn when necessary. J.B.	
	15			
	16		Visited all Companies – No 466 in the worst condition as regards ground. Horses in all companies in good dry standings, but badly in need of tracks to water – no material available. All supply work at railhead working smoothly. Beginning of unloading from railway trucks 7 A.M. – everything cleared away easily by 10 A.M.	
	17		Suggested to H.Q. that when the Divn. moves to rest area, the train horses stay in present billets when they have dry standings, instead of moving on to new ground which under present weather conditions will quickly be churned up. Cases of "mud fever" amongst horses rapidly increasing. J.B.	
	19		Very heavy bombardment in early morning in front, followed by air raid – many bombs dropped in & around POPERINGE – casualties & very few considering the number of	

1875 Wt. W593/826 1,000,000 4/15 J.B.C. & A. A.D.S.S./Forms/C. 2118.

WAR DIARY
or
INTELLIGENCE SUMMARY
(Erase heading not required.)

Army Form C. 2118

Place	Date	Hour	Summary of Events and Information	Remarks and references to Appendices
	19th (Cont)		of bombs dropped. Heavy firing during day, and enemy shelled POPERINGE from noon until night. JM.	
	20		Shelling of POPERINGE by enemy continued during whole of night until this morning. Intermittent firing during day & POPERINGE again shelled in the evening, all companies full of repairs for repairs. Coal again short, none up to-day JM.	
	21		No coal up to-day – last lot issued. 1 truck arrived late in evening. Arranged to borrow 20 tons from 14th Group if necessary. JM.	
	22		Complaints in about issue of maize in too great a proportion, causing sickness among horses. JM.	
	23		20 tons coal from WAUDRECQUE & 10 tons from minor – all issued to-day – none left for to-morrow. Going into question of repairs & transport, in anticipation of move. JM.	
	24		Serious increase in sickness amongst horses, chiefly mud fever & front bite – saw A.D.V.S. who hopes that with a change in weather conditions his Vet. Officers will be able to quickly change matters. 1 truck coal in, all issued JM.	
	25		Visited all companies and saw all ranks doing their best to make things cheerful & comfortable. No coal to-day JM.	

WAR DIARY
or
INTELLIGENCE SUMMARY
(Erase heading not required.)

Army Form C. 2118

Place	Date	Hour	Summary of Events and Information	Remarks and references to Appendices
Dec	26	5.0	Two of coal to hand – half issued. Issued fever amongst horses still rampant, but not on increase. Had preliminary discussion re coming move of the Division. /µ	
	27		Detailed instructions received for removal of 148th Inf. Brigade to rest area. Made all necessary arrangements re Supplies & Transport. /µ	
	28	3.0	Two of coal came this afternoon none in stock previous to its arrival. Arranging details for supplies & transport to 147th & 146th Brigade. 80 remounts advised to arrive at GODEWARSVELDE and 72 at CAISTRE to-day – the former advised late as arriving to-morrow – the 72 came in here 12 midnight owing to delay at CAISTRE. Advice received of further 95 remounts coming to-morrow. /µ	
	29		Divison block of traffic this morning owing to 16th & 49th Divisions dumps on same ground at same time, due to some mistake – arrangements made for 49th to refill on POPERINGE – PROVEN road to-morrow. 466th Brigade C.T. marched to STEENVORDE. /µ	
	30		M.T. 464 Coy marched to HOUTKERQUE after delivering supplies to Units. 2nd H.Q. also moved to ESQUELBECQ. /µ	

Army Form C. 2118

WAR DIARY
or
INTELLIGENCE SUMMARY

(Erase heading not required.)

Place	Date	Hour	Summary of Events and Information	Remarks and references to Appendices
	Sep 31		463 Coy and 465 Company marched to LEDRINGHAM and HERZEELE respectively after delivering supplies to their units. Clearing up camps and handing over to rear of D.A.C. H⁰Qrs preparing to move to LEDRINGHAM to-morrow A.M.	

Joseph C. Chambers
Lieut. Colonel,
Commanding 49th (W.R.) Divl. Train.

49 Div Train
Jan 1916
Vol X

WAR DIARY
or
INTELLIGENCE SUMMARY
(Erase heading not required.)

Army Form C. 2118

Place	Date	Hour	Summary of Events and Information	Remarks and references to Appendices
Jany 1916	1		H.Q. Train marched to new area — Whole train now settled down, and reported same to 2nd H.Q.	
	2		Visited 463 Nº 464 Companies — all satisfactory both thereof trains. 463 Coy had 1 horse casualty on route, managed to get it to destination, but destroyed by order of V.O. this morning.	
	3		Received instructions from D.A. + Q.M.G. VI Corps re inspection of Trains by Corps Commander on 5th Inst. — Visited 465 Company — satisfactory.	
	4 to 6th		Routine work — Visited DDS+T and DDR with D.A.Q.M.G. Inspected the 463-464 +465 Companies ft	
	7 to 9th		On partial sick list due to cold. Corps Commander inspected 463.464 +465 Cos. and expressed satisfaction.	
	10		Received orders for Companies to move at of LEDRINGHAM. owing to outbreak of Diphtheria.	
	11		Preparing to move — arranging billets for 464 Coy with its Brigade in WORMHOUDT and for 463 Coy in ESQUELBEC, ARNEKE.	

WAR DIARY
or
INTELLIGENCE SUMMARY
(Erase heading not required.)

Army Form C. 2118

Place	Date	Hour	Summary of Events and Information	Remarks and references to Appendices
Jan'y	12		Refill at WORMHOUDT and HERZEELE an hour later. 463 Coy marched to ARNEKE and billeted in area outside the town — 464 Coy also marched to billets in outskirts of WORMHOUDT. Train H.Q. moved to ESPUELBEC. W/c	
"	13		Arranged new billets for 465 Co: in outskirts of WORMHOUDT.	
"	14		465 Co: moved to new billets an afore. A.D.O's meeting at Office of D.D.S.&T. Second Army 5.P.M.	
"	15		148th Inf: Bde & 466 Co. arrived from HERZEELE. 147th Bde & 465 Co: moved from billets in HERZEELE to WORMHOUDT. 146th Bde & 464 Co. A.S.C. commenced march to CALAIS. Inspected billets of 463 & 465 Co's & left to night in BOLLEZEELE.	
"	16		Refilling for 146th Bde: & 464 Co: at BOLLEZEELE at 6-30 A.M. after loading wagons this Co: marched with its Brigade to ZUTEKERQUE & billeted for the night.	
"	17		Refilling for 146th Bde: 464 Co: at ZUTEKERQUE at 6.30 A.M. after loading wagons this Co: marched with its Brigade to CALAIS. Conference of Co: Commanders. Adjt. S.S.O. & D.A.Q.M.G. Div: arranging the system of Supply Transport in the event of a sudden move forward. Interview with C.R.A. re above subject.	

WAR DIARY
or
INTELLIGENCE SUMMARY

(Erase heading not required.)

Army Form C. 2118

Place	Date	Hour	Summary of Events and Information	Remarks and references to Appendices
	18		Inspection of 464 Co. by Adjutant at CALAIS. JCA	
	19-27th		Routine work - inspected 463 Co: all satisfactory. JCA	
	26-27		Routine work - Inspected all Companies during this period JCA	
	28		Returned from leave. JCA	
	29		Mostly in Office. JCA	
	30		Army Commander intimated that the Division is moving in few days. JCA Divisional Commander distributed known to Officers mess in the Divn at WORMHOUDT. Divisional Commander inspected horses of 463, 465 & 466 Companies JCA. all satisfactory. Discussed details of move	
	31		Visited refilling point at HERZEELE- all satisfactory. Discussed details of move with D.A.Q.M.G. and S.S.O. JCA	

Joseph C. Allsopp
Lieut. Colonel,
Commanding 49th (W.R.) Divl. Train.

CONFIDENTIAL.

War Diary of.

Lieut Col J. C. Chambers. C.B. V.D. Commdg: 49th.(WR) Divl Train

From. Feb: 1st: 1916.   To Feb. 29. 1916.

(Volume XI).

Army Form C. 2118

WAR DIARY
or
INTELLIGENCE SUMMARY.
(Erase heading not required.)

Instructions regarding War Diaries and Intelligence Summaries are contained in F.S. Regs., Part II. and the Staff Manual respectively. Title Pages will be prepared in manuscript.

Place	Date	Hour	Summary of Events and Information	Remarks and references to Appendices
1916 Feb.	1		Arranging details for removal, as conversation with supplies for the Division which is going during the 2nd, 3rd, 4th & 5th. Inst.	
	2		147th Brigade entrained at ESQUELBEC for AMIENS. & 148th Brigade entrained at CALAIS for same district.	
	3		Div: HQ & 146 Brigade entrained travel during night to new area.	
	4		All A.S.C. Companies settled in new area &billets. Arranged details for supplying of Units & refilling points.	
	5		Removed 464 Co. & 465 Co. to PICQUIGNY to be nearer the Units for supplies. Also 466 Co. to LE MESGE. Altered refilling points to more suitable positions and advised H.Q. of same.	
	6		Visited new area which will be occupied by Division in a few days.	
	7		S.S.O. & Asst. at new area arranging details for billeting companies. 29th Am. Park came on to our strength for rations from to-day.	
	8 & 9		Routine work — refilling altered each day, owing to Divn moving.	
	10		146th Brigade marched to PIERREGOT & 148th Brigade to PICQUENY.	
	11		148th Brigade do do do – Baggage train companies accompany their respective Brigades. Part of H.Q. Company also marched to PICQUENY. to accompany Divl. Troops to-morrow.	

Army Form C. 2118

WAR DIARY
or
INTELLIGENCE SUMMARY
(Erase heading not required.)

Instructions regarding War Diaries and Intelligence Summaries are contained in F. S. Regs., Part II. and the Staff Manual respectively. Title Pages will be prepared in manuscript.

Place	Date	Hour	Summary of Events and Information	Remarks and references to Appendices
Feb	12		147. Brigade marched to destination; 147. Bde/Sigs & 7 HQ Coy — all well. Remainder of HQ Coy marched to PICQUENY. Jr. PIERREGOT, also Jr. 7 second half of HQ Coy	
	13		147. Coy & half of HQ Coy marched to destination — all well. second half of HQ Coy marched to PIERREGOT. Jr.	
	14		Remainder of HQ Coy reached destination all well — Train now complete in our area. Visited all billets detailed to. Jr.	
	15		All men billets inspected and various alterations made. Jr.	
	16		Routine work Jr.	
	17		Visited refilling points. Made alterations in positions which were to exposed. Also attended Army H.Q. to see D.D.Q.S+T. Jr.	
	18		Refilling points again changed — discussed same with D.A.Q.M.G. Jr.	
	19 & 20		Routine work. Endeavouring to obtain billets for 28 horses + 16 men in SENLIS, engaged in carrying R.E. stores to shorten daily journey which is excessive & affecting horses severely. Jr.	
	21		More transport required for loading store to tr. R.E. — arranging with D.A.Q.M.G. to get civilian transport — part promised, and endeavours being made to augment from train & other known is difficult owing to number of sick horses. Jr.	
	22		Got 3 promises for Civilian transport, which however was later withdrawn — The inhabitants show no disposition to help. Now trying to hire wagons alone, and arrange for artillery horses for same. Jr.	
	23 & 24		Made other arrangements for dispensing with civilian transport. Routine work Jr.	

Army Form C. 2118

WAR DIARY
or
INTELLIGENCE SUMMARY
(Erase heading not required.)

Place	Date	Hour	Summary of Events and Information	Remarks and references to Appendices
	Feb. 25		Snow fell put fresh - roads bad, and transport much interfered with. All work completed but mostly late. Convoy of wagons with forage from railhead to VADENCOURT reached destination at 11.0. P.M. 5 hours late. Having been out 17 hours — roads very difficult this places required 16 horses to 1 wagon. ft.	
	26		M.T. Column withdrawn owing to thaw. 20 teams came from R.F.A. units to assist — made arrangements with 93 wagons to load up at railhead to-morrow — 16 extra wagons sent by H/Q Sec. to draw fuel from railhead to-morrow. 40 wagons complete expected from reserve park now not available. Horses taken from yesterday's Convoy resting to-day. ft.	
	27		All supplies from railhead to dump carried by H.T. — 123 wagons used. All work complete except 8 tons of ordnance stores which was left over. ft.	
	28		Supplies in H.T. wagons parked overnight at dump. Off loaded at 9.0. A.M. & proceeded to railhead, and again brought up supplies to dump. All work completed but 6 tons of ordnance stores and 10 tons coal left till to-morrow. 84 wagons used for supplies — 15 for ordnance — 3 for mails & 21 for coal.	
	29		Supplies and all surplus fuel brought up from railhead — 149 loads of ordnance stores taken to SENLIS — 29 loads of fuel taken to dump in WARLOY. 92 loads of supplies and 4 loads of mails. ft.	

Joseph C. Arnett Lieut. Colonel,
Commanding 49th (W.R.) Divl. Train.

CONFIDENTIAL

WAR DIARY

of

Lieut. Col. J. C. Chambers. Commdg. 49th Bn'l: Train.

From: 1-3-16.   To 31-3-16.

(Volume 12.)

WAR DIARY
or
INTELLIGENCE SUMMARY
(Erase heading not required.)

Army Form C. 2118

Place	Date 1916	Hour	Summary of Events and Information	Remarks and references to Appendices
March	1		All supplies brought up from railhead by train. Pack train 4½ hours late. D.D.R. inspected horses which units unable to cart.	
	2		Routine work. Received orders to prepare to move on 4, 5, & 6th.	
	3 & 4		Refilling point removed to West of WARLOY, and have changed. Considerable alteration in supply details owing to moving of troops. Instructions received to move train to MIRVAUX on 6th.	
	5		Arranging billets at MIRVAUX - visited railhead - Orders received to move train to SENLIS to-morrow p.m.	
	6		Train H.Q. moved to SENLIS. Nos. 463 & 466 Companies unable to move to MIRVAUX owing to other troops being there, so moved to WARLOY.	
	7		Nos 463 & 466 Companies moved from WARLOY to MIRVAUX - Visited refilling points.	
	8		Instructions received to move to MIRVAUX to-morrow p.m.	
	9		Train H.Q. moved to MIRVAUX. Conference with all Officers re details of probable entraining scheme. — double refill to-morrow, after which Train supply wagons will push full each night for Brook refill tank place, and supplies for 12th parked in supply wagons in Train lines for supplies delivered to Units & refitted 6.0 P.M. for 13th Consumption. Saw A.A. & Q. M.G. in reference to irregularity of coal supplied. Also pointed out the very inferior quality of coal supplied, which causes higher consumption. Baths, laundries & hospitals take a considerable quantity of coal daily, but the	
	10			
	11			

WAR DIARY
or
INTELLIGENCE SUMMARY
(Erase heading not required.)

Army Form C. 2118

Instructions regarding War Diaries and Intelligence Summaries are contained in F. S. Regs., Part II. and the Staff Manual respectively. Title Pages will be prepared in manuscript.

Place	Date	Hour	Summary of Events and Information	Remarks and references to Appendices
	March 11 (Cont)		This is not allowed for in quantity sent up to railhead. W. Routine. W.	
	12			
	13		Coal supply coming more regularly – visited ACHEUX railhead with view of establishing a coal dump – 30 tons received to-day. W.	
	14		Arranged with R.T.O. at ACHEUX for coal dump, and for an issuing staff to proceed there. All coal will now come to ACHEUX and requirements for CONTAY when a store is still kept, will be transported by road. W.	
	15		Routine – Refilling hour changed from 6.0 P.M. to 12.0 midday. W.	
	16			
	17 to 20			
	21		Routine work – Visited railhead, Refilling points – gave instructions re cleaning of wagons, which is hampered by scarcity of water, more particularly in MIRVAUX when 250 horses have to be watered from two wells. W. Took observations on the above two wells – it seems clear that they both tap the same pocket of water, which appears to be practically inexhaustible. Inspected No 2 Coy; billets & equipment, all satisfactory. W.	
	23		Inspected No 3 Coy; billets, wagons &c – horses in the open, but with top cover. Intimation from H.Q. (Q) of probable move in 3 days. W.	
	24		24 Remounts arrived at railhead, & be distributed to-morrow – also advised that 145 more will arrive to-morrow. W.	
	25		Remounts arrived yesterday distributed – 145 others came to railhead specially distributed – 66 H.D. horses should have been sent to railhead by R.F.A. but only 50 went, due to some misunderstanding. W.	

Army Form C. 2118

WAR DIARY
or
INTELLIGENCE SUMMARY
(Erase heading not required.)

Instructions regarding War Diaries and Intelligence Summaries are contained in F. S. Regs., Part II. and the Staff Manual respectively. Title Pages will be prepared in manuscript.

Place	Date	Hour	Summary of Events and Information	Remarks and references to Appendices
Mar	26		Inspected billets of 67 H.Q. + 466 Companies. Visited refilling point at RUBEMPRÉ.	
	27		Orders received to move to new area on 29th — arranging supply details and re-grouping units for that date.	
	28		Making arrangements for moving to-morrow — Met DA+QMG X. Corps with DAQMG 49th Divn at FORCEVILLE.	
	29		Bulk of Divn moved West — move carried out without casualties.	
	30		Visited refilling point at VARGNIES — also H.Q. Divn re arrival details. Coal dump at CONTAY closed and now at pond at RUBEMPRÉ.	
	31		Routine.	

Joseph C. Chambers
Lieut. Colonel,
Commanding 49th (W.R.) Divl. Train.

49

W R Dio Train

Vol XIII

WAR DIARY or INTELLIGENCE SUMMARY

Army Form C. 2118

Place	Date	Hour	Summary of Events and Information	Remarks and references to Appendices
April	1		H.Q. (A) no special routine matters – visited IVth Army H.Q. with D.A.Q.M.G. No fuel at railhead today.	
	2,3 & 4		Routine work – Still no fuel at railhead. Drew up coal from "Army" dump at CARNAPLES. H.Q. 466 Coy. marched to NAOURS, and remainder of 145 Inf. Brigade to TALMAS.	
	5		No 464 Coy marched to VIGNACOURT together with 1 Batt{n} & Bty H.Q. – remainder of Brigade stopping in present positions.	
	6		Visited refilling point at VIGNACOURT, and inspected 464 Coy billets & transport.	
	7		Inspected 466 Coy billets, transport etc.	
	9 to 15		Routine work – 2 motor cars withdrawn from Coys, to be replaced by bicycles. The two cars sent to Corps H.Q. – Orders received that all T.F. units army abroad are to be on "New Armies" establishment Part VII-1915.	
	16		Stock of coal at ACHEUX handed over to 36th Div{n}. (140 tons) Stock at CARNAPLES gradually increasing – now about 70 tons.	
	18		Inspected clothing equipment of No 463 Coy.	
	19		do No 465 & 466 Coy.	
	21		Making arrangements for supplies to be drawn by units, during 12 days, whilst train men are being inoculated for typhoid. Commencing on 24th – 25% at a time.	
	22		Inspected the clothing equipment of No 464 Coy. – All horses standing very bad, owing to weather.	

Army Form C. 2118

WAR DIARY
or
INTELLIGENCE SUMMARY
(Erase heading not required.)

Instructions regarding War Diaries and Intelligence Summaries are contained in F. S. Regs, Part II. and the Staff Manual respectively. Title Pages will be prepared in manuscript.

Place	Date	Hour	Summary of Events and Information	Remarks and references to Appendices
April 1916	24		All Companies inspected by G.O.C.	
	25 - 28		Routine Work - Personnel of Train being inoculated against paratyphoid - 25% every two days - supplies being drawn by units in meantime, with puppy wagons &c.	
	29		Going into several matters in regard to 464 Coy, which are not satisfactory &c.	
	30		Routine work &c.	

Joseph C. Chambers
Lieut. Colonel,
Commanding 49th (W.R.) Divl. Train.

Vol 14

Confidential

War Diary
of
Lieut Col J. C. Chambers + Major C. B. Haigh
Commanding: 49th (WR) Divl Train.

From 1-5-16.   To 31-5-16.

(Volume 14.)

Army Form C. 2118

WAR DIARY
or
INTELLIGENCE SUMMARY
(Erase heading not required.)

Place	Date	Hour	Summary of Events and Information	Remarks and references to Appendices
1916 May	1		Inspected books and accounts of 463, 465 & 466 Coys. W.	
	2		do 464 Coy.	
	4		Advice received of 29 remounts coming to-morrow to railhead - arranged for party to take over, and for distribution. W.	
	5		Arranged for horses & personnel who have been drawing supplies during introduction of train driver, to return to their units on the 7th inst. when introduction of Train personnel will be completed. 29 remounts received from railhead - went by own transport up - several being sent straight in to M.V.S., and several others not yet fit even yet sent up - several being put to work for some time. W.	
	7		31 Remounts (Chargers and riders) arrived at railhead and brought in to 463 Coy lines. 6 G.S. wagons, 12 H.D horses & 6 drivers being baggage supply wagons for new Batteries & carts received from Base. W.	
	8		Remounts which arrived yesterday duly distributed to-day. Baggage wagons handed over to our Batteries. W.	
	9		Major Haig arrived from England to take over command of the Train - my appointment terminating on May 28 - A.W.	
	10 to 13		Visited all Companies with Major Haig, preparatory to handing over command of Train. W.	
	14		Major Haig took over command of the Train. W.	

WAR DIARY or INTELLIGENCE SUMMARY

Army Form C. 2118

Place	Date	Hour	Summary of Events and Information	Remarks and references to Appendices
1916 May	14		Took over command of the train from Lt Col Chawston. C.B. Posted all Refilling Points Bn.	
	15		Received 18 H.D. Horses from 483 D.A.C. (Remainder) B.H. Arranged to unposted 1st line Transport 146 Inf Bde R.H. Reported AA & QMG B.A.	
	16		Inspected 1st line Transport 146 Bde B.H. Col Chawston departed for England 10AM. to AA & QMG. BA. Copy of orders issued re quick move & dumping of surplus stores, sent into HQs Division 7PM.	
	17		Drew up report on Transport. Arranged details of further inspection 10AM. while on receiving orders to entrain BM	
	18		Discussed settled system of supplying	
	19		Visited H.Q. re the Training Scheme. Saw L.A.D.M.S. officer re Field Amb. personnel. Arranged for inspection of 1 Amb. 1st line Transport 1st line Transport 10AM "Field Rest" to 146 Inf Bde also the Field Ambulance report to Field Rest the Machine Gun. B.A. Attended lecture by the M.O. B.A. into ADMS & Bde HdQn. B.A. Offered all Refilling Points. Made arrangements	
	20		Interview with AA & QMB re entraining scheme. Inspected station for L.A.B.C.Q. in re special car of the Train during the Hot-weather. BH.	
	21		Interview with AADG MS to discussed	B.A.C Train Wagons & Entraining Point of the 146 Bde groups. arrangements also arranged for attendance of the Refilling Point of the New D.A.C Train for Wagons for the New D.A.C Train. Visited C.R. A.S. Office Re actg Hay Magazine 7.A.B yhe Rest Relief Service R.M. Attended Divine Service with the H.Q 1 C Chaplain Hood.

WAR DIARY or INTELLIGENCE SUMMARY

Army Form C. 2118

Place	Date	Hour	Summary of Events and Information	Remarks and references to Appendices
May	22		Inspected pack trans transport of 148th Inf. Bde. 5th Batt. Y.L.I, 5th K.O.Y.L.I. Brigade H.Q. Brigade Machine Gun Company. Visited Divl H.Q. & had interview with D.A.Q.M.G. D.M.	
	23		Inspected 1st Line Transport of 6th Batt. K.O.Y.L.I. & 3rd Field Ambulance. Inspected all Ranks of 465 Co. Dvl. Train in marching order. Visited Co. Rflls. B.M.	
	24		Inspected 1st Line transport 4th Batt. Y.L.I. Regt. Had all Company Commanders of from H. Q. discussed advisability of having each Company officer attached to the Brigade Supply officer, for a course of instruction in Supply work, for one month; this was arranged. B.M.	
	25		Inspected 1st Line Transport of R. 245th (N. R) Brigade R.F.A. 246th 247 & 248th. Visited Co. Rflls. R.H.	
	26		Inspected 1st Line Transport of H.Q. gns. Co. Dvl Train in marching order. Visited H.Q. Hy Regms. re: tie logs & information re moves. B.H. Interview with Q.A. Hy Regms. re.	
	27		Inspected 1st Line Transport 7th W.R. 9th Infantry 464 L.o Enjam. Dramer held & Inspected all Company Rflls. Visited new Refilling point 148th Bde. R.H. marching over.	
	28		Visited all Refilling point li, made arrangements to for a more suitable position for Ho 147th Bde. Deamps. B.H.	
	29		Inspected 1st Line Transport 147th Brigade H.Q. gns & Hq Co. 5th Batt. D.R. Reg.l. 6th Batt. D.R. Rgt. & Brigade Machine Gun Co. R.H.	

Army Form C. 2118

WAR DIARY
or
INTELLIGENCE SUMMARY
(Erase heading not required.)

Instructions regarding War Diaries and Intelligence Summaries are contained in F.S. Regs., Part II. and the Staff Manual respectively. Title Pages will be prepared in manuscript.

Place	Date	Hour	Summary of Events and Information	Remarks and references to Appendices
May	30		Arranged for 463" CO to report to 147th Inf Bde for march across supporting the three of the Brigade. Made out fresh Supply Groups sheet. Came to Divl H.Q. for orders. BH	
	31		465/294 marched to HERISSART under Brigade orders. Buried new Refilling point in forward area to relieve CEY in trench lines in evening. Arranged the new Refilling point in forward area to the 147 Brigade & put our mile into the Supply Groups. BH	Benne a Haugh Major A.S.C.? Comdg. 49 Div. Train

49

Vol 15

CONFIDENTIAL.

War Diary
of
Lieut Col C B Haigh, Commanding 49th. (WR) Divl Train,

From June 1st. 1916.

To June 30th. 1916.

(Volume 15).

WAR DIARY or INTELLIGENCE SUMMARY

Army Form C. 2118

Place	Date	Hour	Summary of Events and Information	Remarks and references to Appendices
June	1		Visited Field Post Office. Visited 464 L° Train Horse Lines at Stable Farm.	
	2		Inspected 1/2 Field Amb. Horse Lines. 1st Line Transport also 1/2 Field L° R.E. Visited CANDAS, with a view to arranging Rest House & canteen for Divn. on its leave. Officer from HQ made arrangements for attention to it.	
	3		Visited 466 Coy A.S.C. Horse Lines at Stable Farm. Visited 464 Coy A.S.C. Horse Lines to inspect mixing of fields. B.H.	
			Arranged for the Royal No 4 2.L. Regt Jefferson to report to O.C. Train 364 Divn. in connection with the decamping of their reserve rations.	
	5		Rifts acute connected with the Supply Column to 364 Inf. Fntg. Shoe & Paul Emit. Bt. LR. Brigades & Regt Jefferson proceeded by the R.E. Diray Shoes. Visited R.E. Reserve Dump. Transport Reserve Dump. & 3rd Divn Res. Rations in Pork Reserve Dump.	
			Arranged for messing stores, equipment, tentage &c for Rest. Camp interviewed the R.E. & A.D.E.S. re the matter.	
	6		Visited Div. Sig. Co. Corps Cyclist L.D. & Div. HQ 9S 1st Line Transport. 9S° Infantry detachment in marching order visited hotels.	
			Visited Supply Column of HQ 9 Coys A.S.C. Horse Lines Visited 466 Coy A.S.C. Horse Lines.	
	7		Inspected 4 L.N.R. Regt. 1st Line Transport in forward area. Visited O.C. 364 The Train re the arrangements to of reserve Dumps.	
			Visited the forward area. Visited Dumping Point. B.H.	
	8		R. Head. & Dumping Point. B.H.	
			Visited Div HQ 4 Judges in Lorries Coats. Broke & Harn. Position of Dump informed area. Ordered for 36 Inf Bde. by the 36th Divn. without informing O.C. 466 Coy A.R.C. B.H.	
	9		Inning of Baggage Wagon 14/9 Inf. Bde. to 11th Bde.	
			Interview H.Q. re Harrassers going out of the Division. Inspected 11° 9/ Coy at Stable Farm. C.C. Sgt. Wheeler unfortunately broke her Leg. B.H.	
	10		Visited Div. Troops & Field Sanit. Arranged for 466 Coy A.S.C. tomorrow to remove to forward area. Interview H.Q. re grouping of units in forward area. R.H. on the 11th inst.	

Army Form C. 2118

WAR DIARY
or
INTELLIGENCE SUMMARY
(Erase heading not required.)

Instructions regarding War Diaries and Intelligence Summaries are contained in F. S. Regs., Part II. and the Staff Manual respectively. Title Pages will be prepared in manuscript.

Place	Date	Hour	Summary of Events and Information	Remarks and references to Appendices
June	11		Lt Reynolds returned from attachment to 36th Ind Train. Attended Conference at Div. H.Q'rs re Movement to forward area. B.H.	
	12		Inspected 1st Line Transport of D.A.C. B.H.	
	13		Attended Conference at Q. Received Area Accelerated Train Z.O.1 Commanders received.	
	14		Attended Conference at Q. Received movement order made arrangements for the Reponing of the Div. when concentrated in the Reserve Area. B.H.	
	15		Arranged for the refilling points in Reserve Area. Issued Div. Troop Rouls. Refilling Points arranged for. Issued march order for H.Q. & 65 Ambs Trans Move on 16th of	
	16		From A.D.S. Lafolly Aveyron to H.Q Train & 46 Zd.Z.O.A.S.C. Move to R.F. Rugot. 464 Zd.Z.O.A.S.C. Move to Resuve Area B.H. Divided from Refilling Point at 1 R.H.B. EMPRIE, No 1 Group & No 4 Group, on Killage. all Billets allotted by divisional inspector by Serial 463.Co — Appointed Lt. Ae Aelq'r as Town Major. B.H.	
	17		Interview at Q. elevis t up the Point. The Facing Cuff. ca at R Hend. Visited 464.Co. Hor. Linn. Mallil. Took Orderly Room Interior area. Visited 466.Co in the Forward Area. Horse Lines Matild. Took Orderly Room Visited 32nd Inf. Train. made arrangements for future R.R.s in forward area division the Railhead & Cuffs quarter generally. B.H.	
	18		Visited both R.R.s in morning. Divis Ervace in evening. H.Q.188 & 1/2 F. Ambulance attended B.H.	
	19		Visited D.A.D.O.S. re Field Forges & Panels for Supply Column. B.H.	

WAR DIARY
or
INTELLIGENCE SUMMARY
(Erase heading not required.)

Army Form C. 2118

Place	Date	Hour	Summary of Events and Information	Remarks and references to Appendices
	20		Made Reconnaissance of by Roads in forward area. Chose site for Divisional Transport lines. Pegged out same. Fixed Division posts & on the Roads chosen. Drew Motor & plan of same & sent up to Q. Visited No 464 & 2 Horse lines with the S.O.C. who explained later points at the improvement in the horses. B.H.	
	21		Interview with Q. re Rusheed & Refilling arrangements. Fixed time up. R.H.	
	22		465 Coy moved into reserve area. Billeted at Toutencourt, arranged for the collection of Remains from Rusheed. BH. Capt. Scott & 2/Leuven. officers to transfer to R.F.E. forwarded the application. BH.	
	23		New R.P. at Varloy started. arranged to move 148th Bde R.F.A group for the arrival. 465 Coy withdrawn into Reserve Area. Arranged for all transport to be off roads between 9AM & 2PM. allied Refilling time to correspond, informed all concerned. Visited Q. R?.	
	24		Interview Q. re Supplys arrangements made for the move of the Division. Caused by Trenches, made arrangements to 36th Div'l Train as relieving the Guards left on Dumford Cutter. BH.	
	25		Interview Q. re change of loading arrangements. Col Rusheid. made arrangements accordingly Visited 465 Coy Horse lines Billets at Contay. BH.	
	26		Visited all Billets in Forward Area. Arranged for 209 Horse lines. Chase R.P. for 2/ Gmt. Interview Q. re Divisional move. Interview A.R.M. re assault on Dump Rents. BH.	

WAR DIARY
or
INTELLIGENCE SUMMARY
(Erase heading not required.)

Army Form C. 2118

Place	Date	Hour	Summary of Events and Information	Remarks and references to Appendices
June	27		Train moved to Forward Area, Forceville. Visited all Billets & Horse Lines. Visited new R.P. arranged for Major Lines. All Coys concentrated A.B.H.	
	28		Arranged for Train to load at R.HQ in place of S.C. Interviewed all Coy. Commanders re the Non movement of Suffy. arranged for letter. R.P. orders issued accordingly. B.M.	
	29		Train loaded at R.E. H.Q first time. Suffys. Train + Reserve Cate. Refilled on Company lines in lieu of a Scale of Mules. Visited Refilling Points. Interview with all O.C. Coys. re Traffic routes, Bicycles, Messages to the Reynolds to ascertain the Agst. of the Capt. Mounts to take up Suffy. Work. B.M.	
	30		Changed R.P. from Roan to Mesnil. Weather having improved. Suffy. Train arrived very late at R.E. H.Q., 2 Batts 4685 L.H. Crews Supplies in y.s. to first train RHQ.	

Bernard Haigh Lt Col
Commanding 49th Div Train

30/6/16

D.A.G.
G.H.Q.
   3rd Echelon.

Secret.

Herewith my War Diary for the month of July; please;

Bevan o Haugh
Lieut. Colonel,
Commanding 49th (W.R.) Divl. Train.

31/7/16.

Vol 16

CONFIDENTIAL.

War Diary

of

Lt Col G Hugh Commanding 49th. (WR) Divl Train:

From July 1st. 1916.   To July 31st. 1916.

(Volume 16)

WAR DIARY
or
INTELLIGENCE SUMMARY

(Erase heading not required.)

Army Form C. 2118

Place	Date	Hour	Summary of Events and Information	Remarks and references to Appendices
July	1		Interview Q. re materials, Traffic Routes, & time for using same. B.M. Inspected Divisional Transport Lines. V.S. Interviewed T.O. M.L.F. Re Transport Officers re starting wagons & horses etc. Train without rations. Inspected Baggage Wagons starts in by train G. B.M.	
	2		Inspected Railhead. — Suppr Train still very late. Dr. Train much delayed in consignees. Inspected a bogged Wagon of M.P. L/Bde. Interviewed C.O. 3rd Mountain Y.A.Co for his Baggage Wagon to return to his Regl. Lines. Arranged for supplies to be Sent back moving from Lines, as to delay of Supplies previous night. B.M. He gathered Rations. Inspected Regl Transport as they proceeded to the Mule in trenches. B.M.	
	3		Making arrangements to examine R.E.'s asked to help up on the communication Pipes. M.F. Arrived at Railhead. B.M. "Coaling horse". Distributed Rations G. B.M. Picked R.P.	
	4		Used Railhead at earlier charge times with the 36th Division. B.M. Managed with Q. to get Rock Train up earlier. Change to V.S.	
	5		Interviewed Q. to arrange change of Road for Supplies to go to V.S. Inspected 466 Cy Office Books. Thanx B. Mels. B.M. Reconnoitred new road to V.S. Instructed O.E. Corp to continue old route. Inclement weather. Was visited by A.A. & Q.M.G. re Supply position, showed him copy of Ref. orders given out in accordance to his wishes, received from him on the subject. B.M.	
	6			

WAR DIARY or INTELLIGENCE SUMMARY

Army Form C. 2118.

Hour, Date, Place	Summary of Events and Information	Remarks and references to Appendices
July 6	Inspected 463 & 464 Coys. Offices, Cook & Pickets. BH	
" 7	Interview O.C. re making up of Reserve Dumps to supp Returns, also to the 36th Divl R.F.A being stationed by the Train. Inspected loads to Y.S. issued orders to take to track. Found the Cloas [Class] woods to Y.S. issued orders to take to track across the field close to Ammunition Dump. BH	
" 8	Interview O.C. re Forward Reserve Dumps. He wired O.C. 465 Coy Train to take over acc 36th Divl R.F.A. Baggage & Supply Wagons. 2 Officers & O.R. from 36th Train engaged in on unloading with the interim unit O.C. 2nd DT [Divl Train] Coys & latterly in Coran? & not in Covien Droom & acting fatigues BH	
" 9	Interview O.C. made arrangements to be reinforced also 328 D.A.C. Offices going to Brea and Train. BH. Wired R. Heads. BLG. Received instructions from 2Lt P.B. Slingsby to return to by land issued orders accordingly. Capt F H Shaw reported for duty from 13 H.T. Depot H.M.R.C. posted him to 463 Coy to act under the perm OC as assistant transport officer BH	
" 10	Interview O.C. re Offices duties. Reserve Dumps &c. Slingsby left for England. Capt G.C. Storehouse reported to duty from 13.H.T.D. Posted him to 466 Coy to assist present OC. Reinforcements arrived & are with Coys.	

WAR DIARY or INTELLIGENCE SUMMARY

Army Form C. 2118

(Erase heading not required.)

Place	Date	Hour	Summary of Events and Information	Remarks and references to Appendices
July	11		Interview O. Visited R. Points. Received instructions that Lt. Mackley was to report to the M.T. School at Gt. Omega. J.S.O.I. called & gave instructions re the reinforcements. Made arrangements accordingly. BM.	
"	12		Interview O. Made arrangements to deal with unfit Reinforcements. Appointed Capt. Shaw as Town Major in place of Lt. Reynolds. Inspected 485 Coy Office Books & Billets. Visited R. Points. Visited Horse Lines of 36th & 2nd R.F.A. Despatched Reinforcements to their respective Bdes. BM.	
"	13		Interview O. Received instructions to form 1 Motor Cart. to French Batty. 4.5 inch. Motor Cart. despatched to D.A.C. at Hedauville for the Batty. Arranged for 4 G.S. Wagons to call at Town Majors Office on return journey. BM.	
"	14		Interview O. Made arrangements for the expresses made: being checked in the office. Visited all R. Points. Checked to alter position of same, views action accordingly. BM.	
"	15		Interview O. Received instructions that we are the checking of Reinforcements to Major Parker. Refilled at New R.P. BM.	
"	16		Interview O. Handed over the Reinforcements to Major Parker. Church Parade. all 4 coys attended. BM.	
"	17		Interview O. Routine work. BM.	

Army Form C. 2118.

WAR DIARY
or
INTELLIGENCE SUMMARY.
(Erase heading not required.)

Hour, Date, Place	Summary of Events and Information	Remarks and references to Appendices
July 18.	Interview O.R. Troops in FORCEVILLE & O.C. Train from 6.30 a.m. O.C. Troops arranged for their passages & to put on to Train Major & O.C. Rail Transport Schools R.M. Visited the R. Rowels B.H. Interview arranging to carry passengers from W.O. to English Patrol Train P.M. Left report with Lieut Roth.	
19.	Interview MAYOR of the New Train Established received recruits to keep the Engines 3 F C's going in Green Station work being done by Transport & men sent to storm & Co's unload supplies convert to also in evening.	
	Moving AEDAUVILLE Close Route. Received orders accordingly. B.M. Visited all supplies points. B.M.	
20.	Interview O.C. Wagged orders cancelling orders. Laws Hardenville from road. Received orders accordingly. Recommended new road. & got consent of the R.F.A. & from the C. de F. at 132	
21.	Interview O. Renche noch. officer & Co. Harrison taken by the R.F.C.	
22.	Interview O. also I.D.S.T. Reserve Army, re Trsp. Shun. returns to R.M.	
23.	Interview O. Head I.D.S.T. Reserve Army to alter party. Interview 50% Front Truck Yppend, allowed and O. R.T.O. Train	

Army Form C. 2118.

WAR DIARY
or
INTELLIGENCE SUMMARY.
(Erase heading not required.)

Instructions regarding War Diaries and Intelligence Summaries are contained in F. S. Regs., Part II. and the Staff Manual respectively. Title pages will be prepared in manuscript.

Hour, Date, Place	Summary of Events and Information	Remarks and references to Appendices
July 23 (to 14)	Inspected all 2043 Horse lines at Stable Hour from Inspected all feeds & Sam the issue of same. 13H/ Forwarded R.L. Hade application for transfer to R.7.C. 2pt R.7.C. 10/	
24	Interview with O. the 101st to SENLIS being discussed. Recommended new road be made beyond MEDAVILLE, shelled too heavily at present. the road was inspected this morning & reported by Capt Preston. Forwarded to 464 L.Q. B.H. that left the road in report from the scene in place of Harrison. Postal items to 464 L.Q. B.H.	
25	Interview O. Printed Dispensed Transport Lines. R.H.	
26	Interview O. Mounted Repatton of Pouls, Hoorner and horse lines 4th 35 L.D. coming up in place of H.D. Rgt Inspected the 35 H.D. who returned to No 2 Armored Remount Depôt B.H.	
27	Interview O. discussed the question of Pulling of the Mounted detch. Rifles in H.Reel Area aut. C.T.S. Column for Ra-Town	

WAR DIARY
or
INTELLIGENCE SUMMARY.
(Erase heading not required.)

Army Form C. 2118.

Hour, Date, Place	Summary of Events and Information	Remarks and references to Appendices
July 27. (Contd)	3 S. L. Ds arrived from Rouen to replace some numbers of M.D. inspected them & distributed them to the four Companies 17 to H/Qm 20 & 6 each other 20/. B.H.	
" 28.	Interview Q. Inspected H.Q. & No 2 Advanced Remount Depot. Ending 27. Strength B as instructed by O.D.i. B.H.	
" 29	Interview Q. Made arrangements & reconnoitred ground & positions for train horses to & take to in the west of the village being shell'd. used orders accordingly. B.H.	
" 30	Interview Q. Routine work. Work commenced on Ingant for the No. 5 Draining Station. B.H.	
" 31	Interview Q. Inspected the new Water Trough. to Ingant. Yesterdays B.H.	

Bernard Haigh
Lt Col
Commanding 49 A.Vet.Train
31/7/16

49

49 Div Tran
Vol 17

CONFIDENTIAL

War Diary
of
Lieut Col C.B. Haigh Commanding 49th (WR) Divl Train.

From: Aug: 1st 1916.   To August 31st 1916.

(Volume 17.)

Army Form C. 2118.

WAR DIARY
or
INTELLIGENCE SUMMARY.
(Erase heading not required.)

Instructions regarding War Diaries and Intelligence Summaries are contained in F. S. Regs., Part II. and the Staff Manual respectively. Title pages will be prepared in manuscript.

Hour, Date, Place	Summary of Events and Information	Remarks and references to Appendices
August 1st	Inspected all C of S at Railhead. Horses, Harness & Wagons of Supply Section. Baggage Wagons of units returned. Visited Motor Trough at watering time. Quite fine. Urgent representation to R.E. about the property of motor & urgent representation to [?] 13H	
2nd	Interview Q. Inspector Park Roy late unit to Portwater of Reg. to M.A.G.M.E. Van led Dug but at Steenie & took Cpt Cameron to take order. Arranged to have men [?] from R.E. 13H	
3rd	Interview Q. Inspected note through. Received instruction re arrival of Remounts. [?] from 4 hours late causing great delay in movement to troops taking Returns into trenches & counting of them 13H	
4	Interview Q. received accessibility of Money Regt Transport Div. Question of late Supply train. Every bit up & were sent back to Corps H.Q. Remounts arrived R.H.A & distributed 13H. 2 Yeoman accepted by R.F.C. 13H	

WAR DIARY
or
INTELLIGENCE SUMMARY.
(Erase heading not required.)

Army Form C. 2118.

Hour, Date, Place	Summary of Events and Information	Remarks and references to Appendices
August 5.	Lieutenant Q. Capt Shaw left for Wireless Station & Rate br Lt Jackson taken on & Town Major one. Lt Fry appointed C/off office to 455 & 4. Marched Turkhud & Upthng Points B.H. Received instructions at 10.0 P.M. to start moving tomorrow R.H. has been attached to 3. A. M.	
6.	Train booked at R.H. at 3.15 A.M. Lt C/off taken our own loading train himself. There was no brake van own along the work. Had trouble of toy commander who cancelled new arrangements. I settled new times to Capt Robinson & C/offs Escorts, come to Forever to early morning duty. Held Brig. arrived at C/of attended Capt Reeves 2.7 later to service B.H. Lt Trevor Q R.H.	
7.	Lieutenant Q. received instruction to Clear Reserve Dump & supplies from MARTINSART. Discussed matter of Machining this to offices from É.S. Major from Train to report at North wound on out to 6 É.S. Major for support Dump at 2.30 P.M. also Lt J.S. Major Major for support to report same place. evening. B.H. The Dump was cleared by	

Army Form C. 2118

WAR DIARY
or
INTELLIGENCE SUMMARY
(Erase heading not required.)

Place	Date	Hour	Summary of Events and Information	Remarks and references to Appendices
August	8		Interview O. Foden at 4 P.M. All wagon class of R.D. by 9 P.M. Visited Horse Lines in Y's intitled by Enemy, moved them to kilter position. BH Discussion at Question of Pirates & Train officers' Billets	
"	9		Interview O. Visited New Dug out, inspected HQ Train line Good supply now that the new Water pump is in working order. BH Arranged for surplus supplies to be brought back from THE PEAL Wood to MARTINSART Dump. BH	
"	10		Interview O. Visited Transport lines 467.493ds x 148 M.Oc which have been moved from V.S. to present position now being 148.806 Y4.A.1.c. 147.1 P.34.2. 146.5 P.35.a.re. Inspected 484 coy Y 463 coy Horses & Horse lines at stables hour. 464c's outlying elsewhere. Feeds were well mixed. The King & the R.O Motor passed through the village today, all traffic being stopped between 1 Y 2 P.M. BH from the R.H.E Dump to Administrate Dump.	
"	11		Interview O. re Supplies for Rations being drawn from our R.H.E Dump to Administrate Dump arranged to clear same from the latter place. B.H.	
"	12		Interview O. Inspected A.465 Y466.coy Horses Horse lines at Stable hour. These horses are in excellent condition, & the feeds well mixed. BH	

WAR DIARY or INTELLIGENCE SUMMARY

Army Form C. 2118

Place	Date	Hour	Summary of Events and Information	Remarks and references to Appendices
August	13		Interview Q. Pushed to New Day Out. B.H.	
	14		Interview Q. Pushed Railhead 6.30 A.M. Now east coy. Has same flank out well.	
			Many promotioly. B.M.	
			Interview Q. Received instruction to send 6 of the Share note book I to 11th Corps.	
	15		Interview Q. Received orders meeting 5. B.M.	
			H.A. issued orders accordingly. B.M.	
	16		Interview Q. Discussed training of Reserve Bn from Material to Reserve Tom Major	
			Management. B.H.	
	17		Interview Q. Discussed the question of the Home side Reserve Area, H.Q. H.Q. 29 Train to stay at FORCEVILLE	
			462 Y & Bde at PUCHEVILLERS. 464, 465 Coys at ARQUEVES. Discussed how Supply will Arrive.	
			Also problem of New R.P.Y. Charge P. Railhead. Received the operation orders & carried over to	
			O.C. all trains in the morning. B.M.	
	18		Interview Q. Railhead not yet allied. Explained importance of Amy co. 466 Co. Manded	
			to Puchevillers. B.M. St train with OC 258 Bn. Train, he charge over. B.M.	
	19		Interview Q. Railhead not yet allied, although Divisions out of area. 464 Y 465 Coys Marched	
			to Leabury. Aqueous infantry. the infantry Bns took up the new position. Any	
			144th Puchvillers. 465 LasBricas, & Laleur, 147th Argurs. et. Div. H.Q. at ACHEUX.	
			Moved in decided opin New Refilling Point L. PUSSLA the 3 Bde Cage in New Areas. B.H.	

WAR DIARY or INTELLIGENCE SUMMARY

Army Form C. 2118

Place	Date	Hour	Summary of Events and Information	Remarks and references to Appendices
August	20		Lorreur Q. Dn. H.Q. at ACHIEUX. Incurred the Railhead being moved. Picked up 46509 in new area, but our Battln. have gone forward. Bttn.	
	21.		To Corron Q. & R.E. Visited the Note Dump at Packerillers. the note is now being all right - Vacated the Village. Arranged for 46609 to keep the 2 Horsing all night - Vacated the Village. Arranged for R.H. RA. G.S. Baggage began to arrive in Lorry journeys by R.H. RA.	
	22.		Lorreur Q. Received information that 46609 by not moving will forward over used orders according to O.C. 46609 to move to Forceville on 23rd the Horses of 46609 the are going forward with them. O.C. called respected the Horses of 46609 the 10 & 15 & to be O.C. called respected meanwhile cancelling move of the 10 & 15 & to be conclusion. BH. Received instruction cancelling move at 10.30 P.M. Both warned O.C. 46609. by Special messenger at 10.30 P.M. ...	
"	23		Lorreur R. Visited 46409 at Leerrillers. upheld their observations. Mobile to Remains	
"	24.		To Lorreur Q. Presence in the Army fast. Learned general Questions in the Remains Back to in the Train. Received information that two Battalions of 46609 The Knew of ? & a walk of some will await instruction to O.C. 46609 march to Forceville moving 7.30 A.M. make arrangements with the remaining Battlns. to join a Horsfare Points.	

Place	Date	Hour	Summary of Events and Information	Remarks and references to Appendices
Augur	25		Interview Q. Arranged for 466207 to stay at Pushvillers & attack the supply wagon & 464207 to work the two Battalion manys on to R. Area. Received verbal information concerning the grouping for supply with A.R.A.S. Received orders to keep on of the men of the Divison into R. Area. Med. our to O.C. coys to keep in touch with their Bde H.Q.	
"	26		Interview Q. Discussed the question of responsibility of Bde. H.Q. Agine over moving to A.S.C. coys, also asked for Capt. of Brewer and officer into a pilotent to Train H.Q. explained importance of doing Co. D.H.	
"	27		Received information that we are to take on an est. 3 Bdes R.F.A. & D.A.C. of the Australian Division. arranged from Repelling for 289 conscription for their feeding accordingly & drew all necessary supplies from R.H. with reception of R.M. which will be issued from Divisn supplies from Montreuil.	
"	28		Interview Q. Canadian R.F.A. did not require rations for teams. Issued for contemption on 29A. Had interview with O.C. Canadian Div. Train. Made arrangement for team H91 91 20 to be attached to Drougline & Attornmento to be to the Train. 13 O.R.	
"	29		Interview Q. Cap L. Black Canadian Supply, O. for Div. Troops reported & took up Suppy, Duties, B.H.	

WAR DIARY
or
INTELLIGENCE SUMMARY

Army Form C. 2118

Place	Date	Hour	Summary of Events and Information	Remarks and references to Appendices
August	30		Interview O.C. Major Cameron Canadian Coy. H.Q. Coy Been informed was informed of the Lift by arrangements & Hrs Position of Gen Artillery lines. Capt. Cameron informed that his Coy 466 had arrived at Forceville on the 28th. Coy list Capt Rempfer 466.29 informed his Horse Lines & Field & intercurtable B.H.	
"	31		Interview O.C. H.Q. Coy Canadian Divisional Train en route to see Johns to sea. Mule Transport Lines. 466.29 Horse Lines & Horses Shelled by the Enemy no casualty 466.29 know his lines & Field to West of Village Field 466.29 & 466.29 ordered Capt Cameron to move his lines further West. Order Capt Rempfer in New Position B.H.	

Bernard Haugh Lt Col
Commanding 49th Divl Train

31/8/16

CONFIDENTIAL

D.A.G.,
  G.H.Q.,
    3rd Echelon

        Herewith my War Diary for the month of September please.

30/9/16

                        Bernard Haigh
                            Lieut Colonel.
            Commanding 49th Divisional Train.

HQ Div Trains
Vol 18

CONFIDENTIAL

WAR DIARY

of

Lieut Col. B. Haigh.

From September 1st, 1916   To September 30th-1916

(VOLUME 18.)

WAR DIARY
or
INTELLIGENCE SUMMARY
(Erase heading not required.)

Army Form C. 2118

Place	Date	Hour	Summary of Events and Information	Remarks and references to Appendices
Sept.	1		Inspected all Refilling Points. 466 M.T. Cops settled in new position on the fore ville Varennes road.	
	2		Interview D.A.H.Q.M.G. re the extra 3,000 R.M. R.B. which were then issued to supply men. The required authority was not granted & the whole matter cancelled. Probably a mistake on the part of D.Q.M.G. Interview Q.R. "Clearing Service" re the Troops been to Canaples to bring lorry loads from.	
	3		In Canaples. ABC. IIC Corps went to the Field Depot, issued these 5 Ab Morgades in the afternoon of. Falta A.M. Brought on 10 days bread on the death of the B.S.C. Canadian Division, re drawing of supplies from England. Had conversation with 8 Co. 1 Canadian Division.	
	4		Roll Epehe. Enemy shelled village at night from 8.30 P.M. to 9.30 P.M. houses of 463 Coy. they took shelter, turned all the horses out & stood & horses until 10 P.M. B.M. of 463 Coy. & the Railhead behind us. the at 1.50 A.M. Enemy again shelled village & the Railhead being put-y put out of action. 50 shells come over. by No1 Caton kite Balloon being hit. y put out of action. 463 Coy R.P. to the Varennes - Hedanville	
	5		Visited Refilling Point. y managed to change P.Coy to the kite Balloon position when near the front place being y exposed to kite Balloon shelled at 6.30 P.M. A.M. it is reported by the Enemy W.Terreur Q. the village shelled at 6.30 P.M. A.M. against 1, the Enemy Refilling Point. In Divisional though, this village shelled during	
	6		Interview Q. visited new Refilling Point. no casualties. most of the night 6 - 7.	

WAR DIARY
or
INTELLIGENCE SUMMARY
(Erase heading not required.)

Place	Date	Hour	Summary of Events and Information	Remarks and references to Appendices
Sept	7		Visited 463 2"y Rifyilling point. Visited 464 2"y Horse Lines & Mobile in LEAVILLERS. Arranged for 466 2"y Horse Lines further South into less exposed place. R.H.	
"	8		Inspected R.E. the Village heavily shelled got horses all away without casualty. Interview w/ A.A.Q.M.G. re moving them further back — the request could not be sanctioned by Corps. ordered all men & horses bivouac in the fields. The HQrs train moved into the fields.	
"	9		Dug out. 463 2"y moved into fields, most of all telephone exchange. Interview Q. HQ Green office in fields connected with the lot, the pound in the green area. All companies bivouac there are indeed (?). The last companies parked R.H. at tent canvas with tents & canvas panels. R.H. All comps in camp.	
"	10		Completed arrangements in the fields. Inns [?] 4 P.M. 464 attending. B.A.	
"	11		Interview Q. Inspected & made suggestion re the Lewis Gun implacement. ordered shafts etc attached to the axles. R.H.	

WAR DIARY
or
INTELLIGENCE SUMMARY
(Erase heading not required.)

Army Form C. 2118

Place	Date	Hour	Summary of Events and Information	Remarks and references to Appendices
Spt	12		Interview Q. Discussed the question of Horse Standings with AA & QMG. Issued orders to all Coy Officers to get Gun Standings prepared. H.Q. had interview with D.D.Q. & D.D.O.S.T. Received instructions to move Capt Shaw & Lt Moore & move off the strength of the Train. BM	
"	13		Inspected the Office Rooks. Work books, Impest A/cs re of 463 Coy found all correct & the books & registers being well kept up to date. BM	
"	14		465 Coy I found all correct & kept up to date. BM Inspected 466 Coy & 464 Coy Trans. Officer Books, Registers, found all being well kept up to date. Then Area was shelled us 5–7 P.M. and 15 go-off in the R.E. Park behind us BM	
"	15		Interview Q. Received A.O. instruction informing us that all T.T. A.S.C. are to be transferred to the Regular A.S.C. BM	
"	16		Interview Q. The Railway & R.E. Depot behind us were shelled at 8 A.M. this morning BM	

WAR DIARY
or
INTELLIGENCE SUMMARY
(Erase heading not required.)

Army Form C. 2118

Place	Date	Hour	Summary of Events and Information	Remarks and references to Appendices
Sept.	17		Routine work. Very wet day. R.H.	
"	18		Interview O. Very wet. Inspected billwacs of 465 Coy there were a poor state. Many being swamped out. Improvements suggested. 466 Coy bivouacs were in excellent condition each man having a bed of boards raised from the ground. All were dry. Work continuing in progress. Apparently in getting the full Winter Home Standings in progress. Approval from R.E. R.H.	
	19		Inspected 463 Coy Horse Lines. These bivouacs, owing to the continuous wet weather both here and a very muddy state. Reparations and in hand for overall Horse standings. The lines being marked out & timber being drawn from R.E. The horse beds were improved by raising from the ground. R.H.	
"	20		Interview O. Re the return of 2/Lt. Roberts & Lt. Jackson. Preparation of Winter Home Standings in progress. This Village again shelled at 3.15 to 4.0 P.M. R.H.	

WAR DIARY
or
INTELLIGENCE SUMMARY
(Erase heading not required.)

Army Form C. 2118

Place	Date	Hour	Summary of Events and Information	Remarks and references to Appendices
Opt-	21		Interview Q. 2/Lt B. Lampton went into Hospital 1/day. having a slight Influenza, pending Captft made permanent DH Replies, short in accommodation for Lampton.	
"	22		Interview Q. Received information from Reserve Army of intended move of the Division, no definite instructions RH.	
"	23		Interview Q. Information from Army that Railhead Changes on 25th. No definite instructions as to future Railhead or move from Q. RA.	
"	24		Interview Q. Received information that the Train HQ Qn will move 2 S.R. Instructed O C 466 Coy to march to Lama Area Today also 465 Coy, 463 Coy & 464 Coy to Remain behind & be attached to 18th Divisional Train to drawing supplies. Railhead moves to SANITY morning of 25th instructed OC's 466 & 465. to draw supplies. on arrival in New Area. arrival of Troops & dative kitchen on arrival in New Area. Both their companies Marched To Warlincourt arriving in the evening. RH.	

WAR DIARY or INTELLIGENCE SUMMARY

Army Form C. 2118

Place	Date	Hour	Summary of Events and Information	Remarks and references to Appendices
Sept.	25	—	Train HQ QM marched to Marlincourt then at 10.30 A.M. visited new Refilling Point. Supplies drawn from new Railhead SAULTY. Supplies held by Column to be dumped & arranged for the Reserve Supplies to the units on that day morning of 2.6.2 x to issue two days supplies to units. Owing to uncertainty of time of arrival of Pack train being too uncertain to rely on getting loaded in time for troops to receive rations when in the trenches. Inspected Horse Lines. Men Rumours Militi'y Offrens quarters &c. 46S & 46 BCoy. Very satisfactory. Officers Lines being all covered with good hard standings, all supply arrangements carried out well & satisfactorily by the two Coys concerned. Divisional H.Q moved to R.H.S today 146th & 147th Inf Bdes (VIIth Corps) to day. B.H. groups arrived in New Area for 146th & 147th Inf Bde groups.	
	26		Interview Q inspected Refilling Point. Authority not y/c received for the issue of Column Supplies. Visited III Army Cr Pol interview there with D.A.D.S. re the issue of Column Supplies. R.H. is informed him that 146 If Bde is to be issued Railhead received orders to 464 Cy to in Lower Q. Visited Railhead.	
	27		Corps. up to the Area on 27th	

WAR DIARY or INTELLIGENCE SUMMARY

Army Form C. 2118

Place	Date	Hour	Summary of Events and Information	Remarks and references to Appendices
Sept	27" (cont'd)		to march to WARLINCOURT on 28th & draw supplies on morning 29th	
	28		at SARCY. 25 Teams of Hay & about today on Pack Train ReH. Supply education most unsatisfactory. Pack train coming up short of water. Hay & oats. today. No oats or bran which means drawing again from R.H. in afternoon. The transport turn out @ 1 A.M. each morning & at present men horses are working both day & night. Authority for issue of the Quinine Ration in Column not yet hand. Submitted that Scheme to A.A & Q.M.G. B.H.	
	29		Interview @ 4 & 4 207 Moved from YARENNES to MARTINCOURT the 164 EI/730 orders to move to HAILOY on 30th R. AM.	
	30"		Received orders to move to SAM D.12.MP.T.B. on Oct 1st. Adj. Quartow to run ahead & 14.6 MP.B cancelled & allowed to own most of area due this to no accommodation. Move of 14.6 MP.B & poss. & but information to Q. Railway line. Visited industries to view refilling point.	

Bernard Haigh Lt Col
Commanding 49th Div: Train
30/9/16.

CONFIDENTIAL

Headquarters
49th Division

Herewith I beg to forward my War Diary for the month of October in accordance with D.R.O. No 2379.

1/11/16

Bernard Haigh
Lieut Colonel.
Commanding 49th Divisional Train.

Vol 19

CONFIDENTIAL.

War Diary
of
Lieut Col B Haigh Commdg. 49th (WR) Divl Train.

From 1.10.16. To 31.10.16.

(Volume 19).

WAR DIARY
or
INTELLIGENCE SUMMARY
(Erase heading not required.)

Army Form C. 2118

Place	Date	Hour	Summary of Events and Information	Remarks and references to Appendices
Oct	1		Handed over the command of the Train to Major Montgomery while I am on leave. B.H. Visited Div. H.Q. on to moves - Train H.Q. moved to LA BELLE VUE. 464 Co. to 2m. De LA BREFFAYE near COUTURELLE 465 Co. to LA BAZEQUE Fm. 466 Co. to HUMBERCAMPS - ⟨sig⟩	
"	2		Refilled at new Refilling Points - Column dumped reserve of supplies held in lorries - Received instruction that G.O.C. Division wished to inspect Train Co: at 2.30 P.M. Inspection postponed owing to adverse weather conditions. Visited all companies. Notified that 463 Co: would be marching north with Div: R.A. & that it would be attached to 46/15 Div. Train to rations Visited Div: H.Q. ⟨sig⟩	
"	3		Refilled at 9 A.m. for all Groups - Train drawing Supplies from Railhead to Refilling Points - Units drawing their supplies from Refilling Points with their Reg.t Transport. Supplies drawn by Train to remain at Refilling Points all night - Supply wagons convoys not remain loaded all night owing to loading at Railhead being at 3. A.m. Visited D.H.Q. Notified that the Divisional Commander would inspect Train Co: at 2 - P.M - A.O.C. Division + A.A.& Q.M.G. inspection 464. 465. 466 Co in Company Lines. 463 Co: A.S.C. arrived in this area.	⟨sig⟩

WAR DIARY or INTELLIGENCE SUMMARY

Army Form C. 2118

Place	Date	Hour	Summary of Events and Information	Remarks and references to Appendices
Oct.	4		Supply Train arrived 6 hours late – Visited Refilling Points – Made arrangements to Ration 33rd Divl. R.A. Routine work. Visited Divl. H.Q.	
"	5		Made arrangements to Ration 12th Divl. R.A. Divl: H.Q. moved to COUTURELLE. Notified that 10 remounts would arrive 6th inst. Issued orders to Co. Commanders re Traffic Control at Railhead.	
"	6		Loading at Railhead altered to 7. A.M. Visited 465 Co. M.S.C. & H.Q. 147th Bde: re Rail Transport. Notified that 464 Co. must leave DE LA BREFFAYE Fm., the same being in 48th Divl: Area, arrangements made with Divl: H.Q. to Coy: to move to SOMBRIN on 8th inst.	
"	7		12th Divl: R.A. left us to join Reserve Army, rations up to 8th inst. Visited Refilling Points - Attended Divl: H.Q. General Routine.	
"	8		All moves postponed – Visited Companies –	
"	9		Attended Divl: H.Q. Instructions received for 464 Co. to move to HUMBERCAMP. 466 Co. to COULLEMONT on 10th inst. adjusted Supply groups accordingly – the water lorry reported for duty with Divl: H.Q. Issued instructions to 147th Bde: Refilling Point the move to non-army adjoining BAZEQUE FME.	

WAR DIARY
or
INTELLIGENCE SUMMARY
(Erase heading not required.)

Army Form C. 2118

Instructions regarding War Diaries and Intelligence Summaries are contained in F.S. Regs., Part II. and the Staff Manual respectively. Title Pages will be prepared in manuscript.

Place	Date	Hour	Summary of Events and Information	Remarks and references to Appendices
OCT-TER	10		Pack Supply Train arrived 6 hours late at Railhead - Attached Div: H.Q. Visited all Refilling points with D.A. & Q.M.G. Moved Refilling Points of 146th Bde & 33rd Divl: R.A. to side road adjoining. Attached Corps H.Q. Authority received from A.Q.M.G. for 147th Bde. Refilling Point to remain at LA BEZEQUE. Authority received to issue Soap to French Rations. Authority received from Corps to the the transported daily by Lorries. B.M.O.	
"	11		Visited all Cos: Refilling Points - Issued orders re Surplus Baggage Stores to be dumped in case of sudden move. B.M.O.	
"	11	7.30 p.m.	Col. Haigh returned from leave.	
"	12		Handed over Command of Train to Lt.-Col. B. Haigh. D.S.O. Took over Command of Train. Visited H.Q. Reported my return. Visited Refilling Point 148th Bde Group. arranged for instructing the 1st Line Transport 147th Inf Bde. B.M.	
"	13		Visited 148th Bde Group R.P. also 464 Cy Horse Lines Thrown Retuble in Humbercamp. Visited 147th Bde Group R.P. & 465 Coy Horse Lines Thrown Retubl at La Bazeque Farm. Issued order for 464 Coy to make provision for Major Evans throw over to all Spare poles to be carried on Gde of Major. B.M.	

Place	Date	Hour	Summary of Events and Information	Remarks and references to Appendices
Oct	14		Visited Q. Inspected 46668 Horse Lines & Horse Public. Inspected 463 204 Horse Lines. Horse Hosp. The Coy is attached to 33rd Divi Train & is at Sony on Motor DH.	
	15		Had conference with the three Bde Coy O.C.s went through Divisional Administration before reported out the various important points. Had interview with O.C. Divisional Troops Coy 33rd Divl Train, which is attached to the Divl. Pointed out importance of wearing Civil Helmets carrying water turns on G.S. & having Harness & Wagon Clean & having Civil Cloth drawn for Cols. Ribbon stuck by the Major Montgomery was presented with the M.C. Capt Shaw A.V.C. & self attended. VII Corps Commander. Capt Mulcow. presentation Btty	
	16		Visited Q. Interview Staff Capt R.F.A. re the Baggage Wagons. Horse & Coming up 463 20 to a through overhaul. This was agreed to but will not be able to take place until the F.A. come out of the Line	

WAR DIARY or INTELLIGENCE SUMMARY

Army Form C. 2118

Place	Date	Hour	Summary of Events and Information	Remarks and references to Appendices
Vet	16 (Cont.)		Received information that the G.O.C. will inspect this Unit Sec 466 C0 Stating at 2.30 on the 17th inst. Issued instructions to the 3 Cos. Inspected 147th Lt. Bde 1st Line Transport. Horses suffering from neglect of grooming. Harness not clean. Wagon in poor condition but many required nothing. BH	
	17		Sent report of transport inspection to H.Q. G.O.C inspected 463 C0 464 C0 & 466 C0 & expressed his satisfaction with the state of all three Cos. Received information from 148th Lt. Bde. that the inspection of their 1st Line Transport on 19th would be impossible as the Bde. had moved. Received orders to move; agreed to postpone & await information from H.Q. Bde. BH	
	18		Received information that 2 Batts. 147th Bde. are tomorrow to WANQUENTIN. Made necessary supply arrangements to 146th Lt. Bde. relieves 147th Bde. 147 Bde. to move to "E" area on 19th. Above moves cancelled in afternoon. BH	

WAR DIARY or INTELLIGENCE SUMMARY

Army Form C. 2118

Place	Date	Hour	Summary of Events and Information	Remarks and references to Appendices
Oct	19		Unknown Q. Received instructions that MFG Rde is to move to SOUASTRE. Div. H.Q to HENU & Train to WARLINCOURT. Made necessary arrangements. Guided OC 46th Train, settled R.P. & Supply Scheme for new area. Railhead on 22nd WARLINCOURT. Pack Train to arrive at 9 A.M. R.H.	
"	20		Interview Q. Lovered Supply & Transport Scheme into Q. Made arrangements for Refilling in WARLINCOURT, Train HQrs. to move on 21st. 46CCo to to move on 21st about necessary orders. Lt Reynolds Acty: went on leave. Cpt. information to Q & Learn of landing Acting Adjt. in his absence. Railhead hence Sept 25th R.H.	
	21		Train HQrs moved to WARLINCOURT. together with 46CCo 46CCo R.P. moved to St AMAND. Moving of R.H. put off until 26th B.H.	
	22		Visited Q. arranged with Q to carry on with present Supply Scheme/s until R.H. changed, when the new scheme comes into action. B.A.	

WAR DIARY or INTELLIGENCE SUMMARY

Army Form C. 2118

Place	Date	Hour	Summary of Events and Information	Remarks and references to Appendices
Oct.	23		Visited Q. Informed them of difficulty of getting the remaining C/s into the Village, with present troops now occupying the Villch. Made arrangements to clear Village. Visited VII Corps R. Division. the greater of the detached HQrs & G Train & then return 213 A. being rendered to the Organal Train. HQ Gs. Also the point issue of the popr Channel of 17773 J Corps Troops & Army Troops. He checked with Field return. PH	
	24		Visited Q. Issued order for 464 & 465 Cos to move to MARLINCOURT. 240 A Bde R.F.A not yet moved out of their lines 13A. Visited 25th usual instruction re situation of R.P & R.H. to take place on 28th. Interview with OC HQgs Co 465 Ind Train now attached to the Train. 13A.	
	25		Visited Q. 464 Co & 465 Co moved to Marlincourt. Horses not on standings. 240 A Bde R.F.A not yet moved out of their lines 13A. 464 Co R.P. at BESSUE. 465 Co R.P. Marlincourt. 13A.	

Army Form C. 2118

WAR DIARY
or
INTELLIGENCE SUMMARY
(Erase heading not required.)

Place	Date	Hour	Summary of Events and Information	Remarks and references to Appendices
Oct.	26		Railhead changed today to MARLIMCOURT. New system commenced. Inspected 464 & 465 Cos Horse lines in the open. New Picketts & Huts in a very dirty condition when taken over. Horse lines very exposed. 465 Cos R.P. having been used for Horse Room & loose horses kept in a very disgusting condition. Received information from Q that 1st line transport of 148th Inf. Bde. is staying at GAUDIENDRE, the means that the R.P. at ROSEANE is in a bad position, made arrangement to find a more suitable place. Inspected 148th Inf Bde 1st Line Transport & Chew up Report. for Div H.Q. 13H.	
"	27		Visited Q. Inspected Ripley Pont & Pos Coy 48A. Train. Issued instruction. re Method of loading at R.H. & Chitraying to Troops. 13H. Q. Coy broke down reached Loerk.	
"	28		Started to visit III Army Q. Army Park reported for duty with Train 10H. O.C. Cie 27 A. Bourne.	
"	29		Interviewed the New A.A. Q.M.G. re inspection of 1st line Transport. & the S Co. Visited III Army Q. Discussed New R.P. with A.A.Q.M.S. 13H.	

WAR DIARY
or
INTELLIGENCE SUMMARY

Army Form C. 2118

Place	Date	Hour	Summary of Events and Information	Remarks and references to Appendices
Oct.	30.		Visited D.D.S. YT. IIIrd Army, discussed question of No 1 Coy being detached to other Divisions, difficulty of getting Officer r.o.R. reinforcement. Baggage Wagon coming into Train, & new R.7. A. organization, the question of the 9 Train Wagon being sent in to A.H.T. Appt. B.H.	
"	31.		Interview Q. Visitid. 464 Co. & 465 Co. Horse lines, Iron Huts re o/c Stable Guns, horses evening fit, conversing the expanded position, inspected Cook houses at Tea time B.H. Capt. Milner returned from leave.	

Bernard Hough Lt. Col.
Commander of 49th Divl: Train

Vol 20

CONFIDENTIAL.

War Diary
of
Lieut Col G. Haigh Commdg. 4-9th (AR) Bril Siem

From 1.11.16
To 30.11.16.

(Volume 20.)

WAR DIARY or INTELLIGENCE SUMMARY

Army Form C. 2118

Place	Date	Hour	Summary of Events and Information	Remarks and references to Appendices
No 1	1		Inspected N.C.O 1st Line Transport. Picked 466 2nd in picked Horse Lines, Wagons & Harness. Iron Mills & Kitchen Bt.	
"	2		Inspected 1st & 3rd Field Ambulance. Motor Transport. Inspected 146th Infantry Brigade R.P. 13th. Made out report for Div'l H.Q.	
"	3		Picked Rations, met H.A.A.A M.G. & went round the Horse Lines 7 Mules. Picked 465 cops. Inspected Motors Transport of 146th Inf. Bde with reception of one mule, sick 0.4 L.S. the result was satisfactory. Made out report for O.Bt.	
"	4		Inspected R.P. 46th Div'l; Inspected the Mules & cover for them Supplies. had a visit from H.A. r O.M.S. discussed the issuing of Reinforcements. Made arrangements in the Town Major for 2 Mules to be received & informed R.T.O. 13th.	
"	5		Picked Q. discussed Army Forms to be used for men off-duty for commencers received instructions from O/C more Records, that the Supplies N.C.O Supply Rents are not going to be allowed at present, Hay Ration reduced 2 lbs, they coming to A.H. & 13s, the remainder to be purchased. 13th	

WAR DIARY
or
INTELLIGENCE SUMMARY

(Erase heading not required.)

Army Form C. 2118

Place	Date	Hour	Summary of Events and Information	Remarks and references to Appendices
Nov	6		Inspected 2nd Field Ambulance 1st Line Transport, on the whole satisfac[tor]y. Made out & sent in report to Q. Inspected 147th Inf Bde 1st Line Transport, visited all the Horse Lines. Wagon lines & Horses were much improved. Horses were very clean & I then made out & sent report to Q. Decided that excess Horses purchased by Capt Stonehouse was not fit for issue. BH	
"	7		Visited Q. discussed the question of G.S. Wagons taking the place of lorries in the event of front followed by Shaw, advised that 26 extra G.S. Wagons would be required apart from Baggage Wagons; Was w/oman that owing to reduction of R.E. work in Trenches. The Baggage Wagons can not be returned to Train, in cases where the A.S.C. horses are suffering from overwork the R.E. are to (supply) teams, the Wagon to be sent in for overhaul to the A.S.C. says issued instructions accordingly to O.C. says BH	

WAR DIARY
or
INTELLIGENCE SUMMARY
(Erase heading not required.)

Army Form C. 2118

Place	Date	Hour	Summary of Events and Information	Remarks and references to Appendices
Nov. 1	7 (contd)		Spoke to D.D. of S.T. Office re having another Car sent to the Head Capt. 2.C. Stonehouse reported to III'd Army D. of S.T. with Car, for the purpose of forage buying. B.H. then down the train with one Car only. B.H. the lorry Transport, which was in good condition	
"	8		Inspected 19 & 2.7. Batt. 1st Line Transport, which was in good condition. Men out. Went to R. B.H.	
"	9		Visited Supply Column. Interview with O.C. re the evacuation of 7 & 9 the Motor Lorries. His opinion was that they required complete overhaul. Attended Office Train. The memos to be about 6 weeks. Renewal of many important Parts. The memo was considered to. B.H. Application to D.D. of S.T. for another Car still under consideration.	
"	10		Interview received instruction that 14 & 5 P & E R.R. must be moved. Wrote to all new parties rehave new R.R. winner instruction accordingly. I.D. of S.T. inspected the Brigade Coys & Nº 109 L.F.A. Train, Vieilles Refilling Points. I.D. of S.T. inspected the Brigade Coys & Nº 109 L.F.A. Train, Vieilles from Cuire & Hoymes. Horses hoove to. expressed his satisfaction, at condition of horses, to. B.H.	

Army Form C. 2118

WAR DIARY
or
INTELLIGENCE SUMMARY
(Erase heading not required.)

Place	Date	Hour	Summary of Events and Information	Remarks and references to Appendices
Nov	11.		Inspected 1st line transport of I.C. R.E. Signal Co. R.E. & Div. H.Q. & Australs satisfactory but many sets of harness requiring cleaning & oiling. Visited 146th Bde gun R.P. & saw there system of working through lines 149. drawing from R.H. before delivering general. This worked well. Viz., drawing from horse to back in coy limes by 1.30 P.M. & reveille at usual time. BH	
"	12		Remounts arrived 12.30 A.M. Horses distributed at 10 A.M. A poor lot. Inspected the horse limes over by 464 Coy from 462 R.F.A. to be taken over by 464 Coy. Advised 464 Coy R.P. Bttn. issued instruction re careful disinfection. BH	
"	13		Interview O. re lines allotment for He Qr Coy Train, arranged for S.Q.M.S. Green to go to Q Office on probation as Chief Clerk. Received instructions re placing Tin over the Frog when shoeing, experimented with this. Found that Tin cracked & formed jagged edge. Tried leather pads in the better results. BH	

1875 Wt. W593/826 1,000,000 4/15 J.B.C. & A. A.D.S.S./Forms/C. 2118.

Army Form C. 2118

WAR DIARY
or
INTELLIGENCE SUMMARY
(Erase heading not required.)

Instructions regarding War Diaries and Intelligence Summaries are contained in F.S. Regs., Part II. and the Staff Manual respectively. Title Pages will be prepared in manuscript.

Place	Date	Hour	Summary of Events and Information	Remarks and references to Appendices
NOI	14		Inspected New Stampings for 484 Coy. having been disinfected.	
"	15		S.S.O left for England for 10 days leave. Capt. Milner appointed S.S.O. to carry on in his absence. Lt. Reynolds acting as Adjutant. B.H. Interview Q. Inspected Coal Dumps. The Coal being in Stack, arranged for to-day from R.M. Received the question of having the only Car now with the Train to the purpose & by Means asked for 3 lorries to keep also from Arriens reported wheel of the Lorries will turn to protect the feet from Nails. J B.H.	
"	16		Visited 463 Coy at Bus. Inspected Office Books, Horse Lines, Drawn Wells etc. The two Cabs as in a field of Mud without any protection. Inspected 463 & 207 Office Books & Horse Stables, the latter being Established all over the Village B.Ct	
"	17		Inspected 1st Line Transport of the 2/7 Coy & 1/2 7a Coy R.E. Visited 484 Coy. Horse Lines, Inspected Office Books. B.H	
"	18		Inspected 486 Coy Office Books & Horse Lines 13/4	
"	19		Interview Q. Received instructions that M.T. are to be withdrawn from the Roads as for as possible. A.T. to carry on instead, the Fron & Roving Lindon sp. B.H.	

WAR DIARY
or
INTELLIGENCE SUMMARY
(Erase heading not required.)

Army Form C. 2118

Place	Date	Hour	Summary of Events and Information	Remarks and references to Appendices
Nov	20		Interview O. Visited Coal Dump & all refilling points. Received information at 7 P.M. that the G.O.C. would inspect all Company's instructions accordingly. Had conference of the Train at 2.30 & 2.15. Issued instructions accordingly of Coy OC's at 9 P.M. 13H	
"	21		Interview O. Discussed the question of Promotion of Officers & Submitted a list for approval. Discussed the question of No 1 Coy & 48th Train 2.30 P.M. the G.O.C. inspected all 3 Bde Coys & No 1 Coy & 48th Horses. I regret that 464 Coy Horses & referred his dissatisfaction with all he saw, I regret to say with OC Dpts Coy. & Wagons were not clean, I am very disappointed to get things right. 13H at the small effort that had been made	
"	22		Inspected 1st Line Transport of the 72 M. Yds. Improvement shewn in the horses & harness, 10H. Made out report for Q. 13H	

WAR DIARY or INTELLIGENCE SUMMARY

Army Form C. 2118

Place	Date	Hour	Summary of Events and Information	Remarks and references to Appendices
Nov.	23		Visited LA BRAZZAR farm with a J Meur. to getting 463 Coy into the buildings found all barns full. The Horse Standings available. Pilot Railhead examined here. Now thought unfit. Reported to Q. that they should be moved by M.T. on account of their precarious shafed wheels. Visited 57th Coy Field. R.E. 1st Line Transport. Visited Q. re 2nd LA B.S.Q. u 12 Inspected 57th Coy Field R.E. 1st Line Transport, also asked for an 2nd LA B.S.Q. u 12 re the accommodation at La Preffay. B.H.	
"	24		R.P. for an of 49th Divisional Troops. B.H. Inspected 146th Machine Gun Coy 1st Line Transport, improvement shewn. Visited the proposed New Refilling Point at LA BESEQUE for the 49th Div: Troops. 463 Coy marched to WARLINCOURT. The horses will be in the open until 29th inst. when they are to move into the Standings now occupied by No1 Co 48th Train. B.H.	
"	25		463 Coy. Inspected who covered Standings evacuated by the 278th Res Park. though rather crowded, this is a great improvement. B.H.	

WAR DIARY
or
INTELLIGENCE SUMMARY

(Erase heading not required.)

Army Form C. 2118

Place	Date	Hour	Summary of Events and Information	Remarks and references to Appendices
Nol.	26		Visited & inspected 463 Coy horse lines, Thorn straw dugouts & hard work. Inspected 466 Coy horse lines & inspected horses	BH
"	27		Interview Q. Inspected 147º Inf. Bde. H.Q. & inspected a new attachment to coupling two Lewis Carts together, this officer of a small calve	
			Visited Divisional Coal Dump. Noted Horse Lines of 464 Coy Horses are not in good condition. Had interview with Y.O. with regard to them	
			had interview with 46th Dvl. Staff Capt. R.F.A. re the transport of supply arrangements for their move on to reach area.	BH
"	28		Visited Railhead. Pack train came in late afternoon instead of morning. P.M. & B. School. 463 Coy horses retained at Irucing El Hum delivering supplies. Inspected 5th Batt. K.O.Y.L.I. 1st line transport, this was greatly improved,	
			T.O. Long has replaced BM. Sent in report to Q.	BH
"	29		Interview Q. re cheeing to present railpacking up, discussed the question of Major Montgomery going to Div. Q. for a month. also prospective move of Divisional	BH

Place	Date	Hour	Summary of Events and Information	Remarks and references to Appendices
	30		463 coy moved into Horse standings vacated by No 1 coy 463 coy which moved away from this area is now detached from this Train. Visited Q had interview with A.A.Q.M.G. re purchase more of the Divis on I also accompanied him to R.H. to inspect the Snow Ploughs & discussed the question of harness for them. Capt Campbell R.A.M.C reported to Train H.Q". for duty. I was taken round by the present M.O. at the end of the day. Capt Campbell was entertained by us an interview with me, informed me he was not physically fit for the post. he is unable to ride a horse. BH	

Bernard Hough

Lt-Col

Commanding 49th Divisional Train

Vol 21

SECRET.

WAR DIARY.

OF

49th (W.R.) Divisional Train

FOR

December 1916.

CONFIDENTIAL.

WAR DIARY

OF

Lieut Col. B. Hugh. Commanding 49th (WR) Divl Train.

From: 1-12-16.   To. 31-12-16.

(Volume 21.)

Place	Date	Hour	Summary of Events and Information	Remarks and references to Appendices
1915 Decem b	1		Received warning of the Move of the Division to begin on the 4th inst. Operation order received at night. D² Campbell R.A.M.C. started then. Acts as M.O. to the Train. Meo. D^n Carr gone to 135-70 Ambulance Bee.	
"	2		Made necessary Transport & Supply arrangements for the Move. Attended Conference at VII Corps Q. discussed the question of M.T. replacing M.T. in case of thaw often front, also advisability of clearing reserve of M.T. being required, also brought up the question of M.T. being required. had that 3 days, also during the move. B.H. In supply work during the move. B.H.	
"	3		Division Q. received information that Railhead changes to Bonneumaison on 5th Inst. issued Train operation order No 21 to all companies in the MTC. and VII Corps to use of Column to draw at new R.H. on 5th B.H.	
"	4		Had visit from O.C. 46th Train, to see Billets that he is taking over, discussed the question of R.P.ts with him, received information that 180 Reinuments are coming to R.H. in the morning. B.H.	

WAR DIARY or INTELLIGENCE SUMMARY

Army Form C. 2118

Place	Date	Hour	Summary of Events and Information	Remarks and references to Appendices
December	5	—	Interview O. discussed the question of Train H.Q. being in NEUVILLETTE. Which LEHOUX & preferred Billets there, there being most unsatisfactory, went to NEUVILLETTE & found Billets place. 464 Coy marched to BOUQUEMAISON. 466 Coy marched to COULLEMONT. 49th S Column drew from BOUQUEMAISON, railhead to first time, & we now revert to original system. Column drawing at R.H. & then dumping at the R.P. the following morning stations R.P. are 146th Bde Group at HALLOY. 148th Bde Group at COULLEMONT. Div Troops & 4.5" Div Artillery at LARHEUX, served by the H.Q. on 465 Train. 147th Bde Group at BOUQUEMAISON. B.H. Received Telegram authorising H.Q. Train to use NEUVILLETTE Billets. B.H.	
"	6	—	465 Coy marched to HALLOY. H.Q. of 49/49th Train remain at WARLINCOURT. 49th Div Artillery always in the R.P. at WARLINCOURT. The R.E. H.Q. for this group changed to SOUTY on 5th inst. Inspected 463 Coy Billets & Horse lines in WARLINCOURT. also visited the 49 Div. Art R.P. Visited R. 13 H.	
"	7	—	Hd Coy marched to NEUVILLETTE, arriving at noon. Office opened at that time. The Train visited New R.H.Q. & 146 Bde Group R.P. B.H.	

WAR DIARY or INTELLIGENCE SUMMARY

Army Form C. 2118

Place	Date	Hour	Summary of Events and Information	Remarks and references to Appendices
Dec:	8		Interview O. Visited 465 Coy. inspected Horse Lines, Mens Billets & Workshops. Confirmed to the R.P. for 465 & 13th Bde Group, found that the best had been made of the accommodation available. Visited 464 Coy. inspected Horse Lines, Mens Billets, Workshops also the R.P. for 145th Bde Group. Look to find fault with various points & informed the O.C. Coy. to have fuller reports rendered by the orderly Officers. Clearly many small details having obviously been overlooked. Bh. Received Gallantry card from Div. H.Q. to O. Emmerton 13th Bh.	
"	9		Routine Office work. Returns &c.	
"	10		Visited 465 Coy. at HALLOY. inspected Horse Lines, Mens Billets, Workshops, had Parade of Coy. & read out extract from Divisional Orders stating Act of Courage by Dr Emmerton, & presented "Gallantry Card" to him. The horses are much scattered & he returned to train. 13th Bh. Div. orders the Baggage Wagon in small Battles.	
"	11		Baggage Wagon were returned to train, picked up N.P.E. Column & took Q.O's Coy. in to Whails. 13th.	

WAR DIARY
or
INTELLIGENCE SUMMARY

Army Form C. 2118

Place	Date	Hour	Summary of Events and Information	Remarks and references to Appendices
Bac	12		Inspected 1st Line Transport of the Hd Qrs 146th Inf Bde, 6th & 8th Battns West Yorks Regts & 146th M.G. Coy. Interviews with the Brig. Gen. re the Transport of his Brigade. B.H.	
"	13		Inspected Q. discussed the question of Chaff Cutters & absence of Brakes on all limbers. G.S. left copy of correspondence re the latter. Inspected 1st Line transport of 5th & 7th West Yorks Regt. Both very unsatisfactory. Made out report to Q on the result of Bde inspection. R.H.	
"	14		Visited 464 Coy, 465 Coy & 463 Coy at Bouquemaison, Halloy & Marlincourt. Lapce Coy. B.H.	
"	15		Capt. Hull was ordered for a week by Lt Reynolds. Visited 464 Coy & discussed the question of the Baggage Wagon. B.H. at Coullemont 12.15 AM Oct.	
"	16		Visited 466 Coy, inspected Baggage Wagon Horses which Battery Horses received information that the 49th Ind Art will exchange places with the 46th Art. Saw Capt. Pearson who is acting the Hd. Qrs. Coy 469 Train at Lucheux, with regard to taking over their Hd. Qrs. Horses private on 23rd; R.H. to change on the 23rd and 10th.	

WAR DIARY
or
INTELLIGENCE SUMMARY.
(Erase heading not required.)

Army Form C. 2118.

Instructions regarding War Diaries and Intelligence Summaries are contained in F. S. Regs., Part II. and the Staff Manual respectively. Title pages will be prepared in manuscript.

Hour, Date, Place	Summary of Events and Information	Remarks and references to Appendices
Dec 17	Visited R.P.s. & 464 Coy, RH.	
18	Visited 465 Coy. Saw Baggage Wagon Horses, Batt.	
19	Inspected 147th Inf. Bde. 1st line Transport, 4th & 5th L.N.R. Regt. & the 147th R.E. Coy, with the exception of the 4th Bn. the Transport was in a satisfactory condition RH.	6th & 7th N.H.R. Regt.
20	Inspected remainder of 147th Inf. Bde. 1st line Transport the 6 & 7 Batt. Both were satisfactory, made out reports for Q. BH.	Q. BH.
21	Interview Q. A. & Q.M.G. & Barker, I.S.S.O. going to Q. Office for instruction, arranged for the 26th inst. 463 Coy marched w/o L.Col & Heads from Martinsart. Visited U.T.3 Central St Divisional Wood cutting position. Visited 466 Coy & 465 Bac R. Point at Coulemont, Visited 465-209 at Malloy & 147th Bac R. Point. BH.	

WAR DIARY
or
INTELLIGENCE SUMMARY.
(Erase heading not required.)

Army Form C. 2118.

Instructions regarding War Diaries and Intelligence Summaries are contained in F. S. Regs., Part II. and the Staff Manual respectively. Title pages will be prepared in manuscript.

Hour, Date, Place	Summary of Events and Information	Remarks and references to Appendices
Dec: 22nd	Obtained Q. re the authority for issuing 2 days supplies on the 24th inst. Visited 463 Coy in LIEUCHEUX. Horses outside & in very bad position. 2/3 men in billets the rest in tents. Visited the Troop Refilling Point. Visited the I.O.M. SANITY. re Baker for L.G.S. Very unsatisfactory result. He cannot supply any fowls. Ptt	
" 23rd	Interview Q. Authority granted for issue on 24th of 2 days rations. Visited R. Pauli. Division and Troops, received necessary instructions for the double issue. Ptt	
" 24	Issued 2 days rations to troops. Ptt	
" 25	Visited all companies of the Train, the arrangements for the Xmas entertainment were most satisfactory; all having a very good dinner. Ptt. The G.O.C. called to wish all of the Train the compliments of the season. Ptt. Members	

WAR DIARY or INTELLIGENCE SUMMARY

Army Form C. 2118

Place	Date	Hour	Summary of Events and Information	Remarks and references to Appendices
Iec	26		Visited R.P. 46424. Major Montgomery went to Q. 49.b. Division for one months staff course. Capt Milne took over the S.C.O. work. 2/Lt Reynolds to Adjt. work from the date. Pitt	
	27		Visited Q. Inspected 464.c.09 Horse Lines, Wagon Park, Hothorse Lines are in a very bad condition all horses outside. Visited 463.c.07 Horse Lines, Wagon Park, Hothorses were not in a very good state, the chewing back of flooring, the position is very bad lies lying & terribly muddy, also visited to Div. Troops R.P. Pitt	
"	28		Inspected 1st Line Transport & M.G.S. Battn Y.&L. 148th inf Bde, batteries in a satisfactory condition. Made out report for Q. Pitt	
	29		Visited Third Army H.Qrs. Took Capt Cameron to be interviewed by DDG.VS. with a view to his promotion. Also discussed the question of the proposed alterations in the shoeing of various Officers	

WAR DIARY
or
INTELLIGENCE SUMMARY.
(Erase heading not required.)

Army Form C. 2118.

Hour, Date, Place	Summary of Events and Information	Remarks and references to Appendices
Dec 29th (contd)	Sent in report to Third Army re Major Montgomery being temporarily attached to Q 49th Div. Staff. Inspected 1st line Transport of the 4.5th & 5th Batt. K.O.Y.L.I. & the 148th M.G. Coy, the Transport was in a satisfactory condition.	
Dec 30th	Sent in to D.A.Q.M.G. T. Third Army proposal form for reporting of Officers of the Train, also a request that Capt. Stonehouse be returned to the train. 10th.	
" 31st	Interview Q re the new area to be taken up by the Division. Visited 463 Coy interviewed applicants for Commission in the Infantry. Inspected 1st N.R. Field Ambulance & their Transport, made out report for Q. 10th.	

Bernard Haugh Lt Col
Commanding 49th (N.R.) Divl Train

SECRET.

Vol 22

WAR DIARY.

OF

49th (W.R.) Divisional Train

FOR

January 1917.

CONFIDENTIAL.

War Diary
of
Lieut Col C.B. Athigh. Commanding 49th (WR) Sigd Train.

From 1-1-17   To 31-1-17.

(Volume 21)

Army Form C. 2118.

WAR DIARY
or
INTELLIGENCE SUMMARY.
(Erase heading not required.)

Hour, Date, Place	Summary of Events and Information	Remarks and references to Appendices
1917. January 1st	Inspected the 1st line Transport 1/2nd & 7th Ambulances, the Turn out was Visited 463 Coy & the Ind. 7s Refilling Point. Interviewed A.A.Q.M.G. re the move of the Division & got details of Coys in the new area.	Turn out was very satisfactory. BH
" 2nd	Inspected the 1st line transport 1/3rd & R 7s Ambulance the Turn out was satisfactory. Interviewed A.A.Q.M.G. re the move. Visited HQ & 305 Divl Train, on. O.C. saw new Bell's Tells taken over, made all arrangements re the coys of the Inspective Trains changing places with one another. I made necessary arrangements on the 5th, 4th, 464, & 466 to move on the 5th instant. BH Interviewed O.C. 465 Coy to move by Train Train.	
" 3rd	Interviewed A.A.Q.M.G. Observed Transport Plan & HQs arrangement, applied to hand over train to him. Asked for Lt. P. BARKER to W/O.C. 463 coy whilst Capt. Wells is on leave. Made out new Duffs Transport Train Orders re. arranged for Baggage Wagons to returned to Train on the 5th inst. BH	CAPT. CAMERON
" 4.	Interviewed A.A.Q.M.G. the Pro. & A.I.G.S. for Divl School. Visited 463 Coy. Visited 466 Coy. Details of made arrangements w A.I.4.Coys Amb. to take them in. Spoke re his lorry on one & G.S. to hand to Divisional School from 463 Coy. BH sent to Divisional School from 463 Coy. BH Baggage Wagons reported back to their Coys in forward area. BH	

Army Form C. 2118.

WAR DIARY
or
INTELLIGENCE SUMMARY.
(Erase heading not required.)

Hour, Date, Place	Summary of Events and Information	Remarks and references to Appendices
January 5th	Interview Q. Noted 463 Coy discussed the question of the Forage Wagon, going well to R.A. Bns. on its reorganisation. 465 Coy marched from HALLOY to LARORET. 464 Coy discussed the question of Chaplains and that No C. also a armed him about the march discipline.	going well B.H.
6th	Interview Q. 466 Coy Moved to LARBRET. 464 Coy Moved to Germans to METZ	B.H.
7th	Train H.Q moved to BAYINCOURT. Railhead changed to SANCTY. Noted 463 Coy R.P. 463 Coy remain at LEBEUENEUX attached to the 30th Division. 13H Move of Division completed 13H in New Area	
8th	Interview Q. Visited all Refilling Points & Railhead. Visited 463 Coy. re the proposal early move of the 449 & 72 Artillery. Interview the DDQMG Third Army, re alteration in the posting of Officers commanding No 1 No 4 Companies, sanction given for the change over of these two. also discussed the question of Major Montgomery being attached to for Q. Staff work also being left in my hands, 13H.	

WAR DIARY or INTELLIGENCE SUMMARY

Army Form C. 2118.

Hour, Date, Place	Summary of Events and Information	Remarks and references to Appendices
January 9th	Interview ATQMG re. necessary lorries required for transport of Supplies. A.T. now drawing from R.H.Q.; gone full information re T & S arrangements. Leave granted by G.O.C. from 12th.	
10	Interview Q. Sent in request for lorries to help during move of the 49th German Flak Plaa on 14-15.	
	Visited LA BAZEQUE & took particulars of Horse accommodation in covered standings also Officers Mess accommodation. Made out report for Q. Arranged with Major Montgomery to take command of Train in my absence on leave, wrote to him accordingly.	
11	Inspected 14th Divn Transport Q., Dvl. H.Q Q?, H.Q. R.E. Signal Coy ½ & 2/, T.S. ?, A Field Coy R.E. Made out report for Q. Handed over Command of Train to Major Montgomery whilst on leave.	16th Lt. Col. B. Haigh R.M.O
12	Took over Company command of Train from Lt. Col. B Haigh whilst on leave to England	

Army Form C. 2118.

WAR DIARY
or
INTELLIGENCE SUMMARY.

(Erase heading not required.)

Instructions regarding War Diaries and Intelligence Summaries are contained in F. S. Regs., Part II. and the Staff Manual respectively. Title pages will be prepared in manuscript.

Hour, Date, Place	Summary of Events and Information	Remarks and references to Appendices
12 -	Visited 465 - 466 Cos: Inspected billets - Pack Train did not arrive at Railhead until 10. P.M. losing 11. P.M. Orders issued re movement of R.A. wit found arm. BMc	
13 -	Pack Train late - Commenced loading 5.30 P.M - Visited 464 Co: Inspected stable billets - Horses suspected of mange visited nostrils. BMc	
14 -	Pack Train late. Commenced loading 4-30 P.M - Mange becoming serious - Visited 465 & 466 Co: 465 Co: clear - Mange - 466 Co: several suspected cases isolated. 463 Co: report being made to move without assistance on 1st visit: arranged for spare yhorses to sent them from other Co: BMc.	
15 -	Pack Train late - Commenced loading 5-45 P.M. Visited BAZEAUE HOUSE where 463 Co: Train H.Q. will move to tomorrow. 463 Co: moved from LUCHEUX to BAVINCOURT. Reported to Division that we were unable to have 23 wagons owing to shortage of horses - evacuates & isolated through mange - asked for 8 lorries transit with drawing supplies - BMc.	

WAR DIARY
or
INTELLIGENCE SUMMARY.
(Erase heading not required.)

Army Form C. 2118.

Hour, Date, Place	Summary of Events and Information	Remarks and references to Appendices
16th Train H.Q.	463 Co: moved from BAUNCOURT to LA BAZEQUE V.O. inspected horses of 463 Co: visitated 6 Riders +44 H.D. a suspected cases of Mange – H.Q. Co: 15 H.D. deficient. Reference 1 Train Riders 5 – H.D. 39 – L.D. 3 – Reference 1 Train Riders 10 – H.D. 69 – L.D. 3 – Isolated Riders 2 P.M. Pack Train late – loading commenced 2 P.M. Informed by Div: H.Q. that Corps Cares only allow 4 lorries & 15 G.S. wagons from 27th Reserve Park to assist in drawing from Railhead.	
17th Pack Train late – loading commenced 4 P.M. Heavy fall of snow during night 16/17th – made arrangements for drawing supplies from Railhead with the limited amount of Transport available – many wagons having to do double journeys. This was possible as Refilling Points were near Railhead. Received orders to be prepared to move at a few hours notice. 3 Co: 1 Train & BAZEQUE at a few hours notice. In reply to enquiry from Division reported unable to move 37 wagons in case of Division being required to move at short notice – and informed Division that we should require 56 wagons to supplies fuel & 14 wagons to Ordnance Port should all M.T. be taken off roads in event of sudden thaw. Wired to Division asking if we could evacuate 8 G.S. wagons with drivers & horses ren. by surplus through re-organization of S.S.O. instructed to undertake woods cutting arrangements. 1 R.T. Attended XVIII Corps. Horse deficiencies – 2 Riders – H.D. 45 – L.D. g. Horses Isolated sick 13 Riders – H.D. 65 – L.D. 3 –	

WAR DIARY
or
INTELLIGENCE SUMMARY.
(Erase heading not required.)

Army Form C. 2118.

Instructions regarding War Diaries and Intelligence Summaries are contained in F. S. Regs., Part II. and the Staff Manual respectively. Title pages will be prepared in manuscript.

Hour, Date, Place	Summary of Events and Information	Remarks and references to Appendices
18th	Pack Train late - Commenced loading 7.45 P.M. Visited XVIII Corps re rationing Item - in view of Item being on our Ration Strength asked for Pack Train to be increased - No more cargo of Mange reported. All suspected horses still isolated. BMcC	
19th	Pack Train late - Commenced loading 1-45 P.M - Visited XVIII Corps re wood cutting arrangements - BMcC	
20th Jan.	Commenced loading 4-45 P.M. Wire from Div: H.Q. stating train in the event of a train of 15 wagons from 27th Reserve Park would be withdrawn and that 30 wagons from No 3 Sec: (work) be placed at disposal of Train - BMcC	
21st Jan:	Commenced loading 4-30 P.M. S.S.O. instructed to take over wood cutting from XVIII Corps - Visited 464 Co: with V.O. only 4 horses isolated 466 Co: 12 H.D. isolated sick and 7 rifero - 46st Co: 1 r.D. isolated BMcC 463 Co: 31 H.D. isolated sick and 4 riders.	
22nd Jan:	Commenced loading 12-30 P.M - S.S.O. attended XVIII Corps H.Q. re Wood cutting BMcC Issued instructions to Cos: re action to be taken in the event of Railhead being Shelled - Handed over command of Train to Lt. Col. A. Haigh on his return from leave BMcC	

WAR DIARY or INTELLIGENCE SUMMARY.

Army Form C. 2118.

Hour, Date, Place	Summary of Events and Information	Remarks and references to Appendices
Jan 23.	Took over Command of Train on Return from Leave. Visited 466 Y & 465 Coy at LA BRET. Inspected Horses. Then Rolli. Inspected Horses (Mange) were affected. 5 466 & 40 465 Coy. L'ênieur Q. re. Horse of Pole Carts, as their are in good covered standings, it is hoped the necessary wield out arise, at AntiRhumalerys are not yet finished at LA BAZEQUE. Pack Train arrived Railhead 1.30 P.M. The Mange appears to be now in Command. Inspected 463 Coy Horses & standings. The spreading of Mange is now restopped. B.H. tops to being all pupes on action for H.T. B.H.	
" 24.	Rung to the Horse Front. great difficulty experienced with the Mules, 25 strut now on a special Train. Pack Train arrived at 2.30 A.M. the Horses are to be fitter	
" 25.	Reported continued late arrival of Pack Train to Division Q. gathed for the matter. Got up with the Higher authorities. Visited Divisional Troops R.P. at LA BEZEQUE. then Coy. got Jan Lid. 464 Coy. appeared to have suffered most owing to the lack of Sheds, but is should up on the Morale trite & its good. Their Coy. & majority of Horses in poor condition. The condition of Horses are distinctly getting Horse Standings, when Rolli; Cake is available. & the Rains are properly feeding Stuffs. No Rain or General delayed 2 hours, owing to shunting. Withdrawed Pack Train arrived R. Head 7.30 P.M. loading delay 10th.

WAR DIARY or INTELLIGENCE SUMMARY

Army Form C. 2118.

Hour, Date, Place	Summary of Events and Information	Remarks and references to Appendices
Jan 26.	Interview O.C re Personnel for Remounts, due to arrive 10 P.M. received warning of the G.O.C's inspection of the Train on Tuesday and the 30th inst. issued necessary instructions to O.C. Coys. Capt MILLS taken over to Adjts work whilst Lt Reynolds is on leave. Lieut HOGENMEYER on attachment to a Staff for instruction in Staff duties. Front Still very quiet. Lieut MONTGOMERY/SHAW on attachment to R. Head. B.H. Pack Train has not arrived at R. Head. B.H.	
Jan 27.	At 9.45 A.M. as no Pack Train for Y'day has arrived, Spoke to O.C. asked to authorize to draw supplies from nearest Reserve Field Depot. Received instruction received that the C. Half will be attached to the Train in place of Capt. F.C. SCOTT, who is to depart to the M.O. for trains for to the R.F.A. Officers lid. Capt. MANTLE as temporary C.O. No 2 Company in place of Capt Scott. Second application for Capt J.C. STONEHOUSE to return to train sent to D.D.Q.M.G. He is required to command No 2 Company. Remounts arrived at R. H.Q. 2.30 A.M. 9 der hebrueled. 31 being for the Train. 10.30 A.M. received information that the Pack Train is broken down in broken Clown at MAN VICON T. arranged to Remount to be sent by lorry to Repelling Point. later straw forage from SAUCY R.H. for the demands of the supplies to be sent during the day. 465 2n Repellug Point. Clothes during the morning one troop woman and 3 even over by Stansfield & S. pain. Att. windows in 465.29 Officer Anmard of the Repelling shed blown up.	

WAR DIARY or INTELLIGENCE SUMMARY.

Army Form C. 2118.

Hour, Date, Place	Summary of Events and Information	Remarks and references to Appendices
Jan 27 (cont)	Remainder of Supplies finished refilling at 6 P.M. No news of Today's Pack Train.	
	The Divisional Troops Group finished refilling at 9 P.M. B.H.	
" 28th	At 10 A.M. no news of yesterday's Pack Train, reported to D.Q. at 10 A.M. Reported the departure to England of Capt. F.G. Scott, to transfer to the R.F.A. to D. Pack Train for the 17th. Arrived 1.30 P.M. at Soulty R.H.Q. Refilling completed at Base 2nd 8.45. D.H.T. @ 7 P.M. No news of Today's Pack Train.	
	Inspected roads in vicinity with a view to fresh Refilling Points. Received instructions that all Coys are to move to LA BEZEQUE by the 31st inst. Received instructions B.H. to G.O.C.s instructions.	
" 29th	Yesterday's Pack Train arrived at R.H.Q. 2.30 A.M. Had meeting of O.C. Companies re the G.O.C.s instruction. tomorrow also their new billets atrium standings at LA BEZEQUE.	
	No news of today's Pack Train. B.H.	
" 30th	Yesterday's Pack Train arrived at 11 A.M. Refilling completed by 4 P.M. G.O.C. inspected the Train today & expressed his satisfaction & pleasure with all he saw. Today received the 15 G.S. Wagons of the 27th A Reserve Park. Interview A.A.Q.M.G. re the withdrawal of the 15 G.S. Wagons to the Train when the Straw comes. Also the allotment 7.30 G.S. Wagons to the Front Field. Very keen today, high fall of snow. B.H.	

Army Form C. 2118.

WAR DIARY
or
INTELLIGENCE SUMMARY.
(Erase heading not required.)

Instructions regarding War Diaries and Intelligence Summaries are contained in F. S. Regs., Part II. and the Staff Manual respectively. Title pages will be prepared in manuscript.

Hour, Date, Place	Summary of Events and Information	Remarks and references to Appendices
Jan 31st	Interview A.A. & Q.M.G. re hosting of the Promoters of Officers Reid & on the 22.12.16. Inspected 1st Line Transport of the 19th Batt. Loco Fus. Pioneer Bath; on the whole fairly satisfactory 464, 465 & 466 Coys moved to LA BEZEQUE. The Train now being concentrated for the 1st time of the Companys all Officers being billeted in the Chateau meaning together. No news of todays pack train; 2 baggage wagons for each Batt. Bn ordered to report at Bde HQ to assist with the move of the Battalions, they are to return to the Train. The Pack Train arrived at 8.30 A.M. on Feb 1st. 2nd Bn in 14 Hours.	
31.1.17		Bernard Haugh Lt Col Commanding 49th Inf Train

SECRET.

WAR DIARY

OF

FOR

1917.

SECRET.

WAR DIARY.

OF

49th (W.R.) Div'l Train

FOR

February 1917.

Vol 23

CONFIDENTIAL.

WAR DIARY

OF

Lieut Col: G.B. Haigh. Commanding 49th. (WR) Divl Train:

From Feb: 1: 1917. To Feb. 28. 1917.

(Volume 23.)

WAR DIARY or INTELLIGENCE SUMMARY.

Army Form C. 2118.

(Erase heading not required.)

Hour, Date, Place	Summary of Events and Information	Remarks and references to Appendices
February 1st	Yesterday's Pack Train arrived 9.30 A.M. New Repelling Points used today for first time. Visited the new positions which are rather exposed gave instructions for improving them. Received authority from R.E. to draw total 7 Stores & Stakes. Soo for making to form standings for No 3 Coy. Wired XVIII Corps Q. Re concentrator is expected to phone for Officer.	
	Managed to turn in another application. Today's Pack Train arrived 7.30 P.M. Transport late loaded at R.H. retempted at R.P.	BH
2nd	Interview O.C. discussed to question of the 48th Army Field Art Not becoming attached to the 49 Brigade. Transport of supplies from Railhead to R.P. being the main point. Visited 14 A.L. Train interview O.C. re the hants of the transport & THE228.20.19 on the 3rd inst. 3 E Wagons arrange for them to Commence at 4.70 P.M. Pack Train arrd Railhead 10.15 P.M. Loading to commence at. all Wagons turned out Accurately 5	BH
3rd HQ	R.d. Train arrived 2.30 P.M. Arranged for Trucks & Stocks to House Standings 486 coy. made arrangements with AA79 M.S. to have a further 60ft of trough for watering. Trade allow purp to chateau got 3 new lengths of hose pipe. the Engine to pumping Hoppes at the Chateau began to pumping	

Army Form C. 2118.

WAR DIARY
or
INTELLIGENCE SUMMARY.
(Erase heading not required.)

Instructions regarding War Diaries and Intelligence Summaries are contained in F.S. Regs., Part II. and the Staff Manual respectively. Title pages will be prepared in manuscript.

Hour, Date, Place	Summary of Events and Information	Remarks and references to Appendices
February 4th (contd)	Strafe has been closer for several hours today	
5th	The Pack Train arrived Railhead at 9.15 P.M. leaving at 10.15 P.M. Issued all Repelling Points & Meteorological Cool Damps employed the Motor Engineer Ent. LM.B.T.R.Q.A.F. went on his leave in the Company of the New Capt. Tonight organised the Park who are using their Trough. R.E. should keep to the alarm Trough Pack Train arrived 2 P.M. leaving again 6.6. 5.15 P.M. Time table of Material Announced. CH	
6th	Pack Train arrived 8.30 A.M. was here until 9.30 A.M. Repelled 664 Co. Mountain Workshop. Then Multi. 1887 466. Col. Pinkshop, Horse Lines, Water Supplies & Good houses. To that an meeting completion Enquires Stores & Stores. Inform O.C. 141 Co. R.E. to the Water arrangements have appeared to have the importance of keeping it up & 10.30 received instructions that attached units are to be returned by the 30th Bren having been informed to carry out special arrangements made direct with the S.S.O. 30th Division Capt. Nelson then decided on leave for fourteen days. Leave started on the 9th until 23rd.	

Forms/C. 2118/10.

WAR DIARY
or
INTELLIGENCE SUMMARY.
(Erase heading not required.)

Army Form C. 2118.

Hour, Date, Place	Summary of Events and Information	Remarks and references to Appendices
Feb 7th	Interview Q.M. Graham re R.G.S. He states Carrier on G.S.; it being arranged that the general idea of carrying the Water Tins be carried out on all G.S. Wagons. Gave L.O. the G.O.C.'s orders accordingly. Pack Train arrived today at 12.15 P.M. Cpl CAMERON & 25 REYNOLDS returned from leave. B.H.	
8th	Pack Train having commenced today 1.15 P.M. Pte REYNOLDS took up duty as duties. Pack train arrived today from leave B.H. 2.30 P.M. Received Telephone message that Major MONTGOMERY will return 9th Train. Shall try Hen. R.H. Tomorrow to see him. Attached to Q. Staff pours Jacobson. Turk &c.	
9th	Interview A.M. & Q.M.G. discussed the question of return of R.G.S. from 463 Train. Returns to him. B. C. HALL reported for duty with the Train from 27th Reserve Park. Interview R.E. de Girels & Shaik for home landings. Maj L.E. MONTGOMERY rejoined duty from travel at 1 A.M. & assumed the S.G. of Supply. Pack Train arrived 1 A.M. Commenced loading at 2 A.M. Convoy of 10 Raced R.H. Starting loading at 2 A.M. 11th	
10th	Pack Train arrived 1 A.M. Convoy of 1 A.M. 11.2 loading & leaving to break up. B.H.	
11	The continual night work is telling on Esc.H. Horses Pain, this morning the Convoy returned to H.H.L. between 4.30 & 5.30 A.M. B.H.	

Army Form C. 2118.

WAR DIARY
or
INTELLIGENCE SUMMARY.
(Erase heading not required.)

Instructions regarding War Diaries and Intelligence Summaries are contained in F. S. Regs., Part II. and the Staff Manual respectively. Title pages will be prepared in manuscript.

Hour, Date, Place	Summary of Events and Information	Remarks and references to Appendices
Febuary 11th (contd)	The roads today are getting soft. Made arrangements with Telephone to the H.T. going to M.T. work during the Thaw. Come from 27 Feb. Rail Head to be attached to his train. Attached to this XVIII Corps. 1 F.S. Cole sent to DAD Railways	HT 9 n 5 on the Thow. 30 I.S.C.T. 3 T which are to be
7 A.M.	No news of Pack Train 18.H.	
10.30 A.M.	No news of Yesterdays Pack Train. It would be much better had we a system of Capt. Depot O.C. Railhead for the Divisional Trains to draw and from. The continual between R.M. Butts Pack Train is getting very serious. Held meeting of Officers. Telephoned the recent 4 7 Supporters to M'n Leon or for instruction in Div. No A/16/98. Yesterdays Pack Train arrived at Railhead 3.15 P.M. loading commenced 4.15 P.M. Supply Train finished 7 h 7.30 P.M. Tin Twenty 8.0 P.M. Men is getting very nearly to extreme limit as the Supplies are for tomorrow consumption. Wired all from Conjohans Officers yesterday Let all Officer Books to 2nd Class they were more pronounced.	

WAR DIARY or INTELLIGENCE SUMMARY

Army Form C. 2118.

Hour, Date, Place	Summary of Events and Information	Remarks and references to Appendices
February 12th (contd.)	The C.R.A. 49th Division visited the Motor Transport & expressed its appreciation & made. Shaw gave three left trough & frame better. Battery horses through the day. The Engine is working better. Batt.	Sent the tipster that Shaw gave three from 2.000 to 2.400
13th	No post from around today. Commenced trading 4.30 A.M. on 16th inst. Frost at night. BH.	
14th	Post train arrived 12.30 P.M. Issued a at 2 P.M. closed the Yard at 12 noon 20 hours	
15th	This is the first time for G.S. Wagons Bt. H.T.P.M.S. together with the new D.A.Q.M.G. Issued from H.Q. & the new horse standings were down. Also the Rations arranged by Today Post Train arrived 8 P.M. Issuing commenced 7.15 P.M. Batt.	
16th	Today's Post Train arrived at 12-15 A.M. on 17th inst. Loading Oc 58th Batt. Train called their Rebels & horse train with a view to taking our when the moves. Rev. Fred Hollier for our horses 17 hours 61.0 P.M. these vehicles loaded on the Yard Batt.	
17th	Horse Train out from 12.30 A.M. to 4.30 A.M. The Thaw is now Rel in & the road is in a bad state. Had a visit from D.A.Q.M.G. XVIII Corps. explained the Motor Cutting system. Also showed him the Horse Lines here.	

WAR DIARY
or
INTELLIGENCE SUMMARY.
(Erase heading not required.)

Army Form C. 2118.

Hour, Date, Place	Summary of Events and Information	Remarks and references to Appendices
February 17th (contd)	Received notice of arrival of Removals 296 all classes due at MARLINCOURT at 8 A.M. tomorrow. No H.D. available at present. Made arrangements for collection & distribution.	
18th	Today's Pack Train arrived at 2.30 A.M. on 18th. Wagons returned from R.P. at 5.30 - 6 A.M. Inspected all Corps Horse Lines & Horse Hosp., Cook Houses &c. The Mud is getting bad. Off. Received Operation order No. 96 from Q. issued from O.O. M. 23rd accordance with M.Q. 21st. Was received from Q. Received Train Instructions for Lorries. 7 A.M. to 7 P.M. 21st Off. Today's Pack Train arrived at 5.30 P.M. Loading commenced at 6.30 P.M. Off.	
19th	In General O. is proposed move of the Division ascended to transport supplies Supplies from Railhead. Arrangements to be made, as that for Lorries to draw supplies from Railhead at LA MEZEAUE, R.P. Paul for 146th Bde. Group. on 20th one Lorry to carry up supplies on L.F. Switch area to which to Railhead for the supplies wagon have gone to the other to load up but not to the other, as baggage wagon have gone Authority granted for the Co. Lorry but not for supplies from Railhead to Refilling Point - hence it will be difficult to draw 146 Bde supplies from Railhead, arranged to use as many of the 21 Reserve Park Wagons as possible for the work these supplies will be taken to R.P. & then picked up by the Lorries Token to L.F. Switch area. Pack Train arrived at 8.30. P.M. & Turned out at 9 P.M. returning midnight. Off.	

WAR DIARY or INTELLIGENCE SUMMARY

Army Form C. 2118.

Hour, Date, Place	Summary of Events and Information	Remarks and references to Appendices
Feb: 18th (contd)	On receipt of Rw Ratwohim, 21 G.S. wagons reported from 27th Reserve Park. 3 Put at the disposal of Corps Troops Supply Officer, 1 Sent to Div: Laundry & to the use of Balance S/ Section Postal S/ for Fuel. RH	
20th	464 COY marched from LA BEZEQUE to LE SUICH. Reported from 27th Reserve Park. unexplained delay with the first party, and Capt. Mouton & a corporal moving off. very dissatisfied with the first party, and Capt Mouton & a corporal unexplained to them the importance of turning & correctly. Have notified the Co. when up to 6.30 p.m. the Rest did not arrive for issue a talk until 11 p.m. B.H. Today's Pack Train arrived not arrived up to the time may P.S. wagons not arriving	
21st	Interview O.C. concerned the question of transport of supplies from Railhead to the issue to the 146th S/ Bde Park kept all morning to pt. kept the T.A.C. plan the supplies & authorized authority for the case & obtained the required authority for
2 P.M.	Rang up XVIII Corps & explained urgency of Pack train arrived Railhead 5 P.M. Loading started 6.30 P.M. 13th
5 P.M.	Pack train arrived Railhead	

Army Form C. 2118.

WAR DIARY
or
INTELLIGENCE SUMMARY.
(Erase heading not required.)

Instructions regarding War Diaries and Intelligence Summaries are contained in F. S. Regs., Part II. and the Staff Manual respectively. Title pages will be prepared in manuscript.

Hour, Date, Place	Summary of Events and Information	Remarks and references to Appendices
Oct 21st (Contd)	Received Divisional Operation orders for the Move of the Division to the 1st Army Area. Made out Train & Bus accordingly. Operation Order No. 24. Bt.	
22	Supplies/with B.A.C/Pats at L.G. Sweep drawn from 58 Divl. Railhead BOUQUEMAISON. Rum & Tea & Pack draw own Pack at SAULTY. Pack Train arrived 7 P.M. Drawn Rations & horses stall on picket until 7 A.M. the 23rd with Bt.	
23rd	Pack Train arrived 3.30 P.M. Made out Railhead Supply Table for the Move. Authority received for use of Column. B.tt.	
24th	463 Coy marched to L.G. Sweep. Pack Train arrived at 10 A.M. the Supply Point being taken from 27th Reserve Park attached to this Train. One hour & one hour's being held from 1st Army. Pass out of those pro found to be warm off. March Table from 1st Army made out & Train for L.G. S.Q.G. Received. Had visit from O.C. 58 Divl. Train to the Relief Tomorrow, arranged with him to stay at Chateau. Btt.	
25th	Train Hd Qrs moved to LUCHEUX. 463 Coy marched to LUCHEUX. Officers & horses Billets very poor. Bt.	
26	Packed Divl. H.Q Q. deliveries of Billets, Area, arranged for Adjt to Regt RAMECOURT. Tomorrow. H.Q. Divl. marched to LUCHEUX. W.M.	

WAR DIARY
or
INTELLIGENCE SUMMARY
(Erase heading not required.)

Army Form C. 2118

Place	Date	Hour	Summary of Events and Information	Remarks and references to Appendices
Feb.	27.		Move of Division continued. 146th L.F. Bde marched from BERNES Area to First Army Area. Visited 13th Field Ambulance inspected transport. Seat report to A.D.M.S. this Army. Lignières 3 Remans to bring up to strength, one horse has to stay with Farm for observation + two others are in very poor condition; otherwise 3 L.D. from 148th M.O.C. Rlt.	
"	28.		Div. H.Q. marched to RAMECOURT. 148th Bde to BOUGAINVILLE Area N° 1. Train H.Q. to SAUCHIN. Inspected. Transport of 14/15th H.C. Co. & 3rd & 4th L.L.D. on 1st inst. A Visited III Army Hd. Qrs. No record 147th Inf. Bde. 466 C.T.Y. marched to CROISETTE. B.H.	

28/2/17.

Bernard Haigh Lt Col
Commanding 49th Ind. Train

Vol. 24

SECRET.

WAR DIARY.

OF

49th (WR) Divisional Train

FOR

March. 1917.

CONFIDENTIAL.

WAR DIARY

of

Lieut Col C.B. Heigh. Commanding. 49th (A.R) Siril Train.

From 1-3-17.

To. 31-3-17.

(Volume 24.)

WAR DIARY or INTELLIGENCE SUMMARY

Army Form C. 2118

Place	Date	Hour	Summary of Events and Information	Remarks and references to Appendices
March	1st		Visited Q. discussed the further move of the Division. Div. H.Q. & Train H.Q. near St Pol. B.H.	
"	2nd		Train H.Q. marched to PERNES. also Divis. H.Q. & 146 H.of Bde. H.Q. Visited Q. discussed the movement of 147 H. of Bde. received march table, to transfer tr. 145 Coy travel to 1st Army Area & to remain on trains by Tactical Train & the remainder to entrain? B.H. Interview D.D.S.T. re the Train party drawing 2 days rations on entraining B.H.	
"	3rd		Train H.Q. marched to LESTREM. 464 Coy moved to the MERVILLE – LA GORGUE road. 466 Coy stayed at ST. VENANT. 463 Co moved to CALONNE SUR LA LYS. 465 Coy moved to LUCHEUX. Div: H.Q marched to LESTREM. B.H.	
"	4th		19th Coy finished arranged to load this Bn. 2. G.S. M Supplies onto the transport arrive. Visited new Railhead LA GORGUE & all new Refilling Points. Visited Lempire & the horses of Marel were looking fairly well. chance of Gas has not marked. Visited O.C Train 58th Division, discussed all points. & made arrangements. T 463 Cy 464 Cy 466 Co the horse often then Marel were looking fair	

Army Form C. 2118.

WAR DIARY
or
INTELLIGENCE SUMMARY.
(Erase heading not required.)

Hour, Date, Place	Summary of Events and Information	Remarks and references to Appendices
March 4th (Contd.)	Staff over their H.Q. on the B.M. not arranged for O.C. 463 Co. Staff over afrom No1 Co. on 6th P.M. Invited Q.Y. clearance of new Transport arrangement & explained the final system of supplies - arranger for Rfll.'s then issue	arranged for O.C. 463 Co.
5th	to La Gorgue to train H.Q. M.	
6th	In La Gorgue.	
	Train H.Q. moved to La Gorgue. Invited to Echelon of 147 & LS Bde (A Transport Section) at PERNES inspected all Horse Transport of the group which are marching up to 1st Army area. Made out report for Q.. 463 Co. at PERNES are this day Bty.	
7th	Divisional H.Q. moved to La Gorgue. 465 Co. Mackay to th Colonne area.	
	146 Co. moved to the position LESTREM - MERVILLE took yesterday Relieved Headquarters. 2009 S.&d. Divisional, all Co except 465 Co are now in their final position in LA GORGUE - LESTREM - ESTAIRES area.	
8th	Interview Q. re the new arrangements for dealing with the Corps & Divisional Transport requirements.	

WAR DIARY or INTELLIGENCE SUMMARY

Army Form C. 2118.

Hour, Date, Place	Summary of Events and Information	Remarks and references to Appendices
March 8th (contd)	Inspected 3rd & 4th Bns New Yorks Regt & 1/H.Q. 146 B[riga]de Transport at LAVENTIE. B.H.	
9th	Had meeting of C.O. Commanders. discussed the stowing out of new Horse & Wagon March Discipline etc. Inspected the Bells & Horse Lines of H.Q. No 3 Co. 58th Train.	
	Mr Capt Ren from to the gun of taking over H Capt Ren from to the gun & taking over 7th & 8th Bns High Rgts & 146th Machine Gun Co. at Inspected 7th & 8th Bns. High Rgts. & 146 MG Co at LAVENTIE. Made out Report for Q. B.H.	
10th	46520 took over the Position of the No 3 Co 58th Train B.H.	
11th	Routine Office Work. turned action for X1 Corps standing open to be accepted	
	throughout the train B.H.	
12th	Had order Room Charge & Drunkeness against a Driver of 46600 Charge	
	made & N.D.	
	Pearls Inspected 46620 Horse Lines arm Bills & Workshops Inspected 146th Infs[a]de Transport. H.Q. 146th M.G. Co. Y.S.R Yrs. first improvement all round B.H.	

WAR DIARY or INTELLIGENCE SUMMARY

Army Form C. 2118.

Hour, Date, Place	Summary of Events and Information	Remarks and references to Appendices
March 13th	Visited Railhead at Lozinghem today being the first day for the train to draw there. The work was completed in 1½ hours. Made arrangements for the flag system the corner and visited the Refilling Points, not satisfied with flow, asked O.R.E. for 3 more Supply shelter to put up also more grease. Visited Q.M. Green D.A.Q.M.G. & S.A.H.O. Corps & 4th Divs. Inspected MT's at Hrs. 1st line transport of have yet seen it. The transport now in the best condition I have yet seen it. Made out report for Q.B.H.	
14	Took over charge of Brenham bought 3 M.R. made out full report of same for A.D.M. Had note from D.A.Q.M.G., S.E.M. Matthew 4662 to be attacked for 1 lorries Coy. month non open to S.E.M. Matthew 4662 1 Batt. Interview 4664 Co. to two tenth to M.C. of S. 1 Batt.	BH
	Interview D.D.D Sup. 1st Army at LILLERS. discussed the formation of officers pool in 7th Oct 16.	BH
	Received A.F.A. Bar. Pool Captain & Exchange Adviser Park being attacks kit teams	BH

WAR DIARY
or
INTELLIGENCE SUMMARY.

(Erase heading not required.)

Army Form C. 2118.

Hour, Date, Place	Summary of Events and Information	Remarks and references to Appendices
March 16th	Inspected Motor Transport of the 1st West Rgg Field Ambulance. Made out report for A.D.M.S., I.Q. Completed return asked for by Lt Coll Ruston R.H.	
17th	Visited Railhead at Ouderdom S.C.S.O. re time of trains. Working up. Librarian D.A.Q.G. discussed the question of men helping in the French C.S. Visited 46320 Employment and Workshops from Re Ulls. Horse Lines re. Mules considerable mud. Showers Horses regards moving a coveny 9pm.	
18th	Interv. A.D.M.S. re the two mares submitted as suitable officers for the Junction. T.E.R.C. re a Russian Ambulance two names. Bate	
19th	Picked & inspected the New Repelling Panel for Duncand troops, Escorte 9 to 163 M.S./132 Group econsistent the Horse Lines her Bell C. Workshops re of 46320. The is a very good position, with stables. She is a Home stamp. The D.A.Q.M.S. was with me. Bate	

WAR DIARY
or
INTELLIGENCE SUMMARY.
(Erase heading not required.)

Army Form C. 2118.

Hour, Date, Place	Summary of Events and Information	Remarks and references to Appendices
March 20th	Received notification that all Sport Horse are to be attached to us and 32 horses lent on any Establishment. Made out return for Q. Received verification of the shortage of Horse Shoe Nails. Huggs Remarks for B.H.	
" 21st	Inspected 2nd HR Transport at Lime Transport at YEU CHAPEL. Horses in very poor condition. Horses begun more patching. Received a visit from 142 M.S. Cleveland. The question of mountings of officers with spare mounts explained & the system to be carried out, arranged for R.E. 30.Y.460R Atd attached to Train when advancing. Such A.O.C. 24th Train at NOEUX. M BETHUNE. Together with the five company Commanding Stowe Remarks to O.C. American Park Saade attached with	
" 22	1. Horses Aug. 1. Rembukat. 3 Cait 4140H Kips. 10H. Just Q & Camp for this New Hook Rental & arranged for a Remount to be at Lovesits. 10H	

WAR DIARY
or
INTELLIGENCE SUMMARY

Army Form C. 2118

Place	Date	Hour	Summary of Events and Information	Remarks and references to Appendices
March	23		Inspected 1/3rd Field Ambce; 1st Div Transport; Post at all Watering to Condition.	
"	24		Afternoon being very fine, saw O.C. 6th Reserve Park, arranged detail for taking Reserve Mnt. from his Section to be attached for instructn. in drawing Supplies at Railhead. BM.	
			Invited 1st Army HQ for interview with DDOS Offr. in Charge, an Offcr. for Charge(?) who has been posted T.o.t. 2nd Train, discussed the carrying of Station Pack Mules in the event of an advance.	
			Drew O. & a.q.M.G. conference of the situation in the improved Pack March advancing. Rtt carrying a notice on Relief Train for troops when advancing. arranged to place S.O.C. the Demonstrated to DAQMG for new Pack arrangement. BH	
"	25		Same on 27 Anvil.	
			Visited reinforced No 2 Coy at Stable how 4.15 PM. Horses seem to be Improving. This Coy. shew improvement in stable discipline. BH	
"	26		Made enquires re Purchase of Goats required for new Pack System. Met out Estimate for Agreement, for New Pack arrangements. BH	

WAR DIARY
or
INTELLIGENCE SUMMARY
(Erase heading not required.)

Army Form C. 2118

Place	Date	Hour	Summary of Events and Information	Remarks and references to Appendices
Havre	27		Demos held to G.O.C. the improved Pack Saddle for Supplies. Correspre. Made.	
			9/C Remount Shell Corps, visited Railhead & inspected all Companys Horse Lines, inspected the Hay & Oats train ordered by XI Corps. this is being carried out according to instructions.	
			Attended conference at Q. office, arranged with Staff Capt to attend instruction conference Q. Adm^{re} Z.L. Bn. re alterations with the new Pack arrangement to be on the strength of the A.V.A.Bdes.	
	28		Received authority to 2nd Line Transport Personnel Horses to be on the strength of the A.V.A.Bdes. travel on the train. Visited 46 & 2 Coy & inspected the M.V.C. Horse Transit in Ambulances Bttt	
	29		Major Montgomery went on 14 days special leave today. Visited the Base Supply depot Boulogne with a view of getting tracks for Attach annuals, P.M.	
	30		In Evening accompanied by Major S. Matthews visited Railhead at Loading Zone also Marched to R. Pean the LA BASSÉE Road Pytt	

WAR DIARY or INTELLIGENCE SUMMARY

Army Form C. 2118

Place	Date	Hour	Summary of Events and Information	Remarks and references to Appendices
March	31		All monthly return made out. Received instructions re the transfer of 2/L. Laughton & 2/L. Kings, Roi: 304 Train. Arranged for Car to take Laughton & return with Kings. Field A.C. Labour Batn. to Fatigues here. Field abs. Co. 10A	

Bernard Stevely Lt-Col
Commanding 49th Divl. Train

March 31st 1917.

Vol 25

SECRET.

WAR DIARY.

OF

49th (WR) Div'l Train

FOR

April 1917.

CONFIDENTIAL.

War Diary

Of

Lieut. Col. B. Haigh. Commanding 49th Divisional Train.

From 1.4.17.

To 30.4.17.

(Volume 25).

WAR DIARY
or
INTELLIGENCE SUMMARY
(Erase heading not required.)

Army Form C. 2118.

Hour, Date, Place	Summary of Events and Information	Remarks and references to Appendices
Apl. 1st 1917.	Sent in refs of full details of Promotion of Officers, this was first sent in in November. Had word from Capt. BARNE. D.R.B. 1st Army who is now on the Strength of this Train. arranged with him to forego 2/Lt. Shingly reported for duty, nee 2/Lt 2nd Lt gton who went to 34th Amb Train & 2/Lt SLINGSBY posted to No 1 Coy. 2/Lt POWELL posted to No 2 Coy, in place of LAUGHTON.	
" 2nd "	Instd Pack Saddle Ammunition on No 15 & 16 1st Army of BARLIN. Also instd XI Corps Q. re 13" Gun Ammn infantry this train. You again tracking the Packhorses notes continued. Received instructions that the D.O.C. will inspect the train on Friday next. M.	

Army Form C. 2118.

WAR DIARY
or
INTELLIGENCE SUMMARY.
(Erase heading not required.)

Hour, Date, Place	Summary of Events and Information	Remarks and references to Appendices
Apl 3d	Interview Q character Park Cooke suggests the programme for "FO 2" inspection by Director of Supplies Inspected 197th F. Coy at LAVENTIE. Franks was a good crowd. with Hames & Higgins a few cent more attention. But Reports to Q. Practical repair of Park Noted. Remarks to Q. Bt	
Apl 4"	Practised with the Horse Dumps of the 1st Army Pershore Remns, mules thrust all the horses & HQ. 11 Army. to 9 PM this army is after. Threat Officers & HQ 11 Army. Contract with III & Army which Carried out & is in fact contract with The LILLIERS Line 700 Tons It returned to D. The Church Yard at MERVILLE 900 Tons. BETHUNE had a few of the bathroom at MERVILLE will hold 450 Tons & Bala Straw has now In it Room which I will fill up. Bt been filled up. Bt	

Place	Date	Hour	Summary of Events and Information	Remarks and references to Appendices
O/L	5th		Field D. rehearsed the parade for the G.O.C's inspection tomorrow. Wired recovery instruction to Bn.	
	6th		The G.O.C inspected the Train — all wagons & horses being on the road to Estry Lectures at Railhead & Noyelles-les-Humières — LA GORGUE — MERVILLE Road. & expressed his pleasure with the whole turn out — in my opinion this is the best show we have had — * Published my thanks & appreciation to all Ranks in T.O.'s 10th.	
	7th		Received letter from G.O.C expressing his pleasure at the result — of the Inspection; he says "I consider that the appearance of the Horses Vehicles & Great Coat covered of the turnout of the Horses Vehicles do each company this letter sent down to each company historian Q to the material for making to road for carrying stocks to R.P. Two Btns.	

WAR DIARY or INTELLIGENCE SUMMARY

Army Form C. 2118

Place	Date	Hour	Summary of Events and Information	Remarks and references to Appendices
Apl	8th		Visited 146th L.F. Bde 175th L.F. Bde Reporting Pon. & On. La Bassée Rd. Also the dumps. Have seen Genl. the necessary shelters up & are much improved him a Catafarcing condition.	B.A
	9th		Shu. as the 2nd inventory of the Divisional Staff coming to France, compens up (A.R.P.) to the D.A.P. & C. Staff Captain & the S.C.O. Myself being the Lotto formed arrangements to B.H.	
	10		Interview Q. took up patterns of lights frames to carry. Two of them on Pack-ladder. Sent in report to the photos. are being taken away last night. Rent in report to the photos. car being taken away from the HQ on	10H
	11		Interview Q. re the charge of taking a photo. Car away from the HQ on also interviewed the A.P.M. re the forms being sent away by M. Roberts. Inspected 147th M.G. Coy. Satisfactory result. Made out report to Q.	B.A

Army Form C. 2118

WAR DIARY
or
INTELLIGENCE SUMMARY
(Erase heading not required.)

Instructions regarding War Diaries and Intelligence Summaries are contained in F. S. Regs., Part II. and the Staff Manual respectively. Title Pages will be prepared in manuscript.

Place	Date	Hour	Summary of Events and Information	Remarks and references to Appendices
Opl	12		Made out report for F.G.C.M. for Dr. Roberts, charged with being drunk & disorderly with his equipment &c. B.H.	
	13		Interview O. Received Telegram from Major Montgomery, informing one of having Interview with 3 Parcs. at Halloy & 3 Parcs. at Havre. Sent from Roberts B.H.	
			Move. Due to illness	
			Interview A.D.M.S.	
	14		Vis'd 147th Bde Refilling Point at Teen Chapel, although we have no Platoon up at the point it is in a good position & has high wall at the back. V'std 2nd/7th Bn Lond. Div at the point it is in a good position & has high wall at the back. V'std 2nd/7th Bn Lond. Div	
			Had Dinner from Staff Officer of the Portuguese Division, & shewed them the whole working of a Divisional Train, going first to Railhead Keystone. the System of Refilling them & the loading up of the G.S. Wagons. The Systems of Refilling Points & the Filling Points & explained at each one	
	15		Visited three of the Refilling points & explained in detail game them copies of System of issuing to the Units in detail game them copies of A.F's. B.255, B33,16 & B37.17, & explained the channel of including to the Pof offrs from the Units to the R.S.O. to Army R.E. accompanied was R.L.	

WAR DIARY or INTELLIGENCE SUMMARY

Army Form C. 2118

Place	Date	Hour	Summary of Events and Information	Remarks and references to Appendices
Apl	15 (Contd)		Received letter from Major Montgomery informing me that owing to illness he had applied to M.O. for a further 14 days leave. Discussed the question of the horses of the R.E. being away on other duties & rather than collected together again in the eas't the difficulty of getting them collected together again in the east. & also the M.R.O.M.S. a letter on an urgent advance, & shewed the M.R.O.M.S. a letter on	
"	16		Budget received from O.C. 69th S. Division R.H. Visited 464 Coy. Inspected Supply & Baggage section in Marching order very satisfactory. Horses, harness, Dragon being very clean being just convalescent. Inspected Office books of the Coy. Visited 463 Coy. Inspected Horse Standings, also inspected Office books. Interview A.A. & M.S. re water tin carriers for Bed. Saddles, arranged to tie up with the R.E. to make 112 Supplies, also reported that Major Montgomery is detained in England owing to illness. R.H.	

WAR DIARY
or
INTELLIGENCE SUMMARY

(Erase heading not required.)

Army Form C. 2118

Instructions regarding War Diaries and Intelligence Summaries are contained in F. S. Regs., Part II. and the Staff Manual respectively. Title Pages will be prepared in manuscript.

Place	Date	Hour	Summary of Events and Information	Remarks and references to Appendices
	Apr 17		Interview O.i/c one Captain F.C. Mayers also discussed the question of making it necessary for the Companys for Packeles. Visited C.R.E's Office & discussed the making of the Corpses I took them posters ??.	
	" 18		Received instructions for 24 G.S Wagon to report daily at ESTAIRES WHARF at 6 P.M. to carry stores to A.T Coy R.E. to forward points, arranged to the Supply Column to draw Supplies from Railhead each morning for 147 H Regt Group 12M.	
	" 19		Detailed two 24 G.S Wagons from 465 Coy to report to the A.T Coy R.E. This Coy is relieved from all Supply duties in the mornings 13M.	
	" 20		Applied for the Home Standings lately occupied by Reserve Park to be taken over by No. 1 Coy. Received reply to promotion of officers letter from D.A.O. informing me that no more application for promotion would be considered, the confusion in the Relations 7.7. & Regular A.S.C. become more interesting daily, often five months.	

WAR DIARY
or
INTELLIGENCE SUMMARY

Army Form C. 2118

Place	Date	Hour	Summary of Events and Information	Remarks and references to Appendices
Cpl	20 (Contd)		of recommendation we are now informed that no action can be taken although the train is one huge & three Cafe & below Establishment, than keep so far the fast 6 months. BH.	
"	21		Interview D. Margan S. to new Starage to No4 Coy. Dr ROBERTS No 3 Coy been by S.M. Chaps "Louised to the rank" making any cost Governor to property. Intends to 9 months J.H.L. BH.	
"	22		Interview O a Promoting H.C.S. Officers. Received official notification that hop Montgomery. He had 14 days extended trick leave in England. Enemy Aeroplanes active over this town La GORGUE both morning & evening and Bombs dropped killing one man & wounding one. had them taken to "B" than Bell.	
"	23		Interview cap A.S.C. conductor for Commission. Interview S.S.M. Leyton to Reinforcement for No2 Coy. Instructed him who to report to. Workshops & officer Mess b. of No3 Coy. These are to Lent. Mr L.D. & Knight kept Horse Lines. Mortuary cookhouse & all necessary places to BH.	

Place	Date	Hour	Summary of Events and Information	Remarks and references to Appendices
Apl	24		Visited 1 Wykehn Home Term, Workshops & Officer Books & Mens Coy. Found all in first class order. Capt MANTLE : C.A. when leading two convoys of supplies through LAVENTIE this morning during heavy shelling of the village was wounded in the leg & evacuated to the London No 2 C.C.S. at MERVILLE. Lt P.L. HOLDSWORTH 46529 took on temporary command of 464 Coy. S.S.M. LEYDON was slightly wounded at the horse lines at Capt MANTEL but remains on duty with 464 Coy. The supplies convoy which killed one man, wounded one man (who has since died) and one of our own A.A. shells (aria) on the 22.n.d into from Loton.	
	25		Interview O.M.P.M.I.S. re appointment of O.C. Nº2 Coy in event of Transport for Capt RE break at night. It is now apparent that 31 F.C. Wagon upright weights at ESTAIRE wheuse is very necessary in due course for this Service Batt.	

Place	Date	Hour	Summary of Events and Information	Remarks and references to Appendices
Apl	26		Had interview with J.A.O.M.G. re the transfer & question brought up by the Corps, & discussed the question of posting all Imperial Major to Divisional Mounts attached by the O.C. Train, explained to D.H.Q.'s that this is the system at present being carried out in this Division. Major MONTGOMERY reported back for duty, having had 28 days leave in England, he had 14 being extended sick leave. Received letter from the Corps Commander & the G.O.C complimenting the whole Division on the excellent state of the Transport. RSM	
	27.		Completed Confidential Reports of Hay in LA GORGUE Square. Attended Presentation of Ribbon brooches by the XI Corps Commander at MERVILLE. Capt MAY & Lt STYLES of 463 Coy. A.S.C. A.S.C. receiving the M.M. for Brave & Gallant in YPRES, also G/16 CALVERT attached Div. H.Q Meritorious Medal for Good Service. RSM	

WAR DIARY or INTELLIGENCE SUMMARY

Place	Date	Hour	Summary of Events and Information	Remarks and references to Appendices
OHL	28		Quilid Railhead requested the experiment of loading in detail the Divisional Troops. Group, owing to the various commanders being sent up in various trucks on the move great delay is caused in loading — decided therefore not to continue the system. Between 9 & noon Zed the above, discovered the Frame Water Corner for Road Mule Kennepa to Tent the Rain made by R.E. At 3 P.M. LA GORGUE Railhead shelled for one hour 5 shells making direct hits, some dozen or eight shells also fell in the town of La Gorgue. At 5.45 P.M. Two shells fell near Railhead, during the evening night the Railhead was shelled regularly. — Met Railhead Tomorrow will be MERVILLE Rett. 10.30 P.M. received instructions 148 Bde. Group & Divl. Troops Alm with H.T. the remainder will Quited Railhead MERVILLE, 148 Bde. Group & Divl. Troops Next Tomorrow Rett.	
	29.		Lorries arranged for town to clear Divl. Troops Next Tomorrow Rett.	

Army Form C. 2118.

WAR DIARY
or
INTELLIGENCE SUMMARY.
(Erase heading not required.)

Place	Date	Hour	Summary of Events and Information	Remarks and references to Appendices
Afsé	30th		Enemy continued shelling last night. LA GORGUE & the Railhead. Field Railhead & the new Refilling Point for 146 & 15th Groups on the MERVILLE Road. Our new Turning out 36 G.S. Wagons to R.E. Store work loading of all am new turning out 36 G.S. Wagons to R.E. Store work & M.17. Central. the wagon DESTAIRS WHARF at 6.30 P.M. & taking the Stone to M.17. Central returning to 2.0 hours between 12 Midnight 1 A.M. 465 & 466 Coys Supplies being drawn by M.T. from R.H.Q. & 1st Line Regt Trans. p. drawn from R.P.S.	

Bernard Hugh
Lt Col
Commanding 49th And Train

Vol 26

CONFIDENTIAL.

WAR DIARY

OF

LIEUT. COL. B. HAIGH. COMMANDING 49TH DIVISIONAL TRAIN.

FROM. 1·5·17.

TO. 31·5·17.

(VOLUME 26.)

WAR DIARY
INTELLIGENCE SUMMARY

Army Form C. 2118.

Place	Date	Hour	Summary of Events and Information	Remarks and references to Appendices
In the Field	May 1st		Buried Pte Parker at Merville & the R.P. of the 1/6th Devon Regt. Tested the new water carrier frames made by the R.E's. These proved too weak to take the new water bags, but of shape with result that the tins all came out. New frames would be sent out & shape with... to AA & Q.M.G. & went with him to the Corps. Col. Montgomery was not in to the R.E's to copy. Returned & storage frame for the R.E's to copy. R. afterwards. Major Montgomery had a Sergeant in afternoon who called & DC 14 F.A. Ambulance who & closed them to be. C.O. 8 Norfolks Batt.	
	2nd		Rattled & moved back to Lt. Goneents the morning. T.C.C.R. This morning leading from reports Lt. Majr Montgomerie has been... Moved Q reports Lt Majr Montgomerie to carry on the C.O's work, & Lt. C.C. Reynolds to act a Adjt. Finished C/N Militia.	Btt
	3.		Interview O.C. arranged to Demonstrate the Texas Pack saddle to the AA & Q.M.G. Corps Tnn. H.Q. 66th Division in the afternoon at 4.30 p.m. did so at Corps Ln. H.Q. Had interview with Gen Green the DA & QMG Corps re Promotion of Officers & arranged to send him copy of all correspondence thereon.	

WAR DIARY or INTELLIGENCE SUMMARY

Army Form C. 2118.

Place	Date	Hour	Summary of Events and Information	Remarks and references to Appendices
Merris Q.	May 4th		Inspected 146th M.G. Coy. at Vieille Chapelle. Received instructions to attach 15 G.S. Wagons to XI Corps. The new arrangement to be for Corps R.E. work. Made arrangements for lorries to carry 51 Wagons daily for XI Corps R.E. for 146 Bn Group & transferred balance from R.P. Ry.	
"	5		Accompanied by Major S. & Major S. to L.E. parks No 4 Coy. to be bid inspection of Motor company. Neither of which was at satisfactory. Visited No 3 Coy, in morning Rd.	
"	6		Arranged to also reinforce one of them. Sent instructions to 15 G.S. Wagons to report to Corps R.E. work. Made arrangements for G.S. Wagons to draw at Renescure on 8th and for 3 Groups Atts. straw at Renescure.	
"	7		The above arrangement cancelled by Q. Lorries will continue to train wagons being required for R.E. & Corps Work. Detailed 36 Wagons to Estaires Wharf at 8.30 A.M. daily for L.R.E. & 15 G.S. Wagons for XI Corps Road Construction (Cont'd)	

WAR DIARY
or
INTELLIGENCE SUMMARY

Place	Date	Hour	Summary of Events and Information	Remarks and references to Appendices
May 7th (Cont)			Railhead & Train at LA GORGUE shelled during the evening also Gas attack alarm. Kept up all night. Attack on R.H.Q. Maryhouse heavy. Stopped shortly before on the park R.H.	
	8th		Railhead & train J LA GORGUE. Shelled 6.20 a.m. 4-7 A.M. the line being cut behind the Supply train, delay in trains arrival shells continued until noon.	
			Interview Q. Claimant arrangements re the Corps Commanders inspection of the train Major Montgomerie, Lt Col C.C.S. to base. Discussed quartering Capt MANTLE of the staff of the train R.M.	
	9th		at 5 A.M. Railhead shelled. Slaughterhouse Motor Lorries found it satisfactory	
			Interview Q. Tent. LA GORGUE shelled for two & half hours shells falling at 6 & 15 R.M. LA GORGUE shelled for two & half hours shells falling on on either ends of train H.Q. gr. R.H. Shelling continued through night R.H.	
	10th		Interview Q. & obtained authority to move the train H.Q. on to near No.4 Co at LESTREM. issued necessary instructions. R.H.	

Army Form C. 2118.

WAR DIARY
or
INTELLIGENCE SUMMARY.
(Erase heading not required.)

Instructions regarding War Diaries and Intelligence Summaries are contained in F. S. Regs., Part II. and the Staff Manual respectively. Title pages will be prepared in manuscript.

Place	Date	Hour	Summary of Events and Information	Remarks and references to Appendices
May	10 (a.m)		Train H.Q moved to the LESTREM - MERVILLE road & Estaires commencing line with Div H.O & fixed by 3 P.M. BM	
"	11		Interview Q. discussed programme for Corps Commanders inspection of Train tomorrow arranged for 5 P.M. Maj'd DDQMG 1st Army at HQ DAIN. discussed the question of Capt. Mitchell being appointed S.S.O. Div. Major MONTGOMERY and the question of Alteration of Officers the Corps Commander inspected personnel with many willing RM	
"	12		Interview Q. reported 3 Canadian to new horses due to arrive few days every time to new lines to tomorrow noon. Wired that the two horses next as recommend officers for # S.O.S Waited that the 1st Army DDQMG office had not reached RM	

Place	Date	Hour	Summary of Events and Information	Remarks and references to Appendices
May	13		Visited 4/63 F.M.84 Bn/s & explained what was required for the inspection. Inspects Potable Horse Lines. Had Conference of Company Commanders & discussed details of the inspection. BM.	
May	14		The Inspection. The XI Corps Commander Lt. A. HAKING. inspected the Force. I explained his presence at all he saw. he went as far as to state that having inspected 25 Divisional trains including the Guards Division that this train was the best of all. there was much publicity in Train Orders then encouraging remarks made thanks to all Ranks. & RSM. by the with any thanks to Sophie. Flo An proceeding to Sophie	

WAR DIARY or INTELLIGENCE SUMMARY

Army Form C. 2118.

Place	Date	Hour	Summary of Events and Information	Remarks and references to Appendices
	May 15		On proceeding to England for 14 days leave, handed over the command during my absence to Capt. B.S. CAMERON.	
			Took over command from Lt. Col. B. Haigh on his departure on 14 days leave.	
			Reported to D.A.Q.M.G. Arranged with him and C.R.E. for a restriction of the number of sappers required for duties by 17, to enable the inoculation of the train to be carried out during a period of one week. Recieved "Texas Pack" from "Q" for trial. W.C	
	May 16th		Investigated case of D. Gilliers 4 Coy attached 46y charged with "Striking an N.C.O when in the execution of his office". Remands the case for a summary of evidence to be taken — Summary of evidence taken and forwarded to "A" hbtt	
			Application for F.G.C.M. Tested and reports to D.A.Q.M.G on two Texas Packs. take for the Division which appear satisfactory. but are 6" shorter W.C than those made from Tarr Sacks. Had 100 men from 2.3rd Coys inoculated with T.A.B. W.C	

WAR DIARY or INTELLIGENCE SUMMARY

Army Form C. 2118.

Place	Date	Hour	Summary of Events and Information	Remarks and references to Appendices
May	19th		Interviews 'Q'. Visited 3rd Fd. Amb. with reference to improvising some arrangement for carriage of medical panniers, pack saddles without pack saddles. T.N.B. 20 men No 1 Coy. inoculated.	M/e
	19th		Sett was 'Q'. Present at demonstration of new horse Inspector, by ADVS to Corps Divisional Commander. 193 the issues to the train. 91 men from 2,3 r 4 Coys inoculated.	M/e
	19th		Court Martial on T/2/016816 Dr. Collins. E.J at Pont du Hem – Collins found guilty. Heads on to Cadets of A.P.M. Temp. Capt. G. ALDIS from 2nd Line NORTHUMBRIAN Div. TRAIN reported from B.H.T.D and was posted to 2 Coy. Meeting to be his permanent rank of 2/Lieut. 21 men No 1 Coy inoculated.	M/e
	20th		Interviews 'Q'. Tested arrangement improvised for carrying medical panniers on mule and drive saddle. Explained the methods to O.C.s 2 r 3 Coys. 103 men. 2,3 r 4 Coys inoculated. MT.T.A.B	Ypre
	21st		Visits 2 Coy. Approval of DDyS & T to posting of Lt. C.L. REYNOLDS to be O.C. 2 Coy. vice Capt. G.A. MAULE and Lt. V.S. POWELL to be Supply Officer 2 Coy vice Lt. C.L. REYNOLDS received. 20 men of No 1 Coy inoculated.	M/e

WAR DIARY or INTELLIGENCE SUMMARY

Army Form C. 2118.

Place	Date	Hour	Summary of Events and Information	Remarks and references to Appendices
May.	22ᵈ		Interviews "Q". Visits Railhead. Nominal Roll of Officers' Movements for promotion sent in to 119 Div "A". MC	
	23ʳᵈ		Visited Refilling Points of 2 & 4 Cos. MC	
	24ᵗʰ		Visited Refilling Points of 2 & 4 Cos. 30 Men of No 1 Co. invalids took T.A.B.	
			Demonstrates improvised methods of carrying sick passengers ect and drives saddle to D.A.Q.M.G.	
	25ᵗʰ		3ʳᵈ Fld. Amb. moved to MERVILLE. Mr Chevalets in charge of Train stored. MC 3ʳᵈ Fld AMB. MERVILLE	
			22 men of No 1 Co. invalides with T.A.B MC take over XI Corps Rest Station.	
	26ᵗʰ		Interviews "Q". Visits Railhead 1, 2 & 4 Cos Refilling Points	
	27ᵗʰ		Interviews "Q". Visits Refilling Points. MC	
	28ᵗʰ		Visited 2 Co. & 3ʳᵈ Fld. Amb. 1st Section Portuguese Exp. Force arrives in Div. area. Billets at CHATEAU, LESTREM. MC	

WAR DIARY
or
INTELLIGENCE SUMMARY

Army Form C. 2118.

Place	Date	Hour	Summary of Events and Information	Remarks and references to Appendices
	May 29th		Interviews "Q". Inspects 146 M.G. Coy Transport at ZELOBES.	
	30th		Visits 147 Bde. Refilling Point.	
			Interviews "Q". Visits Refilling Points 146 & 148 Bdes	
	31st		Hands over Command to Lt.Col. B. Haigh on his return from leave.	
	30.5		Returns from leave. B.H.	
	31st		Takes over Command of Brain. Reported to Div. H.Q on our return had interview M.G.O & G.S. discussing Div. Horse Shows & suggested that a Pol. Officer be kept always to further down Lights Railways both as Remounts also chosen to junction of further Lights Railways from R.H.S to R.P.L. BH	

Bernard Haigh
Lt Col

May 31st 1917 Commanding 49th Div. Train

Vol 27

SECRET.

WAR DIARY.

OF

Hqrs (WR) Divl. Train

FOR

June 1917.

CONFIDENTIAL.

WAR DIARY

of

Lieut Col. B. Haigh.

Commanding 49th W.R. Divisional Train

from JUNE 1st, 1917 to JUNE 30th, 1917.

Volume 27.

Army Form C. 2118.

WAR DIARY
or
INTELLIGENCE SUMMARY
(Erase heading not required.)

Place	Date	Hour	Summary of Events and Information	Remarks and references to Appendices
June	1st		Interviewed 2/Lt E. ALDIS. reported to the train from B.W.T.D. informed him of being posted to No 2 Coy. Visited 146th & 148th Bdes R.P's with the C.O. who lent out shelter to this Div's. Army Frdng 31,000 men the Army record these being. 11,000 of the above and the record now being the County. Portuga & E.E. troops. Visited 463 Coy. And posted payments to Divisional Troops R.P's.	
	2nd		Inspected the P.E.T. R.P. at Vieux Chapelle. The Group is now confined entirely of the P.E.T. & is run by the A.P.C. crews & the 75 Suprs. C.O. 147th Inf Bde. The P.E.T, is experienced in handling their special Mail in time which weight difficulty, is at least ½ Ton each. It is hoped that in time the P.E.T. will be able to run their own A.S.C. work on this Ays. Team entails the 147th Inf Bde. Group Co. to have two separate R.P's each day, run by the same number of drawn returns. RH	

WAR DIARY or INTELLIGENCE SUMMARY

Army Form C. 2118.

Place	Date	Hour	Summary of Events and Information	Remarks and references to Appendices
June	2nd (cont.)		Picket inspected Horse & Lines of the M.G. Coy - the Cy. has been having trouble with MANGE again, but I hope that in a week or so all animals will be back at duty again. Resubmitted names for promotion to Acting Rank.	
	3rd		Picket inspected No 2 Cy B.H. Interior Q. attached to the Train as loaders were exchanged so seen. B1. Men today come up from the Base. Picket inspected No 3 Coy horses & lines, the horses are in exceptionally fine condition. B.H.	
	4th		Interior Q. pointed out the position of the Coal Fatigue at present attached to the Train, the question of attached Fatigues being sent back to their Units. B.H.	

WAR DIARY or INTELLIGENCE SUMMARY

Army Form C. 2118.

Place	Date	Hour	Summary of Events and Information	Remarks and references to Appendices
June	4th (contd)		Received information from A.D.M.S. that Lt. L.L. McDONOGH. R.A.M.C. will assume the duty of Capt. T. CAMPBELL as M.O. of the train who will proceed to ETAPLES on the 5th inst. Intimated Capt CAMPBELL accordingly. Handed him his movement order.	
	5th		Interview q. re appointment of C.S.O. Visited the 147th Inf Bde R.P.C. This is the 5th Group R.P. I now have a fearing strength 32 o.r.o Attached Hqrs in the Division. BH.	
	6th		Visited No 7 Con. Hospital. the Recieving Point & Transport. There received information that Major MONTGOMERY, has been admitted to Hospital in England after 10 days sick leave. to Question of getting a C.S.O appointed is now urgent. Capt. J. MUNRO Cleve has been sent in by me on previous occasion.	10H

Army Form C. 2118.

WAR DIARY
or
INTELLIGENCE SUMMARY
(Erase heading not required.)

Place	Date	Hour	Summary of Events and Information	Remarks and references to Appendices
June	7.		Received instructions that One Officer & 8 O.R. to be detailed to proceed to Beuvoigne Army Ho. Renements for the division. Detailed Lt. HOULSWORTH. Visited the D.E.T. Divisional H.Q. Qr. & discussed the question of them drawing their own Supplies from R.H.A. & distributing them to them Units. ascertained that their Supply Column will be at R.H.A. on the 9th. the day they take over the responsibility of the Supplies. Interview Q.re to return of the 16 Supply Clerks who are being made from their Home are Clerks R.I. & the other men are indispensable. Lt. C.C. REYNOLDS & Lt. F.H. JACKSON. gazetted to be Captains in the Times dated 5.6.17. these have been recommended for promotion by me in November 1916	R.H.
"	8		Had a visit from D.D.Q.S.T. 1st Army who inspected all Coys of the Train & expressed himself pleased at all he saw. (R.H.)	

WAR DIARY
or
INTELLIGENCE SUMMARY

(Erase heading not required.)

Army Form C. 2118.

Place	Date	Hour	Summary of Events and Information	Remarks and references to Appendices
June	9		Made preliminary arrangements for Flamertin Horse Show. Debate Dr Hunt back from No 1 Coy received orders to England for commission in Infantry. (B.H.)	
"	10		Held the Train eliminating horse show - won trophy (B.H.) confs Horse Show. The G.O.C. 49th Div. visited the Show & expressed his admiration of all the Turn outs (B.H.)	
"	11		Visited the Field Ambulances 1st & 2nd accompanied by the A.D.M.S. 49th Div. & judged their Transport Turn out & in the eliminating contest for the Div: Show. (B.H.) Interview D. Lieurod details of coming show.	
"	12		Failed No.4 Coy. Horse Show turn out 9, A. 14 7 A.S.C. A.L.A Horse Throughout.	

Place	Date	Hour	Summary of Events and Information	Remarks and references to Appendices
	13		Had conversation with A.A.M.S. & consented to act as Judge in the Infantry Events of the Army Show on 24?. Also discussed the question of finding rest homes to the Corps School after they have been one here for returned with Mange. (R.H.)	
	14		Received Hon. Shaw Stewart big contract for entire going to the XI Corps Show at 4 P.M. the Field Marshall Commanding in Chief much of the Shaw ground & inspecting all the Transport, your complimentary re the Infantry transport & Train Transport. (C.H.)	
	15		Received information of the move of 147? Bde to the BETHUNE area from the 8th Division, made out necessary orders for 46S?O? Kraal to SAILLY LA BOURSE on the 17th with	

Place	Date	Hour	Summary of Events and Information	Remarks and references to Appendices
June	15	(Contd)	Supply arrangements made for the above & orders issued accordingly. Interview O.C. the above.	(BH)
	16		Pulled NOEUX LE MINES & interviewed O.C. 6th Divisional Train reserved the attaching of No 3 Coy to their. Arrested the new arrangements for the No 3 Coy to march from their billets, arranged for the No 3 Coy to march from their billets. This night 16/17 inst. Issued marching orders to O.C. No 3 Coy. and to the 6th & 17th Batton Mach. Rechargs Coy HQ on 147th Inf Bde & to 6th & 17th Batton. to BETHUNE. Supplies delivered by lorry. At 3 Coy marched at 11.15 P.M. on 16th arriving at NOEUX LE MINES 4.30 A.M. on 17th.	(BH) (BH) (BH)
	17			

Army Form C. 2118.
WAR DIARY or **INTELLIGENCE SUMMARY** (Erase heading not required.)

Place	Date	Hour	Summary of Events and Information	Remarks and references to Appendices
June	18		Heat very great. Arrang to move of Baths of 147th Bde. The Train is shew turning out 35 G.S. Wagons for R.E. work. Two Baths 147th Bde train to BETHUNE and back. Supplies for whole of the Bde drawn by 466 Coy at No Eux le MINES. Reqd to stay for first issue. Reorganisation of H.Q. horses at Ecclebrul & abandon A. Echewan. R 7 A 7 B du H.Q. (BH)	
	19		Much of No.2 Coy. Corps Horse Shew proper & No.1 Coy (BH)	
	20		XI Corps Horse Shew. to 49th Div. secured 17 firsts 76 Revenue. The Train got 1st with range of H.Q. vehicle Shew at the Army. Sweepstake ace everything won by Col. Antigus own 1 beyond to 75 allowed to return to their units. (BH)	

WAR DIARY or INTELLIGENCE SUMMARY

Army Form C. 2118.

Place	Date	Hour	Summary of Events and Information	Remarks and references to Appendices
June	21		Capt. J. MILNER acting C.O. Capt. J.H. MILLS. taking over his duties in his absence. 2/Lt. Legge comes to Train H.Q. to study for the adj. C. Por- on June 15th. XI List of an No 1727 d. 21 617 received. A.S.C. officers to transferred to the Infantry. (RH)	
	22		Interview Objection from Bakery 1st Army stores regarding Received instruction from the Adj. C. Por- to act as Steward & take two train officers with me (RH)	
	23		Interview Q. Attended meeting of 1st Army Horse Shows at CHATEAU LA HAYE. Visited No 3 Coy at NOEUX LE MINES now attached to 63rd Division Train (JH)	
"	24		Held inspected 3rd & 24 Fd Ambulance Horse lines at Bruay Stables the Stables of the Horses now available for also the Harve & Offices	

2449 Wt. W14957/M90 750,000 1/16 J.B.C. & A. Forms/C.2118/12.

WAR DIARY
or
INTELLIGENCE SUMMARY

Army Form C. 2118.

Place	Date	Hour	Summary of Events and Information	Remarks and references to Appendices
June	24 (contd)		has not made the slightest improvement, had interview with O.C. 30 yr Ambulance & learned that his M.O. believed an unofficial to his personal rank. (RH)	
"	25		Attached 1st Army Home Shows, acted at Chewar & Theny Show E. to R.A.S.C Army. The M.D. entry No 3209. was not successful in his class. (RH)	
"	26		Interview O. Received information that Major C.E. MONTGOMERY. has been harassed in England & deemed as not being fit for service for 3 months. Yens husband to Stoke his home off the strength of the Train. Capt. J. MILNE R.A.M.C. is appointed S.C.O. Vice Major Montgomery. Received visit from A.D.M.S., discussed the question of the supply clerk	

WAR DIARY or INTELLIGENCE SUMMARY

Army Form C. 2118.

Place	Date	Hour	Summary of Events and Information	Remarks and references to Appendices
	June 26 (cont)		Lieut. R. Clarke of the train been withdrawn in favour of Plan B. Green. I am not at all in my original opinion on this point. Also discussed the question of the P.E.J. two wheeled carts which I am not sent to No 4 Coy for alteration to our pattern. Yours per to home and send. Chough. (BH)	
	" 27		Visited the Coys & Column. Inspected the one day's rations for horse & transport which is held by them, & found a all correct. The supplies are carefully stowed & in sound condition. The horses are showing Visited No 2 Coy. Inspected Horses & Lines. improved condition. (BH)	
	" 28		Interview O. Received information that the 147th Bgde will relieve the Division & be stationed by us for conservation on the 5.4 Visited Town Major LESTREM. Made billets arrangements for No 3 Coy when they return to this area on or about July 2nd (BH)	

WAR DIARY or INTELLIGENCE SUMMARY

Army Form C. 2118.

Place	Date	Hour	Summary of Events and Information	Remarks and references to Appendices
June	28th (con'd)		Visited S.S.M. WELBURN in the C.C.S. at MERVILLE. He is now convalescent & should return to the Coy in about 4 days.	
	29		Interviewed O discussed the new Army Scale with the A.S.C. T.T. Services & held discussed the return move of the 147th Inf Bde made the necessary Supply & Transport arrangements.	
	30		Held a conference at D.D.Q.S.T. Offices 1st Army, & discussed the question of the present system of carrying G.S. wart now received. Portion of the Ammunition in the bags with the R.M.T. also. Received communication from M.S. C.M.P. that a Major will be posted to this Thomas. That Capt. H.S. CAMERON'S recommended promotion cannot be allowed, sent a protest to Q. You had interview with G.O.C. re this question. It was arranged I had better interview D.D.Q.S.T. 1st Army. I sent a letter to Q.A.O.R. protesting against SLINGSBY in the matter of transfer to the 1st July. Acts & D.I.Q.S.T. see the Reply.	

Bernard Haughton Lt.Col.
Commanding 49th Divn. Train

30.6.17.

SECRET.

War Diary
of
49th (WR) Div⁰ Train
for
July 1917.

Vol 28

Army Form C. 2118.

WAR DIARY
or
INTELLIGENCE SUMMARY
(Erase heading not required.)

Place	Date	Hour	Summary of Events and Information	Remarks and references to Appendices
July	1st	—	Sent reply to M.S. G.H.Q. letter re promotion of Capt. CAMERON. Wrote a special Army Order for Officers on tour to the same as Major. Asked No.1 & No.2 Coy's home lines specified the latest Renown's which are on the whole better than usual. Inspected the two wheeled cart belonging to the P.E.T. with a view to altering the Axletree. This cart is now on No.4 Coy workshops arranged for the Axle to be moved further forward to the cart to be let down 30-4 inches room of new Poles & R Bars. During this the file fitted. Received further remark tells & order re the Mobility of the B/att.	(illegible)
	2nd		Received instructions for Officers of the Train to be medically examined for passed to the Infantry. Issued necessary & due down, Asst. particulars of YEsLINGERS to DDGH 1st Army, asking for Him exemption.	(illegible)

Army Form C. 2118.

WAR DIARY
or
INTELLIGENCE SUMMARY

(Erase heading not required.)

Instructions regarding War Diaries and Intelligence Summaries are contained in F.S. Regs., Part II. and the Staff Manual respectively. Title Pages will be prepared in manuscript.

Place	Date	Hour	Summary of Events and Information	Remarks and references to Appendices
July to 1st July Army MALLINSON joined from the Base. Posted to No 2 E.Q.	3rd		Visited 1st Army HQ on short interview with 2 D.G. Sgt. re Cpl CAMERON'S promotion & Lt SLINGSBY'S exemption. Interview Q. suspected looking forward to the Texas Pack Saddle Together with the D.A.Q.M.G. visited the Remount depot & chose the horses required to complete the establishment for the Divis[ion].	CAMERON (P.H.)
	4th		The Officer of the train and 30 gun N.C.O.s here thoroughly examined by O.C. No 73 Ambulance. Further, the exception of Capt SIMPSON none found fit for service with the Infantry the tool batch of Remounts arrived, also brought the train up to full strength M.	(P.H.)
	5		Issued No 1 E.Q. Inspected to Remounts & horse lines. the Train the Texas Pack Saddle Remount held to O.C. 57 & 2nd	(P.H.)

WAR DIARY
or
INTELLIGENCE SUMMARY

Army Form C. 2118.

Place	Date	Hour	Summary of Events and Information	Remarks and references to Appendices
July	6th		Interview O. discussed the light railway system in the area as regards Supplies, also the proposed move of the Division into another area.	
			Visited No 3 Coy, Inspected Remounts & horse lines, horses in good condition.	
			Attention of the Portuguese two wheeled cart to on further draught with two mules from the R.F.T. Forage completed & after talk with G.O.C. & S.O.C. R/e ? Div Conf Ratification, returned home to Q. & arranged for G.O.C. & G.S.O.C. ? Div Conf (off)	
	7th		Interview Q. Discussed the coming move of the Div. in but no order yet. Vacancy of Lane Jeulus.	(PR)
			Visited LA GORGUE. Ratched to the embarkation of BM.	
	8th		Interview Q. No orders yet for the move.	
			Acted as judge for 165th Inf. Bde Horse Show in the morning.	
	9		Interview Q. as usual. Received verbal information that	

WAR DIARY
or
INTELLIGENCE SUMMARY

Army Form C. 2118.

Place	Date	Hour	Summary of Events and Information	Remarks and references to Appendices
Feb 1	9 (cont'd)		Probably the three tpt [trainloads] would entrain at on 12th inst. the Div Artl. to move to new area by the road. No definite orders out yet. Re Railhead or Supply queried Mackie New Area at C.O.X.95. BAINS is Director 19 Division. No definite ordering the Light Relieving the 7th Division or being relieved as they knew nothing of it. Interview O.C. 1st Divisional Train, who knew nothing of interview with S.S.O. 49th Division who informed me by W.S. had interview whether the 7th Div in Reffle that it was uncertain whether he staffed us. or not. Called at XX Corps & saw D.A.Q. 49th Div on informing him was out. The whole of the above area was being shelled continuously he was out. Returned to ola ane at 5 P.M. RM	(BP)
"	10			

Army Form C. 2118.

WAR DIARY
or
INTELLIGENCE SUMMARY

(Erase heading not required.)

Instructions regarding War Diaries and Intelligence Summaries are contained in F. S. Regs., Part II. and the Staff Manual respectively. Title Pages will be prepared in manuscript.

Place	Date	Hour	Summary of Events and Information	Remarks and references to Appendices
July	11		Interview O. received time table for entraining the Division on the 13th & 14th. Made out supply arrangements & submitted them to Q. for approval & publication in administrative instruction. Interview Q at 6 P.M. & received further instruction re to move. Time table for our trains received from Q in morning & also copies accordingly. Train orders & supply instruction issued to all coy commanders & A.S.C. O (att)	
	12		Interview & received information that DUNKERQUE will be reached on 14th inst. Informed O.C. supply Column. Visited No 1 Coy R.P. & had interview with the C.O. re Co. for Dr: trnsp. checking supply goods too for the trnsfer remaining in our area. Supply that I ascertained that the tracing for visited L.E. Column supply & received information that the Detraining Station been a pupil was probably corrected. 6 P.M. Visited Q & received information.	

WAR DIARY or INTELLIGENCE SUMMARY

Army Form C. 2118.

Place	Date	Hour	Summary of Events and Information	Remarks and references to Appendices
July	12 (Contd)		handed to 146 Bde. LOON PLAGE. 147 & 146 Bdes FREYCINET.	(Contd)
	13.		The Divn on march by Rail to DUNKERQUE. Clearing the journey the train with No 3 Co Train was Bombed & attacked by machine gun fire from enemy Aeroplane. Train A.Q. moved by motors to COUDEKERQUE BRANCHE (P.H.)	
	14.		Move & Division continued, & completed by 9 P.M. Units had all refitted. Own & overseas Quitted all Corps in their new position. Units to all refitting have been returned to that all amt. had refilled & that the Supply began has been returned to the A.S.C. Coys. Trains opened issue to St Mephs Dict on 15th day as Emerged Kations. Issue at 1 A.M. on 15th. (P.H.)	
	15.		Unit No 4 Coy & R.P. at 14.45.50. Orders for M.T. Coy at 1AM on the Belle Endeavour move No 4 Coy to move up & take over from 329 Tal Train all unit Brigade Orders 6 P.M. Divn Q referred that all necessary orders are issued for The move on 16th Augt.	(P.H.)

Army Form C. 2118.

WAR DIARY
or
INTELLIGENCE SUMMARY
(Erase heading not required.)

Instructions regarding War Diaries and Intelligence Summaries are contained in F. S. Regs, Part II. and the Staff Manual respectively. Title Pages will be prepared in manuscript.

Place	Date	Hour	Summary of Events and Information	Remarks and references to Appendices
July	16th		11.30 am. Received information that the Div¹ Train H Q will not move into forward area until 18th & then to relieve the 32nd Division. Field H.Q 32nd Train & saw their position in the 2nd Divn. Rlhs moved to Tahigon. No 4 Coy in the forward area which is Bivouacs in the Road. Visited No 4 Coy in the Bivouac area which is Bivouacs in the Road. Drove until the companies & the Coy 32nd Train evacuate, then visited No 2 Coy & arranged for them to move into the 2nd Line in the forward area until their convoy from any Coy of 32nd Train movement. 10.30 PM. Reported to that all supplies arrived today. 3/2 days back train arrived R HQ at noon. today. BH	
	17		No 2 Coy moved to forward area COXYDE town & bivouacked in the 2nd Army. Exchanged with the adjt of 32nd The Train I knew on all coy drove to on the 19th NW G. BH	

WAR DIARY
or
INTELLIGENCE SUMMARY

(Erase heading not required.)

Army Form C. 2118.

Place	Date	Hour	Summary of Events and Information	Remarks and references to Appendices
July	18		No 3 Coy marched to the BRAY DUNES area today. Served men for Train A.D & marched to DE ZOEPANNE on 19th inst. to relieve the 32nd Div. Train.	
	19		Interviewed Staff Captain the morning of the 5th M/W by the 32nd Train, taking over accommodation at 1 P.M. Huts & horse standings being Train H.Q. marched to new area arriving at 1 P.M. places arranged the Canal Junes, good accommodation for all. The Hd Qrs marched to LOYSE BAINES & relieved 32nd Division Hd Artillery Train No.1 Coy stayed 143 B.2./146 & No 3 Coy stayed at BRAY DUNES. at GHYVELDE. Hurled No 3 Coy Horses from standings to horse Ypres huts for the men Dutch Mt. Coy who are harnessed in a field at GHYVELDE All horses completed the march in very good condition	(OH) (OH) (OH)
	20		463 Coy march to forward area. 7.2.C. 465 Coy march from BRAY DUNES – GHYVELDE.	

Army Form C. 2118.

WAR DIARY
or
INTELLIGENCE SUMMARY
(Erase heading not required.)

Instructions regarding War Diaries and Intelligence Summaries are contained in F. S. Regs., Part II. and the Staff Manual respectively. Title Pages will be prepared in manuscript.

Place	Date	Hour	Summary of Events and Information	Remarks and references to Appendices
M	20. (Contd)		Received instructions from O. That all R.E. Transport took it to be detailed by O.C. Train, for this purpose 2 R.E.S. wagons from each Batn. and M.G. Coy. is put at my disposal these together with the Baggage wagons & a certain amount from the D.A.C. will be available.	(M)
	21		Received instructions that H.T. will draw supplies from R.HQ on & after 22nd. March O. & derived the Divisional Trans port question. arranged for the 1st Line Regt. Transport to draw supplies from the R.H.Q. & the Train supply Coy. to draw at R.HQ. The arrangements to make 1 day for transport R.E's to-day cancelled, saw staff came the Train Baggage begun.	(M)
			Gave to G.S. from D.A.C. to R.E. Transport.	(M)
"	22		Visited No.1 Coy on Farmes house, inspected then Refilling Point, thence down Water Ranihad, Reach Leader it will be required tanks more tanks & get more rope.	(RH)

2449 Wt. W14957/M90 750,000 1/16 J.B.C. & A. Forms/C.2118/12.

WAR DIARY or INTELLIGENCE SUMMARY

Army Form C. 2118.

Place	Date	Hour	Summary of Events and Information	Remarks and references to Appendices
July	23rd		Received information that H.Q. 146th Inf. Bde. & 3 Battns. will move from Front line to SHYYEDE & one Battn. from 147th Bde. to Front line. Interviewed O. C. & M.O. arrangement accordingly. Interviewed O.C. of the names of Officers recommended for promotion. Capt. N.S. CAMERON's name sent in G.R.O. 2449.	(RH) (RM)
	24.		Sent application for temporary promotion of 2/Lt. 1899. & Capt. JAMES MILNER whilst holding the appointment. 1. Adjt. & C.O. respectively from 2/Lt. (Temp Capt.) ARTHUR CECIL GRIMWADE. Reported for duty with the squ from the Base. Interviewed him that he would have to revert to his permanent rank & report to & posted him to No 1 Coy.	(BH)
	25		Visited No 4 Coys Office. Inspected the Books. also Horses & harness. these are in a fair condition. Visited No 3 Coy. at GAEYEDIE & inspected Office Books & Horses & harness. the Coy is becoming in the field. Visited No 2 Coy at ZEEPAN. inspected Office Books & Horses & harness. the Coy is showing much improvement. Today's papers from Lt. Col. Mr. Two Gry general in the C in C dispatches.	(BH)

Army Form C. 2118.

WAR DIARY
or
INTELLIGENCE SUMMARY

(Erase heading not required.)

Instructions regarding War Diaries and Intelligence Summaries are contained in F. S. Regs., Part II. and the Staff Manual respectively. Title Pages will be prepared in manuscript.

Place	Date	Hour	Summary of Events and Information	Remarks and references to Appendices
	26		Interview Q. re recommendation of promotion of officers. Discussed return of transport with the D.A.D.M.S. Failed N. L. 207 re TURNER & infested office books & home leave & other sundry army matters. He also supplied me no Battalion relieving 9th 8 P.M. interview A.D.M.S. Re actual return of Muzzle to horses. Division also took return of men at Muzzle to horses. for the Division.	
"	27		Received applications to transfer to Heavy Machine Gun Corps from Capt PEARSON Mills. McPowell. Mitchinson. SMITH RODGERS. FAWCETT. All of whom are under 30 years of age & also wise in the cause of time be taken to the Infantry, forwarded the application & recommended them.	
"	28		Interview Q. discussed the question of reinforcing the Temporary Park Canals to XV Corps Have a return from A.D.O.S. XV Corps & forwarded it with train to Q to the [?] Down to XV Corps H.Q.	

2449 Wt. W14957/Mg0. 750,000 1/16 J.B.C. & A. Forms/C.2118/12.

WAR DIARY or INTELLIGENCE SUMMARY

Army Form C. 2118.

Place	Date	Hour	Summary of Events and Information	Remarks and references to Appendices
July	29		Interview a received preliminary warning of move of 147th Inf. Bde. up to the forward area. (PH)	
	30		Visited XV Corps H.Q. & demonstrated the Texas Pack Saddle to various officers of there. Had interview with Capt. Sam A Son, to see over to La Panne. Received information as to the prospective relief of the division by the 32nd Div. Received application or an No. 118 Reserve Recovery train even in a case of second failure. (PH)	
	31st		Visited _____. Interview a discussing the various points. Received further nos. 10, 119. Second train were executed f. R HEYVECDE. No. 3 Coy Manseka & No. 4 Coy Pellegi at ZEE PANNE. No. 4 Coy Manseka & No. 6 Coy Mariseka. No. 2 Coy Train. I settled details of his taking over from the on 3rd Aug. (PH)	

Bernard Haughton Col.
Commanding 49th H Divl Train

31.7.17.

Vol 29

CONFIDENTIAL

War Diary

of

Lieut Colonel B. Haigh.

Commanding 49th W.R. Divisional Train.

from AUGUST 1st to 31st, 1917.

Volume 29.

Army Form C. 2118.

WAR DIARY
or
INTELLIGENCE SUMMARY

(Erase heading not required.)

Instructions regarding War Diaries and Intelligence Summaries are contained in F. S. Regs., Part II. and the Staff Manual respectively. Title Pages will be prepared in manuscript.

Place	Date	Hour	Summary of Events and Information	Remarks and references to Appendices
Aug.	1st		Interview Q. & B.A.A. & M.S. 32nd Division. I arranged for 1.30.0 Rebus Train & 3,000 Tommy Cookers to be at No1 Coy 49th Train for their collection. Issued Train operation order No 26 & orders for move of Train H.Q. on the 3rd inst.	(BM)
"	2nd		Issued D.R.O. 97. D. Army. detailed with D.A.D.R.S. that Day Troop trips will load at St INESBARD on & after the 4th that on the 3rd inst. the whole Division will load at DUNKIRK & that Night Down un Sea Rev. Troops trips will load at Dunkirk until further orders on the 4th inst. No2 Coy marched from ZISPANNE to GHYVELDE. No 4 " " " GHEVELDE to FIRM STEEN.	(BM)
"	3rd		No1 Coy marched from GHYVELDE TO TETEGHEM. Hd Qr Train marched to ROSENDAEL. Divn H.Q. marched to ROSENDAEL. Pushed Q in ROSENDAEL reported completion of Moves & Supply Services. new R.P's & Routes of Train H.Q. & the Coys.	(BM)
"	4th		Issued No2 Coy at TETEGHEM. Threshold Rebels phone lines. Issued us 4916 & R.P.16 Interview Q.	(BM)

WAR DIARY or INTELLIGENCE SUMMARY

Army Form C. 2118.

Place	Date	Hour	Summary of Events and Information	Remarks and references to Appendices
August	5th		Interview Q. & discussed the allotment of RCHA from Dunkirk to LEFFINCKHOUCKE.	
		10.30 PM	Received wire from R.T.O. BAILLEUL that Regt would be HAEGEDOORNE. The proved to be a mistake but were	(RH)
	6th		Interview Q. re to distribution of surplus rations, authority O.15/2030 & arranged to keep same until Bicycles are obtained	(RH)
	7th		Visited new Railhead, No4 Coy Lanes & R.P.s. Interview Q. & discussed the question of O.C. S Column having dent. regiment for 43 lorries to C.M.T.O. when 24 mgs wine supplies at the R.Head.	(RH)
	8th		"M.C.D." Railhead at LEFFINCKHOUCKE & three transport drawing for 1489 Bde & 146 Bde Group. 146 & 7 Div. Trops drawing from new forward R.Hd at IDESBALD. Interview Q. discussed the question of head guards of forage Nets &, also Accreta Forage. Ration received from A.R.B.	(RH)
	9th		Interview Q. Services tested the Town Pack Horse 33rd Div Train, I.A.D.O.C 33rd Division & the D.A.Q.M.G & Q. etc.	(RH)

WAR DIARY or INTELLIGENCE SUMMARY

Army Form C. 2118.

Place	Date	Hour	Summary of Events and Information	Remarks and references to Appendices
August	10th		Istaween Q. Inspected 7th & 8th Mont. Yorks 1st Line Transport also 146 Inf/Bde H.Q. Ors Transport. The 7th Bn. was not satisfactory. The M.O. attached to the train was offered to return to Bay. Medical arrangements are now made for certain M.O's in areas are to visit the Coys. (BH)	
"	11th		Istaween Q. Inspected 146th M.G. Coy. 6th & 8th Bath. Mont Yorks 1st Line Transport. Made out Report for D. Y/Bde H.Q. (BH)	
"	12th		Istaween Q.	
"	13th		Istaween Q. 2/Lt. A.C.CLEGG reinforcement from base. Further stay at the huts for attachment until advised. The Officer has been commanded 6 weeks is totally ignorant of any 7 am work posted here ZM 3 Coy. (RH)	

WAR DIARY
INTELLIGENCE SUMMARY

Place: August

Date	Hour	Summary of Events and Information	Remarks
13	9(am)	Visited unexpected Home Ybores. One of No 3 Y No 1 Coys on the forward area. The outbreak of Pneumonia in No 3 Coy. seems to still on. No being on the sick lines. No death as yet.	
		No 1 Coys field is in a terrible state having stood up to the continued wet weather. better holds in Ouch. Close to the cantonment it is (RH) used a front field for them. Demonstrated into.	
	4pm	Interview O.C. Capt Milner promoting (applied to corps for authority to more my Coy) and O.C. No 1 Coy to get into Touch with the 32nd Divn. have however don't at COXYDE.	
		Letter TDQRT IV Army re promotion of officers especially Capt. Milner & Lapt Cameron.	
		Returned correspondence re Capt Milner to Divison asking to further recommendation of the Recommendation (RH)	

Army Form C. 2118.

WAR DIARY
or
INTELLIGENCE SUMMARY

(Erase heading not required.)

Instructions regarding War Diaries and Intelligence Summaries are contained in F. S. Regs., Part II. and the Staff Manual respectively. Title Pages will be prepared in manuscript.

Place	Date	Hour	Summary of Events and Information	Remarks and references to Appendices
Anyet	15th		Interview Q re return of R.T.M trackers to No1 Coy. Received information from M.S & C in C that 2/Lt. GRIMWADE & ALDIS in a return then temporary rank of Capt. made out & sent to Pro Col. so they will represent them of the Senior Subaltern of their Tran Coys.	(BH)
"	16th		Received Telephone message that the G.O.C will inspect Trans Coys. Issued instructions to all Coy commanders re the G.O.C's inspection. Interview O. re the retention of the Tem rank of Capt by 2/Lt ALDIS & GRIMWADE. Mett No 2 & No 4 Coys.	(BH)
"	17		Interview Q. re promotion of Offices & discussed the whole question of the 2nd time Officers. Went Hy & spoke to them there. Made final arrangements for the G.O.C's inspection tomorrow & showing the G.O.C inspected Nos 2 & 4 Coys today. Now pleased with the Turn out.	(BH)
"	18	2.30 P.M.	expected No4 Coy. D.D.S.f.T. 1st Army inspected No2 No4 Coys in their Lines	(BH)

Place	Date	Hour	Summary of Events and Information	Remarks and references to Appendices
August	19		Received information from OC No 1 Coy that A/C GRINNADE had been evacuated to C.C.S. (AH)	
	20.		G.O.C. Light Division inspected No 1 & No 3 Coys in the forward area & was pleased with what he saw, especially No 3 Coy. Some of the horse lines on sloping ground of the hard work they have been in day or so. Moved their lines in Battery troops was shelled out of No 1 Coy Lines. Moved them in about 10 P.M. 3 Shells landing within a few yards of the Officers Mess Tent, either 8" or 12" Shells were used. No horses were hit. (AH)	
	21st		On the 19th the Coy moved to a but further. No Led M.T. Coy furnished horse trans., for the Rail Move. (AH)	

Place	Date	Hour	Summary of Events and Information	Remarks and references to Appendices
August	22		Guild Q. visited R.H.Q. & discussed the question of contracts of troops with the R.T.O. & C.R.O. as arranged in Instruction date 11/9/17. (BH) No L.9. Administrative Instructions date 11/9/17.	
	23		Having Q. arranged to cover my inspection of the 108th Inf Bde. Transport arranged for Saturday - Sunday as the S.O.C. is to inspect it on Friday 24. Inspected the 1st 2nd & 3rd N.I. Field Ambulances transport, 14th & are very fair pad. The 3rd is inferior in turn-out to the standard of the others. (RH) Wrote well & Bde concerning inspection of their transport. Made out Report on Field Ambulance transport to A.D.M.S. Wrote H.Q. 36th emphasis medical arrangement. Wrote Q. received information that Lt. 147th Inf Bde is likely to come in a few days. Received confirmation of the appointment of 2Lt. £699 to be Acting & held (RH) Temp rank of Lt. & Acting rank of Captain. Whilst Act.	

Army Form C. 2118.

WAR DIARY or INTELLIGENCE SUMMARY

Place	Date	Hour	Summary of Events and Information	Remarks and references to Appendices
August	25		Lievin R. & Return of Form, being moved spread out that an Motor pt. Make sure to get ice for a fighting tent. Received information that No 3 Coy was shelled out of ye Sheeton & L. Aught have once to another reserve near LaPanne. Received information that 147 St. Bde was from Forward area to H.17.B. operation on NO.12.1. Made necessary supply arrangements to that instruction to all concerned. (R.H.)	
"	26		No 3 Coy marched from ZEEPANNE area to ZOODECOOTE on the way to the Red area near CAPPELLE ST PUNJIN. Mie. issued necessary com to order. The 147 H Bde was something more ? in 2 m on 28th was by here the cobble & The shelling of No 3 Coy at 6 p.m on 28th was by here town been very badly damaged. All riding carts except one were lorries been destroyed the horses were got away in the arms had, damaged from those destroyed thanks to the prompt action of C.S.M. (R.H.) No casualties occurred.	

Army Form C. 2118.

WAR DIARY
or
INTELLIGENCE SUMMARY

(Erase heading not required.)

Instructions regarding War Diaries and Intelligence Summaries are contained in F. S. Regs., Part II. and the Staff Manual respectively. Title Pages will be prepared in manuscript.

Place	Date	Hour	Summary of Events and Information	Remarks and references to Appendices
	Sept 27		Interview O. & received information that 147th Bde will move to LA PANNE on 29th. Issued necessary instructions. No 3 Coy marches back into the former area bivouacked near FURNES – LA PANNE road. No 1 Coy moved to another field near the FURNES – LA PANNE road. Ha had to be shelled during the night. Received information that No 3 Coy is to move to LA PANNE on 29th to the 32nd Division for return & came out the 49th R.F.A. transferred to the 32nd Division for return on 30th of the same. The 2nd Ind. R.F.A. transferred on to me strength for return. Interview O.D.O.T.S.T. & sent him info is on the state of interior effects. 4th Ar.Rg. Regt. with a view to the transfer of the F.O. Transport of A.S.C. very M.T. Coy	29 R 76
	28.		No 2 Coy marched from TETINGHEM – GHYVELDE. Very hot day	

Place	Date	Hour	Summary of Events and Information	Remarks and references to Appendices
Oudp	29		Received instruction from R. Cmdt. that R.H.Q. Change on 31st for that of No. 16 R.M.A. & 1st R.F.A. to ADINKERKE.	
"	30		No 3 Coy moved from FURNES to LA PANNE. Visited No. 2 Coy at GHEYVELDE inspected horse lines & the camp temporarily pitched. Inspected the Rifle Range being prepared for No. 107 H.Bdy on the GHEYVELDE-UXEM Rd. Visited No 3 at LA PANNE, inspected horse lines which are in poor condition. Standings. (1) Major J.B. FOSTER from 33rd Fld. Tren. reported for duty with this Unit. Heavy Cannonading. Capt. CAMERON, MILNER & PEARSON. (BH) Capt. CAMERON & MILNER	(BH) (BH)
"	31		Interview R. McKooter & Major FOSTER promotion of Capt. CAMERON & MILNER made known to them. Received instruction that Div H.Q. & all H.Q. on well move to BRAY DUNES on this [...]. 2/Lt. R.L. HALL & W.B. ROBERTS. deported to England for duty with Lyne 4th (BH) the Infantry. There are the first two Officers to go. (BH) Barrand of Haught Lt Col Commanding 49th Div: Train. 31.6.17	(BH)

Vol 30

CONFIDENTIAL

War Diary of Lt.Col.B.Haigh.

Commanding 49th W.R.Divisional Train.

From 1st to 30th September 1917.

(Volume 30.)

WAR DIARY
or
INTELLIGENCE SUMMARY

(Erase heading not required.)

Army Form C. 2118.

Place	Date	Hour	Summary of Events and Information	Remarks and references to Appendices
Sept.	1st		Interview Q. Wrote to Lord Rawlinson as Colonel of the Regt. Particulars of Capt Emerson & Major F.B. Foster.	
"	2nd		Visited M.T. Coy in forward area. Took over from case, inspected Horses, Limbers, Billeting arrangements at BRAY DUNES. Interview Q.P.	
			The Enemy made prolonged aerial attack on ROSENDAEL lasting from 9.10 - 1.45. Many Bombs dropped in close proximity to these H.Q.s. PM AM	
"	3		Interview Q. & Capt MILNERS application for attachment to R.A.M.C offices. Interview J.D.G. Sgt's. Re the independency of Capt EMERSON by a junior officer of the New Army, A.C.C.	
			ROSENDAEL was again bombed at night for 2½ hours. AM	
"	4		Then H.Q. & Brit H.Q. on moved to BRAY DUNES from ROSENDAEL. Received further instructions to today 4/6 General de Lynn Horse for the Infantry, to train men C-in-C. A. Min.	

Place	Date	Hour	Summary of Events and Information	Remarks and references to Appendices
Sept	5th		Visited No 4 Coy discussed the question of supplying a chief Clerk to Trans H. Qrs Office in place of Sgt Thompson. 2.30 Inspected 147th AT Bde H Qrs & 4-H&S Mountain 19 Guns Transport quite satisfactory with the exception of the 3rd Battery Mule was not as clean as usual. All Ranks H.Qrs Trans H Qrs on the subjects of Heavy Bombing. DMs. No casualties. Air craft between 9 PM & 10.30 PM	
	6th		Held conference of all Coy Commanders re dispatch of the 48 General Duty Spare Drivers. Interview @ re the R.A.M.C. dealing with the A.S.C. attached personnel. Inspected the 6th & 7th A Bn the West Riding Regt 1st Line Transport. Men in a very poor condition Horses & Transport all Report for Div. H.Q. made out	

WAR DIARY
INTELLIGENCE SUMMARY

Army Form C. 2118.

Place	Date	Hour	Summary of Events and Information	Remarks and references to Appendices
Ept:	7th		Received w/instns re Horse show but for Horse Show ANZAC Corps	
			483 Coy marched from ZURNES area to TETINGHEM	
	8th		49th Div. R.E.M. moved back from forward area (BM) Interview O.C. Field Coy. H.Q. on 1st line transport move for the R.T.A. Received R.E.H.Q. arrangement made for another Revision. (BM)	
	9th		Interview O. re the move of No 4 Coy to BRAY DUNES & Move of the LEFRINGOUCHE R HQ. to ADINKIRK 148th L/Ide. (BM)	
	10th		Interview O. re. Rain Women & Drew disposed of by labour Coy without authority No 4 Coy moved to BRAY DUNES. (Arranged for 37th Coy 1st R Fus to draw supplies by 1st line transport (BM)	
	11th		Interview O. Divisional Cavalry Horse Shows held to choose representative of the Division at the 2n Anzac Corps Shows. (BM)	

WAR DIARY or INTELLIGENCE SUMMARY

Army Form C. 2118.

Place	Date	Hour	Summary of Events and Information	Remarks and references to Appendices
Sept.	12		Received for 148th Inf. Bde. Group. Changed to AZINKIRK. All three Groups now drawing from this one R. H. O. The 49th Division to No 1 Coy. Train being attached to 30th Division. New CROIX de POPERINGHE.	Pop
"	13		Thirteen O.C. to the beginning of the Pack Animals according to new Instructions received from 2nd Anzac Corps. Transport inspected by Major FOSTER. & by Robert 199 M. G. C. 101 Inf. 6.15/Capt L. & Pte. T.O. received the new Principal.	Robert
		4 PM	Attended conference at Q. Staff Office ANZAC Corps hqrs. of Divisional Pack Transportation on the ANZAC Corps. i/c Officer in Charge. Handed over Train Animals. Mounsune E/A Lt. HOULDSWORTH to be A.S.C. Officer in Charge between to Major J.B. FOSTER whilst on short leave.	Pop
"	14		Lt.Col. B. Haigh left on short tour to ROUEN - previously having attended Tactical Exercise carried out by 148 Bde. Supervised the fitting of Pack Saddlery & the loading of the "Texas" pattern - suggested that new instruction should therefore meet org. and 17th pattern.	

Army Form C. 2118.

WAR DIARY
or
INTELLIGENCE SUMMARY
(Erase heading not required.)

Instructions regarding War Diaries and Intelligence Summaries are contained in F.S. Regs., Part II. and the Staff Manual respectively. Title Pages will be prepared in manuscript.

Place	Date	Hour	Summary of Events and Information	Remarks and references to Appendices
Sept	15	—	General Routine	
"	16	—	Interviewed O.C. & now of the Field Coys R.E. & three Grenadier Gun Coys & made the necessary alterations in supply arrangement Stores B. Clerks reported from the Base to replace category A. app.?	app.?
"	17	—	Interviewed O.C. fitting of new type Patrol Van for carrying water Visited 3 Coys Lines & Billets & found them in a Satisfactory condition.	app.?
"	18	—	Reported to A on return from Rouen & took over command of Force from Major FOSTER. Received instructions that all Divisional H.Q. is to move on 19th to ROSENDAEL	(H)
"	19	—	Divi. H.Q. Train H.Q. moved from BRAY-DUNES to ROSENDAEL. Interview AAT & M.G.	(H)
"	20	—	Visited & inspected all Refilling Points, the 3 Coys Lorries & Horse Lines, with the exception of No 2 Coy, horses were taken for exe, 18 Lick horses on the train.	(H)

WAR DIARY
or
INTELLIGENCE SUMMARY

Army Form C. 2118.

Place	Date	Hour	Summary of Events and Information	Remarks and references to Appendices
Sept	20. (cont'd)		Received movement warning order from O. Dickens Divn in G. Move on 22nd 23rd & 24th. Interview O.i.e. prospective move of MT Divs to make necessary preliminary arrangements. (RH)	
	21		Interview O. re move. Interview DDOST Office re moving from Fourth Army. (RH) Supp arrangements made out for move.	
	22		Interview O.i.e. Honour Thomas Asquith? Made out list for O.i.e home to England loaded on the Command Ore from the line & Major J.B. Foster. 466 Coy moved from Bray Downs by train to Meyer. (RH) to MMMMMMMM. SYNTHE.Glen. 919	
	23.		Interviewed O. re new fitment for Petrol Tins on G.S. Wagons - Supp tin approved - 4 companies will be instructed to proceed with the work forthwith.	

Army Form C. 2118.

WAR DIARY
or
INTELLIGENCE SUMMARY
(Erase heading not required.)

Place	Date	Hour	Summary of Events and Information	Remarks and references to Appendices
Sept	23 (Ctd)		Inspected New Area - fixed Repairing Point - visited New Railhead. 466 Coy moved from SYNTHE area to WORMHOUDT. 465 " " " LA PANNE " TETEGHEM.	
Sept	24		Trains H4 2 ⁿᵈ moved from ROSENDAEL to LEDERZEELE. 466 Coy moved from WORMHOUDT to LEDERZEELE. 465 Coy " " TETEGHEM to WORMHOUDT. 464 Coy " " OHYVELDE to TETEGHEM.	
Sept	25		Visited Railhead and No 3 & 4 Companies in New Railhd also No 1 Company at Croix de Poperinghe. (Railhead at ERBLINGHEM.) 464 Coy moved from TETEGHEM to WORMHOUDT. 465 " " " WORMHOUDT to BROXEELE.	
"	26		Interviewed O.'s i/c units of two Companies RE. & Pioneers & arranged supply guarding it - 464 Coy moved from WORMHOUDT to NORDPEENE. Temp 2/Lt R.E. CLIFFORD reported for duty from A.S.C. Base Depot & was posted to No 4 Coy. 2/Lt G.F. MITCHINSON ? to Officers Training School. Bedford Eng. 2/Lt H.H. SMITH	

Army Form C. 2118.

WAR DIARY
or
INTELLIGENCE SUMMARY

(Erase heading not required.)

Place	Date	Hour	Summary of Events and Information	Remarks and references to Appendices
Sept	27	—	Entrained P.M. to arrival new to new Area - visited new area & fixed Company Billets & Rejoining Point - 3/2?	
"	28	—	Divisional HQ & Train HQ moved from LEDERZEELE to WIZERNES 464 Coy moved from NORDPEENE to ST MARTIN. 465 " " BROXEELE to HALLINES. 466 " " LEDERZEELE to QUERCAMP. 3/2?	
"	29	"	Entrained P.M. further moves. Visited the 3 Companies in their new positions - 9/2?	
"	30	"	465 Coy moved from HALLINES to QUARIE CAPPEL 9/2?	

9.3. Oct. Tham

fo. Lieut. Colonel
Commanding 49th (W.R.) Divl. Train.

YM 31

SECRET.

WAR DIARY.

OF

4th Sturmwerfer [?]

FOR

1st to 31st October 1917

CONFIDENTIAL

Headquarters

49th Division

        Herewith my War Diary for the month of OCTOBER.   Please acknowledge.

                                            Bernard Haig

1.11.1917.
                                               Lieut Colonel
                                    Commanding 49th Divisional Train

CONFIDENTIAL

WAR DIARY

of

Lieut Colonel B.Haigh.

Commanding 49th W.R.Divisional Train

From October 1st to October 31st, 1917.

(Volume 31.)

WAR DIARY or INTELLIGENCE SUMMARY

Army Form C. 2118.

Place	Date	Hour	Summary of Events and Information	Remarks and references to Appendices
Oct	1st	-	464 Coy moved from ST MARTIN to ST MARIE CAPPEL. 466 " " " OBERCAMP to ST MARTIN.	989
Oct	2	-	Interviewed P.de mives. Train H.Q. moved from Lijerne to HAZEBROUCK Railhead EBBLINGH-EM? 466 Coy moved from ST MARTIN to LE NIEPPE AREA.	989
Oct	3	-	Interviewed P. - Train H.Q. moved from HAZEBROUCK to WATOU. 464 Coy moved from ST MARIE CAPPEL to WATOU area 465 " " " STAPLE " " 466 " " " LE NIEPPE AREA to " "	989
Oct	4	-	Railhead changed to LOSPPENHOEK. Visited 465 Coy in Jr and area. 465 Coy moved from WATOU area to BRANDHOEK area.	989
Oct	5	-	Interviewed P de mives. Visited new area for the purpose of arranging to take over from N.Z. Division.	989
Oct	6	-	Train H.Q. moved from WATOU to BRANDHOEK No.1 AREA. 464 Coy moved from Watou area to BRANDHOEK " " " " " " " 466 " " "	989

Army Form C. 2118.

WAR DIARY
or
INTELLIGENCE SUMMARY
(Erase heading not required.)

Instructions regarding War Diaries and Intelligence Summaries are contained in F. S. Regs., Part II. and the Staff Manual respectively. Title Pages will be prepared in manuscript.

Place	Date	Hour	Summary of Events and Information	Remarks and references to Appendices
Oct	7		466 Company Lines bombed during last night. one building received a direct hit. one man slightly wounded. 7 H.D. killed & 9 wounded, 30 oct. P.D.O.S. Hammers destroyed abt. 10 Saddles, Bridles. - 2/Lt ARGLES, R.M. reported for duty & was posted to Mob. Coy. APP	
			Interviewed O.R. above a supply arrangement.	
Oct	8		Railhead changed from WIPPENHOEK to EDWARDHOEK. Served Unit Transferred to us & 2 Rations. strength fed today 31,000. APP	
	9		Interviewed O. de chauving from Railhead by M.T. Pack Train & Horse late. loading commenced 12 noon. APP	
	10		Interviewed O. re names. Pack Train late - loading commenced 11.30 am APP	
	11		Train H.Q. moved from BRANDHOEK area to WATOU. 466 Coy " " " " to WINNEZEELE area. APP	
	12		464 Coy moved from BRANDHOEK area to WINNEZEELE area. Railhead changed from EDWARDHOEK to WIPPENHOEK. APP	

Army Form C. 2118.

WAR DIARY
or
INTELLIGENCE SUMMARY

(Erase heading not required.)

Instructions regarding War Diaries and Intelligence Summaries are contained in F. S. Regs., Part II. and the Staff Manual respectively. Title Pages will be prepared in manuscript.

Place	Date	Hour	Summary of Events and Information	Remarks and references to Appendices
Oct	13		General Routine. 9B.?	
"	14		Interviewed O or m.c. of 148 Bde. 9B.?	
"	15		466 Coy moved from WINNIZEELE area to BRANDHOEK area 9B.?	
"	16		General Routine. 9B.?	
"	17		Visited 465 & 466 Coys in forward area 9B.?	
"	18		Visited 464 Coy – 2/Lt F.E. CLIFFORD seconded to 10 ELMS C.C.S. suffering from Boils, now due to fall from horse whilst on duty. 9B.?	
"	19		General Routine. 9B.?	
"	20		Visited Companies in forward area – T3/Lt A.V. Rowe reported from Base A.S.C. depot & now posted to No 1 Coy. 2/Lt T/Lt A.P. Barringer T.F. reported from A.S.C. depot Base & now posted to No 4 Coy. 9B.?	
"	21		466 Coy moved from BRANDHOEK area to WINNIZEELE area. 2/Lt R.C. Baxter reported from A.S.C. depot Base & now posted to No 3 Coy. 9B.?	
"	22		General Routine. 9B.?	

WAR DIARY
INTELLIGENCE SUMMARY

Army Form C. 2118.

Place	Date	Hour	Summary of Events and Information	Remarks and references to Appendices
Oct	23	-	Railhead for our units at IPPENHOEK.	
"	24	-	466 Coy moved from BRANDHOEK over to DROGLANDT. Lt. Col. B. Hough returned from leave to England 98.3. Major J.B. Foster handed over to Lt. Col Haigh who assumed command of the train. Took over command of Train from Major J.A. Foster on return from leave. Interview Q. re proposed move of Division to the STEENVOORDE area & Reported My return. Visited No 2 Coy & No 4 Coy Horse Lines &c. (BH)	
"	25		Visited Railhead & No 3 Coys Refilling Point. Visited No 1 Coy & No 3 Coy & inspected horse lines. Threw Bellis.	
"	26		Interview Q re use of Exen boats for Drivers. discussed move of Division to the STEENVOORDE area on the 27th 98R(?) instr. Visited new Area & chose Refilling points for the Brigades. Made necessary Supply arrangements for the move. (BH)	
"	27		Interview the new G.O.C Division re discussed the inclusion of the infantry 1st his Transport + Carrying of Pack Saddles on the Off horses of the T.B.S. (BH)	

WAR DIARY
or
INTELLIGENCE SUMMARY

Army Form C. 2118.

Place	Date	Hour	Summary of Events and Information	Remarks and references to Appendices
Vol:	27	(contd)	Interview A.A. & Q.M.S. discussed the importance of having Lt. BARKER back to train to do Supply Duties, in face of so many new & untrained Officers being sent up to replace the ones going to the Infantry. Lt. G. FAWCETT & Lt. Y.S. POWELL left the train for Inf: trg. to be attached to the Infantry. ⚹ No 4 Coy moved to the STEENVOORDE area (Central) No 3 " " " " (West)	BH
"	28		Train H.Q. moved to STEENVOORDE. Interview Q discussed the question of Lt. BARKER returning to the train for Supply Duties. Visited 2nd Army H.Q., D.D.Q.M.G's Office discussed the question of moving R.H. Had to severely reprimand Lt. D. CARBY HALL for using bad language to Clerk in the office. Fixed up fresh Patrolling Rowls C: for W.S.B. as much was no more suitable places. No 2 Coy moved to STEENVOORDE area (East).	BH
"	29		Interview Q a question of fuel forage. Had interview with Soc Bois & Straw for means this in Fush. explained the position fully. then spoke D.Q.M.G. 2nd Office re the matter.	BH

Place	Date	Hour	Summary of Events and Information	Remarks and references to Appendices
Ftt	29	(10.10)	Hauled Hoffding Room 1. 14 B.D. Batt.	
	30		Hauled N° 3 Coy. (RP) In Tower A. Hauled N°2 Coy inspected Rankfile & took Same &c. from Room H.T. 2/Lt WALTER MURRAY SIMPSON joined from 6TH A Coy temporarily attached/seconded (officer). Posted to 6TH 4 Coy	(RP)
"	31		Major F.B. FOSTER left for England on 14 days leave. Claims issues to units at this rate of 9d & 12th per man in lieu of Straw issued for beds to practical unit from Lower huge to cook &c. utensils arranged for	

31.10.17

Bernard Hughes Col
Commanding 49th Division Train

WR 32

CONFIDENTIAL

WAR   DIARY

of

Lt.Col.Bernard Haigh

Commanding 49th W.R.Divisional Train

From November 1st 1917   to   November 30th,1917

(Volume 32.)

WAR DIARY
OR
INTELLIGENCE SUMMARY

Army Form C. 2118.

Place	Date	Hour	Summary of Events and Information	Remarks and references to Appendices
November	1st 1917		Interview Q. Inspected 1st Line Transport 14/6th Bde Headquarters & 5th Bath K.O.Y.L.I. the latter were in a poor condition generally.	(P.H.)
"	2nd		Interview Q. discussed the question of moving the D.T.'s Group R.HQ from FLAMETINGHE to WIPPENHOEK. Inspected 1st Line Transport of the 4/5th Y & L & 4/5th K.O.Y.L.S. the latter being in a good state throughout. Issued orders for the three supple Groups Coys to draw by horse Transport from CAESTRE R.E. HQ on the morning of the 3rd inst. Lt. E. Hook. No 3 Coy awarded the M.M. Boaty's II "ANZAC Corps order today Oct 5.	(P.H.)
"	3rd		Interview Q. Capt. J. MILNER the S.C.O went on one months special leave to England. Capt [S.] MILLS assumed the duties of S.C.O. in his absence. Bde HQrs moved to day from WIPPENHOEK to CAISTRE. Northead changes Inspected the 5th Bath Y & L & 146 M. Gun Coy. 1st Line Transport made out report on the 146th L/Bde 1st Line Transport for Divisional Headquarters. Visited 147th & 146th Bde Reports & Posn to Vet of Horse Lines No 4. 204.	(P.H.)

WAR DIARY
INTELLIGENCE SUMMARY

Army Form C. 2118.

Place	Date	Hour	Summary of Events and Information	Remarks and references to Appendices
November	4th		Interview O. the move of Division on Bn. 9th roll. Bn. to MM Palon Bunch to Lt. EARLE Hook No 3 Coy, awarded by Z.ANZAC Corps Commander for gallant conduct near YPRES. Cie hom seen. Received morning orders from Q. re prospective move of the Division. Remarks Dr. O'HALERN for latest medical advancing knowledge of here	[BH]
"	5th		Interview Q. re prospective move.	[BH]
"	6th		Invited the new town and interview 2nd AUSTRALIAN Inf. Train HQrs. Re the Coys Transport arrangements to invite the new position for the Brigade Coys, have lines & them that ye. Interview Q. re explained the above arrangements, submitted scheme for approval of the S.O.C. Issued instructions to No 2 Coy re move of the 4 B.G. Inf Bde on the 8 inst.	[BH]
"	7th		Interview Q. received confirmation of the move. H.Q. Train know to forward area on 12 inst. S.S.O. arranged festival dumps to be taken our from the 2nd Aus. Inf. SCo.	[BH]

WAR DIARY or INTELLIGENCE SUMMARY

Army Form C. 2118.

Place	Date	Hour	Summary of Events and Information	Remarks and references to Appendices
November	8th		Interview O.C. Divnl. Sup. Column. H.Q. Coy. marched to the forward area 2000 yards south of POPERINGHE. The Chief of 2nd Australian Coy. A.S.C. 14 D.S./Bn. moved by Rail to forward area in relief of 2nd Australian Coy A.S.C. 14 D.S. who were to be relieved by forces in the supplies located at CAISTRE area to be forwarded by lorries for the Bde. Group. Received wire from O.C. Ch...of Railhead on 10th inst. from CAISTRE to DICKEBUSCH S.S.O. noted Petrol Park in forward area.	(10H)
"	9th		Interview O.C. Supt. Movements. Inspected 35 Renaults in My. Coys. lines before Recce. to Civilian.	(10H)
"	10th		Interview O. C. to BARKER also arriving gazetting of Capt. E. Reynolds. The 30th Anc. Train. C.R.O. & O.C. noted that A.O. with a view of taking over.	(10H)
"	11		Three officers & Br. N.C.O.s, No.4 Coy. Rolls (Lorries) leave Camp. 7703 Coy. & Co. Proceed to forward area. H.Q. of 2nd Australian Train, they are not moving out together. Marched interior with 2nd Australian Train. Recent: field to remain at railhead until 14th inst. Received Order from Authority to stay in place to Rolls until 17th inst. if necessary between O. & Qnl. Army Authority.	(10H)

Army Form C. 2118.

WAR DIARY or INTELLIGENCE SUMMARY

(Erase heading not required.)

Place	Date	Hour	Summary of Events and Information	Remarks and references to Appendices
	Nov. 11	(cont'd)	No 4 Coy marched to forward area, & took over Covered Horse Standings from Australians.	
			Left of Bde moved nr. HIRDENHOEK AVE. (M)	
	12.		Div. H.Q. moved to forward area behind YPRES to the Q knack. Advance H.Q. in YPRES. Train H.Q. not able to move as the 2nd Australian Int Train has not yet vacated their position. Invited Nos 2, 3 & 4 Coys in forward area inspected all Horse lines from Kiels rd. to the Horse lane had entered Stan range. Quite a Q officer 151 ANZAC Corps & attained their consent for to Red Australian Sup train 45 on to move out on the 17th as we can only stay in present Rikke until 17th — 3rd position being so far back. (BH)	
	13d		Visited Railhead at DICKEBUSCH also forward position for Horse lines shown park attached to R.E. work. Lieutenant Q. O.L. BACKIER CAMP. (RH)	

Place	Date	Hour	Summary of Events and Information	Remarks and references to Appendices
November	14		Had interview with D.A.A.G. 30th Divn. re take over Bull & re in GREEN AREA DC. Spoke with D.O. re getting telegram confirming take over. 9th BN AUSTRALIAN Train H.Q. on — Relief Brigade Staff. Must have two days supplies in hand & complete double rlf held. Interview 2nd Army D.O.S.O.	(RH)
"	15		Major T.O.B.M.R. returned from 14 days leave in England & takes on duties of S.S.O. from Capt. G. Moore on the 15th inst.	(RH)
"	16		Issued instructions re relief of the forward Transport Lines for R.E. work. Took relief to coincide with the Brigade relief on 19 inst. Issued orders for the move of the Train H.Q. to forward area.	(RH)
"	17		Train H.Q. moved to forward area S. of POPERINGHE. Inspected horse lines Train Relief of the 18th A.S.C. Train Coy by 9th Aust. Train with a view to moving 704 Coy into them. Decided not to do so, until further notice.	(RH)

WAR DIARY or INTELLIGENCE SUMMARY

Army Form C. 2118.

Place	Date	Hour	Summary of Events and Information	Remarks and references to Appendices
Proven	16th		We now have 12 O.R. Major ought for R.E. work, taking the R. Tovey up to the Support Trenches. 1 Officer N.C.O. is in charge of parties at Horse Lines for this work & all are subjected to long shelling on the road. On night of 15/16 one horse was wounded. Interview Q. received information of a move of the Division in a short 23rd inst. Major J.B. Foster attended the Auction of Q.E.O. in Capt J. Milmer's absence on leave. Visited Horse Lines & then dug-out of the forward position. The horses are in Sand Covered Standings & well protected from the weather. (P.H.)	
	17th		Visited M4 Coy. Hrq Lors now taken over another hut for men accommodation which was improved the position. Visited the proposed new area at RENINGHELST. interviewed 65th Train H.Q. & got permission of their temporaries. 2/Lt MCKENNA reported for duty from Base posted from No 4 Coy.	

Army Form C. 2118.

WAR DIARY
or
INTELLIGENCE SUMMARY.
(Erase heading not required.)

Place	Date	Hour	Summary of Events and Information	Remarks and references to Appendices
November	19 (Contd)		(Contd) for Coys duties at the Dist toady to Lt ALDIS. (PH) Visited New Divisional Area, inspected the positions of 3 Coys, some of the	
"	20		S.M. Inf. Train with a view to taking over from them on or about the 23rd inst. No 1 Coy site at Pioneer Camp is an excellent place. No 2 Coy west of No 4 Coy will remain in their present position. No 3 Coy will move into good hard covered township & from hut for the men. Interview O. re time of G.S. Wagons going to R.E. Dump & re the G.S. Wagons staying up at the R.E. Dumps during the day time. Explained the positions of the Coys in the new area to I.A.A.G. (PH)	
"	21		Visited No 1 Coy R.P. & inspected the Cooks use thus. Visited No 4 Coy & discussed the training of the New Officers & arranged for them each to be attached to the S.O. in turn for instruction. Received information from I.A.D.S. 2nd Army that the present Northland II8kF1305M will remain our R.H.Q when we take over new Area to be of more of Div Area to be 26th inst. (PH)	

Army Form C. 2118.

WAR DIARY
or
INTELLIGENCE SUMMARY.
(Erase heading not required.)

Instructions regarding War Diaries and Intelligence Summaries are contained in F.S. Regs., Part II. and the Staff Manual respectively. Title pages will be prepared in manuscript.

Place	Date	Hour	Summary of Events and Information	Remarks and references to Appendices
Poperinghe	22nd		Interview O.C. re move of 464 Coy & 463 Coy.	
			Visited Area Commander concer- re move of 464 Coy in this area.	
			Visited Lieut Col. Thom Belles O/C 466 Coy garrage in 464 Coy.	6
			Move in on 23rd & to stand "Staples" where he & staff is, plus S.M.	
			Arrangements for both Coys to	
			Visited 2nd Army H.Q. & had an interview with D.D.D.S.	
			Orders issued to move of train H.Q. on to RENINGHELST.	
	23rd		Train H.Q. moved to RENINGHELST.	
			Visited town & Dets H.Q. in YPRES. Street. Deree-in-General of the T.F.	
			& Lieut M.E.N.D.S. C.B. discussed with the latter the question of wrong postings	
			in the Army list of various officers of War Paving A.S.C.	
			Interview with A.A.P.M.S. re the overdraunk of H.D. Nations	
			Lord Scarborough, the Hon Colonel of this Unit visited the overdraunk held	
			an interview with him at 1/P.R.E.S.	
	24		Interview A.A.Q.M.G. re overdraunk of H.D. Nations in YPRES	
			Lt ALDIS left the ninth to be attacked to the Infantry.	

WAR DIARY or INTELLIGENCE SUMMARY

Army Form C. 2118.

Place	Date	Hour	Summary of Events and Information	Remarks and references to Appendices
November	25th		Visited R.P. No 3 & 4th Bde Pipeline Pts. 198th Bde R.P. & 49th Div. Artillery R.P. Examined new positions for future R.P's.	
	26th		Interview Q. discussed the position of the above new R.P's. (BM) Submitted great scheme for transport supply services for the left Bde in the line with the O.M. Stores thrown down in the forward area at School E. of YPRES. Received information that Re Ha. changes on 27th inst from Dickebush to Ouderdom, B., several necessary crews for this change.	
	27		Interview Q. at YPRES. Discussed the question to arrange schemes adopted. No's certificates for moving D.H.Q. action on established. The final scheme for the forward Brigade & the move of its O.M. Stores dragons. Capt. CAMERON who took T.H.Q. for interview re closing of supplies & forming of a composite Coy from two Coys at & take supplies from R.P. to O.M. Stores inl. of YPRES. (BM)	

Army Form C. 2118.

WAR DIARY
or
INTELLIGENCE SUMMARY.
(Erase heading not required.)

Place	Date	Hour	Summary of Events and Information	Remarks and references to Appendices
November	28		Lt Jackson attached to the Div. H.Q. for Staff instruction is attached to this Train for instruction in A.E.C. duties in the piece & spent today with the O.C. Train. Arranged for him to be with the C.E.O. tomorrow. All arrangements for the forward base having its A.M.S. store full of Yprès is cancelled & the original scheme for Suffolk is now being worked.	
	29		Visited suspected Horse standings from Rebels of No 3 Coy. Standing on for a load over towards thelus Rebels are kats yon rich as necu. (AH) Visited suspected No 2 Coy Horse standings Thens Rebels. These are hard covered standings in fair over Rebels also in fair over the is from & huts.	
			Interviewed the Chaplain's from C.R.E. interviewed Lt Mackinnon & C.S.M Houlton.	
	30		No 1 Coy. (AH) Made out reply to C.R.E.'s memo. Received information that 4 wagons had been abandoned after taking R.E. stores to forward Dump. On going to house, found 4 wagons Hayley etc	

30/11/17
Cmdy. Capt Div. Train

WR 33

CONFIDENTIAL

WAR DIARY

of

Lt.Colonel B.Haigh.

Commanding 49th W.R.Divisional Train.

From 1.12.17. to 31.12.17.

(Volume 33).

Army Form C. 2118.

WAR DIARY
or
INTELLIGENCE SUMMARY.
(Erase heading not required.)

Place	Date	Hour	Summary of Events and Information	Remarks and references to Appendices
Decembr	1st		Re TETLOW. 7th M.T. Coys. attached for two days to the Train for instruction in A.S.C duties in the field. Issued orders for them to spend one day with the 6 C.O. & one day with the Adjt. Visited the new Railhead ORDERDOM. Each train one ton & a half late. Worked out the new train instruction for the supplies of the Division. Interviewed D.A.Q.M.G. re-explained the supply position for each of the Trains.	
	2d		Interviewed A.A.Q.M.G. at Train Hd. Qrs. Reviewed the system of supplies during Train Restrictions. Issued instructions to have all R.Ps coralled to enable the supplies to stay overnight & to revert to the normal system of supplies. Held conference of the three Rlhd. Coy Captains. Discussed the necessity of J.C. Wagons in lieu for supply book & R.E. book. Interviewed O.C. 107 Coy. & received information of them gone to Rail Head (BM)	
	3a		Attended conference at D.H.Q. YPRES. G.O.C. discussed the question of available transport for the R.E. Stores for forward dumps. Issued instructions re the above.	

WAR DIARY
or
INTELLIGENCE SUMMARY

Army Form C. 2118.

Place	Date	Hour	Summary of Events and Information	Remarks and references to Appendices
December	3rd (contd)		The Conference of all the T.O.'s on the train & explained the new system of receiving transport for R.E. work. Impressed upon all the importance of getting the stores through.	
	4th		T/F. G.C. Hogan daily are supplied by the train. Inspected 254 M.E. Coy (late, attached to this Division) 1st line transport. Found the mules of a very poor stamp & in poor condition. Went out & reported to Q. & to M.S.O. T.F.L.E. J.P. Roger reported from Rouen upon 2nd No 2 Coy. Inspected the 146 Lt Rec. R.P's. This is in a good position for hard river Coft (Rpt) Rood inspected house Louis. There Bullets of 104 Coy the Stonings are loose but require much pitch & rubble & need its many holes including occupation to obtain license. Made twice from YPRES.	(OM)
	5		Received telegram from Q. instructing me to take 30ty Months precautions. C.S.O. spoke to D.D.S.W. Office re demanding the Iron Rations numbered in A.R.O. 1403. Y. confirmed former conversation by wire. Issued instructions to C.S.O. to clear up R.P. at B'ment, most at Elvern to this. There confirming to the normal system. Capt J. Milner C.S.O. returned from one month leave Friday to H'bert.	R.P.Ts (RP)

WAR DIARY
or
INTELLIGENCE SUMMARY.
(Erase heading not required.)

Army Form C. 2118.

Place	Date	Hour	Summary of Events and Information	Remarks and references to Appendices
December	5th (contd)		Auto does not return the auto of S.S.O. as he is under orders to report at BEDFORD for Infantry Training School. Major FOSTER is still acting as S.S.O. (PM)	
"	6th		Supplies drawn at R.P. to may air dump at R.P's. This issue to units made. We are now on normal System MT the clop between or Dumps, an carry with this L.S.O. reported position to Q. (PM)	
"	7th		P/C. Hall after seeing the A.D.M.S. he has expelf is ordered to the Base on Medical Grounds. This officer is unable to undertake any night duty because of his bad eyesight. (PM)	
"	8th		Capt. MUNCR. left for England for Infantry training. Received 18,000 iron Rations & dumped them in hut near H.Q. Bee R.P. This was done in accordance with the New precautions contained in A.R.O. 1400.	POH
"	9th		Conversation with A.D.M.S. on Phone re: Colonel E.L. Hagan issued instructions for him began life E.P. 3 Coy. Received supply chart from D.A.D.M.S. shewing position of Cliffstin during a Front & Thaw.	POH
		10 PM	Telephone conversation with A.D.Q.M.S. Double Expel to take place tomorrow 10th inst.	POH

WAR DIARY
or
INTELLIGENCE SUMMARY.
(Erase heading not required.)

Army Form C. 2118.

Place	Date	Hour	Summary of Events and Information	Remarks and references to Appendices
December	10		Made available issue to units who now have two whole days pack. Motor Lorries hour Reserve. (P.H.)	
	11		Visited No 1 Coy at PRADELLES. Inspected R.P.s y Horse Lines. Many of the horses are showing signs of over work. The horses are in excellent condition.	
	12		Visited Army Headquarters. Had interview with Brig. Gen. Wilson to D.S.&T. re the appointment of C.S.O. & Vice Capt. MENZIES. Recommended that Major FOSTER be appointed. (P.H.)	
	13		Received information that R.E. H.Q. GULDERDOM will be closed & that on 15th inst. RENINGHELST will be our R.H.Q. Visited New R.E. H.Q. Had interview with R.S.O. (P.H.)	
	14		Lt. Col. EMERY AMERICAN ARMY. attached to this train for instruction proceeded on two days leave to England. The C.O. made arrangements for him to be taken to R.P.G. on the 15th by the S.S.O. Visited No 4 Coy. 170 Coy. inspected Workshops & House Lines. Received information that Dr. ARTHUR ROBINSON M.T. Coy has been awarded the Military Medal for conspicuous bravery when on R.E. Transport work. (P.H.)	

WAR DIARY or INTELLIGENCE SUMMARY

Army Form C. 2118.

Place	Date	Hour	Summary of Events and Information	Remarks and references to Appendices
Dranoutre	15		Lt. Col. LEMLY, U.S. MARINES, visited Bt. HQ & RPs for instruction accompanied by the S.S.O.	
			RHQ changed to RENNINGHELST, trains being run late.	
	16		Visited new RHQ, inspection looking facilities visited Kemphost. The chef is are almost complete & all	
		2Lt T.W.T. ANNETT	three 18" Bde. RPs, the shelters visited the Div. Coal Dump.	
		Joined from B.M.T.D.	RPs all in good positions. Visited new positions air crews on the 146 MG RPs, 9, 10 & 12.	
		Posted No 1 Coy	Got our long machine gun crew for Chopping machine on the Dump & Friction. Jack J. Oats crushed for day.	
			146 RPs being chopped for this week.	
			I Ho. Dr. Coy were shipped up to No.2 Coy I received Ribbon Brooch & TA ROBINSON to the Military Medal. — our teams Hogan, Hogan & Kerr Gain	
	17		Visited No 1 Coy at PRADELLES, inspected Horse Lines & the DTs R Point. Took orderly room charge against I. Engl.	
			Remanded to th for C. Martial.	
			Received instructions for Capt. Pearson to report to the R.F.C.	

Army Form C. 2118.

WAR DIARY
or
INTELLIGENCE SUMMARY.
(Erase heading not required.)

Instructions regarding War Diaries and Intelligence Summaries are contained in F. S. Regs., Part II. and the Staff Manual respectively. Title pages will be prepared in manuscript.

Place	Date	Hour	Summary of Events and Information	Remarks and references to Appendices
December	18.	10	Issued instructions for Capt N.S. CAMERON to take over command of No.4 Cpy. from Capt PEARSON. L. HOULDSWORTH to take over command of No.6 Cpy. from Capt CAMERON. Lt. ARGLES to take over duties of Bde S.O.	
			148th S/Pole from Lt. HOULDSWORTH.	
			Received instructions from G.H.Q. through D.D/S.T. Officer that to obtain treatment of C.R.O. is in the hands of O.C. trains. Major J.B. FOSTER appointed by me to be S.S.O. Division. Received Telegram from D.D/S.T. informing me that Railhead will change to OUDERDOM. on 19th inst. Issued instructions to all concerned. (P.H)	
	19		Railhead changed to OUDERDOM.	
			Made reconnaissance of positions for a Divisional R.P.T. Close to to Light Railway, found a most suitable place near Pioneer Camp. Sent a Report to Q. (P.H)	
			Capt N.S. CAMERON assumed command of No.4 Coy today. Also MWOs taking over westbound signal. (P.H)	

WAR DIARY
or
INTELLIGENCE SUMMARY

Army Form C. 2118.

Place	Date	Hour	Summary of Events and Information	Remarks and references to Appendices
Dunkirk	Dec 20th		Capt. PEARSON. left the train to be attached R.F.C.	
			Lt. HOULDSWORTH returned ????? of No 4 Coy on 18th and showed ?????	
			our certificates signed. Lt. ARGLES transferred to No 2 Coy. Lt. Little Baker	
	21st		visited No 3 Coy inspected the sick horses, suffering from Eye trouble. BH	
	22nd		New regulations re Frau Precautions cancelling to bail scheme out today	
			made out fresh Supply Scheme & Chart stubmiltted same to Q AD today	
	22		Christmas Pudding ration of 1/2lb for Man came up to R.H.Q today	
	23		I has returned to duty. BH	
			Lt. C. came up to D.R.T. explanation of the afficency. BH	
	24		Duck'd unposted Divisional Coal Depot. Charge of NCO'S	
			Visited 146/Mor 147/Mor 146/Mor re Fuelling Pointo, Purchased th Dumps	
			Had interview with MX.Q.M.S. on the Phone, re Thaw Precautions, transport	
			arrangements & Assumed the question of NCO'S being clothed	
			for the C.O.S.	
			Visited No 2 No 4 Coys Mens Xmas dinners, & smoking Consort - all had	
			a Cheery Xmas & Victorian New Year. BH	

Army Form C. 2118.

WAR DIARY
or
INTELLIGENCE SUMMARY.
(Erase heading not required.)

Place	Date	Hour	Summary of Events and Information	Remarks and references to Appendices
Bercks	25		Visited No 2, No 4, No 1, No 7, No 3 Coys. to ask on the employment of horses	
			Issued instructions to revised horse registrations	(AP)
	26		Cleaned the weekly coal train from Rastand.	
	27		2/Lt ANNETT left for duty with Purchase Board Paris. (1st)	
			Visited No 3 Coy Horse Lines & inspected the Horses suffering from Eye trouble. These are showing signs of improvement & the mare on loan above to Eye affection to be having a beneficial result, eight H.3° are off duty.	(AP)
	28		Visited Railhead ORDERDAL to inspect transport & changing supplies from weather & a slippery road. Mares today.	(AP)
			Visited Div. and RE. Camps & the Refilling Point is	(AP)
	29		Handed over Command of Train to Capt. M.C. CAMERON whilst on eight days leave.	
			Took on Command from Lt. Col. B. HACK during his absence on leave. Interviewed "Q"	(V.C.)
	30		Visited Refilling Points and R.E. detachment.	
			re Horse Precautions and issues of frost Caps for horses.	(M.O.)
			Conferred with Company Commanders re Horse Precautions.	(M.O.)

Army Form C. 2118.

WAR DIARY
or
INTELLIGENCE SUMMARY.
(Erase heading not required.)

Place	Date	Hour	Summary of Events and Information	Remarks and references to Appendices
[illegible]	3/9		Epidemic of Ophthalmia. Cases amongst horses of Division. Actg DADVS DADOS re supply of foot Gr. [illegible]	

M Cimenor
Lieut. Colonel,
Commanding 49th (W.R.) Divl. Train.

Vol 34

CONFIDENTIAL

War Diary

of

Lt.Colonel B.Haigh. DSO.

Commanding 49th T.R.Divisional Train.

From January 1st to January 31st,1918

(Volume No. 34.)

Army Form C. 2118.

WAR DIARY
or
INTELLIGENCE SUMMARY.
(Erase heading not required.)

Instructions regarding War Diaries and Intelligence Summaries are contained in F. S. Regs., Part II. and the Staff Manual respectively. Title pages will be prepared in manuscript.

Place	Date	Hour	Summary of Events and Information	Remarks and references to Appendices
	1918			
	January 1st to 4th		Additional to previous notes.	
			List of Names mentioned in the F.C. despatches in December 27/4/17.	
			Lt. Col. B. Haigh. Capt. R.T. Pearson. Capt. A.S. CAMERON.	
			C.S.M. WELBURN. No 3 Coy.	
			Honours awarded in New Year Honours List to:	
			Lt. Col. B. HAIGH.- D.S.O.	
			Capt. R.T. PEARSON.- M.C..	

WAR DIARY
or
INTELLIGENCE SUMMARY.
(Erase heading not required.)

Army Form C. 2118.

Instructions regarding War Diaries and Intelligence Summaries are contained in F. S. Regs., Part II. and the Staff Manual respectively. Title pages will be prepared in manuscript.

Place	Date	Hour	Summary of Events and Information	Remarks and references to Appendices
	1918			
Steenvoorde	January 1st		Steenvoorde "Q". At Railhead and Refilling Points. M.C.	
	2nd		At Railhead, looking about to 8.30 a.m. To New Divisional HQ. Area and new Railhead (ARNEKE) M.C.	
	3rd		Visited No 3 and No 4 Coy. re Ophthalmia cases. Saw DADVS re actively Ophthalmia cases from No 1 Coy into Isolation Stables. Stopped S. apres for horses to remain with Coy. until after move. M.C.	
	4th		At Railhead and Refilling Points. Interviewed Q. Inquiring into Coal Shortage. First 7th and 2nd ant. No 1 Coy moved to NORD PEENE area. M.C.	
	5th		Visited Q.G. Preparing Operation orders for Divisional move. M.C.	
	6th		At Offecame Stw HQ "A" "Q" re move. Lt. Col. Haigh DSO took over command on return from leave. M.C.	
	7th		On return from leave took over command from Capt. CAMERON. Interview with the AA & QMG & discussed the arrangements to meet further precautions. Also the proposed move of the Divis on to Rest Area.	
			Major F.O. FOSTER relieved duties of S.P.O. on return from leave. (P.H.)	

WAR DIARY
or
INTELLIGENCE SUMMARY
(Erase heading not required.)

Army Form C. 2118.

Place	Date	Hour	Summary of Events and Information	Remarks and references to Appendices
January	7		Spoke to D. re Supply returns on these [?] Spoke [?] Thoughts arrangements for D. Board held on shortage of fuel to forward system of taking on charge the Haybilled answer to with no effect for checking the actual amounts. It quite indeed from an accounting point of view, I also the forced taking on of dumps from one Divn on transfer at "estimated" quantity is most unsatisfactory. (PH)	
	8		Visited Railhead. Very bad roads owing to frost. Shows the hole cogs appear to be sufficient, although during a long frost many more will be required thats are at first wanted. Visited 146th Bde R.P.s. Interview Maj. Q.M.G. at Gen. HQ YPRES. Discussed the school on Col. Oliver Taegg, the News TVG arrangements for the move into the field area, &	
	14,7		Bde. Today do not draw Ration from R.P. Thirty lorries up to normal Hystern. (PH)	

WAR DIARY
INTELLIGENCE SUMMARY

Army Form C. 2118.

Place	Date	Hour	Summary of Events and Information	Remarks and references to Appendices
January	8 (cont)		Special train formed & orders to all Coys for the preparation move of Divison to the STAPLE area.	
"	9		Wired New Area that O.C 88? Tea train at MARIE CAPPEL & inspected 1 Bell B Horse home Van No4 Coy & the R.T.O. M? Billière. Discussed the taking over of the Various services with O.C 66 Train.	
			Visited the New Railhead EBBLEGHEM. Between Q.A.D.Y.S. to see any fresh horses & arrange to withdraw & from the M.T.C. Front to the S. effected with Major Gerrard. helm? bemove. Received information that remounts are available CALAIS on 13th not than as at other times, Lens as the Divison will have Coys filled up other [illegible]	
	10		Spoke to A.P.O.M.G. re inspection of horses & Kennel Clapp, for Rev Bolus. Had interview with O.C 66 train & discussed the move of No 3 Coy & what is staying in forward area. Also the Various details of the Train in forward Area. No 4 Coy marched to MARIE CAPPEL. Issued T.H.Q. order for move on 12th inst.	

Place	Date	Hour	Summary of Events and Information	Remarks and references to Appendices
	10		Visited 148 Inf Bde HQ. No rifle Bty. Then inserting back to normal. Keystone the suppliers drawn at RHQ by lorries & dumped at MERRIS CAMEL for thus Bde. for consumption on 12th. (R)	
	11		Issued instructions to O.C 148 3 Coy to discharge Militi Horse trans. with the S&T Jan Train Coy Rd RENINGHELST on the 12th also R.P.T. Transport be exchanged. Spoke ADOMS re the changing of Indian some & changing of lorry to pick up details for Remount Party from No3 Coy to RHEMINGHELST. (R)	
	12		Then H.Q. moved from RHEMINGHELST to ARQUES No 2 Coy marched from " Area to STAPLE area. HH Att: Marsh visited R.P.T. 148th Bde at MARIE CAPPEL. Arrived New Coal Tumps at HONDEGHEM. visited RE HQ at EBBLINGHEM. Trans arrangem. for drawing the coal on the next. Three Precautions on. Reported new location of T.HQ & DH.Q. (R) Interview I.Of. RT. be the prosecution of Lt HOULDSWORTH & Capt. CAMERER (Off)	

WAR DIARY or INTELLIGENCE SUMMARY

Army Form C. 2118.

Place	Date	Hour	Summary of Events and Information	Remarks and references to Appendices
January	13		Thaw Precautions still on.	
			Attended Conference at XXII Corps H.Q. discussed the detailing of all F.S.W. F.S. Wagons by the Corps. as they satisfactory selecting the difficulty of getting the information up to Corps in time & receiving their instructions being evident, it was decided to give the idea a trial for those Divisions in the line.	
			Accompanied by Major A.M.S. visited A.H.Q. had interview with A.M.S. in promotion of Lt. HOULDSWORTH & Capt CAMERON. obtained from M.G.S.H.Q that acting Rank is unanswerable.	
			Visited Div. H.Q. at RENESCURE. arranged for "B" Coys. Supplies to be dumped in the drops.	
			12 D.A.C. wagon reported at EBBLINGHEM from duty to draw coal from on 14th. Issued Detail orders to this L.S.S. wagons to report E.R. & a coal coal on 14th also for train wagon for same duty.	
14			Coal train & to be drawn by H.T. as thaw precautions are still on.	
			Maj. K.C. upon report & look after closing these journey.	

WAR DIARY or INTELLIGENCE SUMMARY

Army Form C. 2118.

Place	Date	Hour	Summary of Events and Information	Remarks and references to Appendices
[illegible]	15		All forage & stopped. Thaw flowing. Received warn from IV Army to accept Thaw Precautions. Spoke Ort re Reserve Forage of 3 days. All this now settled down in New Area.	
			Baggage wagon reported. Beef Cony. 79 Amb Wagon returned. Each 79 Amb. (BH)	
	16		Thaw Precautions. Final. S.F.S. from Fretham detailed for Richmer work. 2 Lorries allowed from Corps Corps for Fuel Road, the Fuel Dump being 3 miles from Rt HQ.	
			Then Rt HQ is too far away from the Billeting Area, & 1 MP is too far from Br. Cor. & is on a foothills & hill makes it very difficult to get round to any of this Rt have transport.	
2/Lt MARDEN			RtHQ. Received Notice releving from DHQ. (BH)	
joined from Base				
Pre Col NOI coy (?)	17		Schedule made out for allot. of any surplus transport transport to various transport groups. Lorries not being available 18 G.S. Wagons turned out to clear Fuel Road from RtHQ. 6 from & 79 Ambulance 45 from Cond Coy No.2 770.4. (BH)	

WAR DIARY
or
INTELLIGENCE SUMMARY.
(Erase heading not required.)

Army Form C. 2118.

Place	Date	Hour	Summary of Events and Information	Remarks and references to Appendices
January	18		Thaw. Restrictions still on. Obtained 2 lorries to bring straw from the CAESTRE area. Received information that coal train with about 90 tons was due at the R.O.D. — Spoke to Rear C. re getting 12 D.A.C. Major's S.S. drawn. Arrangements in drawing. Arranged with D.A.S. to collect the men in STAPLE. —	
	19		2 Tails of horses Transport to draw coal from Re H.Q. Thaw Restrictions still on. 12 DACSC reported for duty. Interview re the Posting of Transport. (DR)	
	20		Interview Sergt No 2. the boys took Billet Room over at each inspected horse lines Wednesdays at No 2. Coy. Supplied R.P.7 168 Bde. Lt Col R.E. CAMERON. gazetted Major Bastham. Nov. 20 1916. Cttee of Gazette 19.1.18. (morning post) (DR)	
	21.		Accompanied the Divisional Commander on his inspection of 1st line transport of 148th Inf Bde. H.Q. H.y.S.R. K.O.Y.L.I. 4/5 Y & L of 148 M.G. Coy. the G.O.C. expressed himself satisfaction with what he saw. (DR)	

WAR DIARY or INTELLIGENCE SUMMARY

Army Form C. 2118.

Place	Date	Hour	Summary of Events and Information	Remarks and references to Appendices
January	22		Received instruction from S.A.S.O. that one lorry only will now be at the disposal of train for supplies at RUYS. Saw instructions withdrawn midnight 23/24.	
	23		Arranged for the MTAC, G.S. Wagons to remain at STAPLE Longest having fuel. Wish to & extra forage from R.H. & R.I. Received information that only one lorry will now be available for supplies and at RUYS.	
	24		2/Lt. D.L. OLIVER reported for duty from A.P.B.and Paris for Tel. & No4 Coy. Supply arrangements made to the Brigades Schools at BORRE. Lt. BARRINGER transferred No. 2 Coy for supply duties. Attached for Duty G.S. Wagons to draw Supplies from EARLINGHEM R.H.A.	
	25		No.7 to take 10 GS — This morning to tent area. — No lorries available.	
	26		Received notification that No. 4 Coy Coal & Oil barge R.H° or R.I. Train 22 G.S. & 19 LS.C from The Pool also 9 lorries from Column to clear No 3 coy moved from RHENINGHELST to MARIE PRPEC area. No 4 coy moved from MARIE CAPPEL area to RHENINGHELST.	

Army Form C. 2118.

WAR DIARY
or
INTELLIGENCE SUMMARY.
(Erase heading not required.)

Instructions regarding War Diaries and Intelligence Summaries are contained in F. S. Regs., Part II. and the Staff Manual respectively. Title pages will be prepared in manuscript.

Place	Date	Hour	Summary of Events and Information	Remarks and references to Appendices
January	27th		The Coal Team did not arrive at R.H.H. today.	
			A Train of fuel Wood was cleared by horses brought with R.A.T.O for use.	
			Arrangements in 8th Corps to draw coal when it arrives.	
			Detailed 2 & 3 S.R.'s + 9 T.S.C. to draw coal in Houses 9. (BH)	
	28		Visited Div. H.Q. interview H.Q.N.S. + A.A.G.	
			Go to D.A.D.O.S. + meet Gans. arranged with A.A.G. to purchase as by total Ticket R.E. Has inspected No 2 + No 3 Coys Horse Mayons.	
			Visited No 3 Coy Horse lines. There are no standings or head cover for this Coy. Arrangements for Horse Clo bte taken first. Hoto arranged to to move.	
			Visited New Coal Dump near Repple.	
			Visited Old Coal Dump + new RPS at HONDEGHEM Parks placed R.P. at.	
			ATKINS CAMP L.	
			Received Telephone instructions from HQ R.M.S. that 19.0. 3.0.O.R 8th R.O.Y.L.I.	
			12.O. 9.0o.O.R 8th W/Yks 1.2.0. 9oo.OR. 5th W.Rdgs. are leaving the Division on	
			30 West. Issued necessary instructions for these troops to be rationed up to 15th Feb.	
			inclusive. (BH)	

WAR DIARY or INTELLIGENCE SUMMARY

Army Form C. 2118.

Place	Date	Hour	Summary of Events and Information	Remarks and references to Appendices
January	29th		Cycled, inspected R.P. & R.H.Q. Horse lines. Horse Pickets, Cookhouses &c of No 1 Coy at NORD PEENE. R.H.Q. at HANDRE.	
			Motor lorry transport standing by & a c/o Corporal on Road had received orders. Horses are standing on a line posed in most bad condition.	
			Lt. ARGLES attached to Train H.Q. O.S. to understudy Adjt.	
	30		Issued 3 days rations to the Troops living turn on reorganization of 146th & 147th Bgdes.	
			Wrote @ rearranged the arrangements for Coy. Coy transport of 14th Bde Lt. LE PEREQUES.	
			Going on musketry course on 1st to 5th to LE PEREQUES.	
			Carted R.F. Hqs Army to Lorries hotel hay from CAISTRE.	
	31		Sent A. No. 1 Coy. & discussed the return of transport required for hot.(PoA) application for the shooting detachment taken & lorry to EPERLECQUES. Received notification that 20 lorries accompanied by B.S.O. & drivers will be attached at R.H.Q. for disposal of Divi Qr. Regimental O.T. to be notified to them daily. (B.H.)	

Kenwood Haig Lt. Col.
Commanding 49th Divisional Train
31/1/18

WR 35

CONFIDENTIAL

WAR DIARY OF LT COLONEL B. HAIGH. DSO.

Commanding 49th W.R. Divisional Train

From February 1st 1918 to February 28th, 1918½

(Volume 35.)

Army Form C. 2118.

WAR DIARY
or
INTELLIGENCE SUMMARY.   40th DIVISIONAL TRAIN.
(Erase heading not required.)

Instructions regarding War Diaries and Intelligence Summaries are contained in F. S. Regs., Part II. and the Staff Manual respectively. Title pages will be prepared in manuscript.

Place	Date	Hour	Summary of Events and Information	Remarks and references to Appendices
1918				
February	1st		Moved to New R.P.s. for Shooting Detachment at HOULLE near ST OMER. The Transport is marching there to-day, the Supplies dumped yards, for tomorrows consumption was drawn this morning by 1st line Transport.	
	2nd		Received notification of 90 Tons Coal due on Sunday 3rd inst. (MM) At Fontein Q. is attached to Pack Locales for carrying Lewis Gun also Tank M.G. detailed because G.S. & S.L. to clear 90 Tons Coal from R? 11ª. (BR)	
	3rd		Coal Train arrived at R?.H? released by H.T.Y.L. lorries. Stinson Q. discussed the run of the shooting detachment from Houlle (RR) Pack Reynolds No 3 Coy Horse Lines to unpicket new rule for Horse Coy	
	4th		at HONDEGHEM. which is about some R.H? — issued washing lines for the move to-day. Arrangements made for the change over of 146 MT S/Bas to Houlle for Motor Tractor Supplies Lorries from left Base taken by Lorry to HOULE from BRAY (BR)	

A6945 Wt. W11422/M1160 350,000 12/16 D. D. & L. Forms/C/2118/14

WAR DIARY or INTELLIGENCE SUMMARY

Army Form C. 2118.

Place	Date	Hour	Summary of Events and Information	Remarks and references to Appendices
Feby	5th		Lt Colonel B Haigh D.S.O admitted New Zealand Stationary H.P. Major J.B. Foster assumed command of the Train 979	
"	6th		Routine as usual. 979	
"	7th		2nd Lieut/A/Capt Conrad reported for duty from 6th Div. Train and was posted to No 2 Coy. R.M.A.	
"	8th		Tested special carriers for Stokes guns and Lewis guns on packsaddles and discussed merits and demerits with 2 branch R.M.A.	
"	9th		2nd Lt D.L. Oliver reported to O/C Canal Supply Office Bruay and was struck off the strength of the Train as from the 9th inst. R.M.A.	
"	10th		Capt. W. Molony reported for duty and was posted to No 1 Coy. 147 Inf. Bde moved from the Moulle Area to Lederzeele. 146 Inf Bde moved from the Staple Area to the Forward Area (Reninghelst). 148 Inf. Bde moved from the Staple Area (Reninghelst) to Staple from Houlle for mobulary practice, 466 Coy R.E. moving into the Staple Area. All the necessary supply arrangements were made for these moves R.M.A.	
"	11th		The 147 Inf. Bde moved from Lederzeele to the Marie Capelle Area, the necessary alterations in Supply arrangements being made. 2nd Lt Maudlen was posted from	

Army Form C. 2118.

WAR DIARY
or
INTELLIGENCE SUMMARY.
(Erase heading not required.)

Instructions regarding War Diaries and Intelligence Summaries are contained in F. S. Regs., Part II. and the Staff Manual respectively. Title pages will be prepared in manuscript.

Place	Date	Hour	Summary of Events and Information	Remarks and references to Appendices
Feby.	12		463 Coy A.S.C. to Abbey O.S.E. to replace 2nd Lt. OLIVER (R.M.A.)	
"	13		Routine as usual R.M.A.	
"	14		Routine as usual R.M.A. Interviewed "L" re carriage of Stokes howitzer from a bookstaller. Submitted.	
"	15		Shortage R.M.A. Visited forward area and made provisional arrangements for the convoy crew interviewing the S.S.O. of the N.Z. Division making arrangements with him for taking over R.M.A.	
"	16		Routine as usual R.M.A.	
"	17		Routine as usual R.M.A.	
"	18		146 Bde moved from HOUTLE area to STAPLE sub-area the necessary alteration in the Supply arrangements being made. R.M.A.	
"	19		147 Bde refilled twice. Ofemondories for the convoys issued to the Coys. being a different Supply pro fro 47 railheads & R.P.s for each day. Lt. MAUDLEN proceeded to CALAIS to collect reinercals. Visited the forward area damaged billets of R.P.s for Train H.Q. the Contains, arranging as to the taking over from the N.Z. Div. R.M.A.	

Army Form C. 2118.

WAR DIARY
or
INTELLIGENCE SUMMARY.
(Erase heading not required.)

Instructions regarding War Diaries and Intelligence Summaries are contained in F.S. Regs., Part II. and the Staff Manual respectively. Title pages will be prepared in manuscript.

Place	Date	Hour	Summary of Events and Information	Remarks and references to Appendices
1918 Feb.	20		No 3 Coy moved to forward area. Supplies from Railhead being drawn by lorry to them near R.P. Capt. W. Molony was evacuated to No 13. C.C.S. R.M.A. interviewed O.C. of Army's reinforcement camp at Rouen Hd Qrs in the forward area. R.M.A.	
"	21			
"	22		Train Hd Qrs moved from Bruges to PIONEER Camp Sheet 28. H.21.b.5.7. 4 Coy moved from STAPLE Sutena to Sheet 28. G.22.C.8.7. No 1 Coy moved from NOORPEENE Sub area to St JANS CAPELLE. Supplies being drawn by lorries from ARNEKE to St JANS CAPELLE. After visiting railhead at EBBLINGHEM interviewed O.C. New Zealand Train &c visited new Refilling Points & Supply Officers in forward area. R.M.A.	
"	23		No 1 Coy moved from St JANS CAPELLE to Sheet 28. H.15.C.4.8. Railhead was changed to OUDERDOM. Retained 2 N.Z. Boxes & their Divisional Artillery, bringing the total issuing strength to the Force to 29,000 men and 9000 animals R.M.A.	
"	24		Routine as usual. R.M.A. Lt. MAUDLEN proceeded to Calais to collect remounts R.M.A.	
"	25		Routine as usual. R.M.A.	
"	26		Attended conference at Q. at transport. Connected into the formation of machine gun Battalion. Lt. H + 4 G.S. in great interest with the Machine Gun Companies. D. will	
"	27th			

WAR DIARY
or
INTELLIGENCE SUMMARY.

Army Form C. 2118.

Place	Date	Hour	Summary of Events and Information	Remarks and references to Appendices
Zelp.	27		Enemy artillery active. Our batteries 2 became busy afternoon. The 1st line Trench in view found from the present in locating enemy Coys in the attached Battalions. R.M.L.	
			No 2 Gun moved to from G.34.b.6.6. to H.20.c.9.1. Sheet 28. Lt MAUDLEN returned from Calais with remounts. R.A.A.	
"	28		Interviewed C.O. re reserve ration in posts in the forward area which had not been inducted by S.O. 148 Inf. Bde. R.M.L.	

28/9/18

J.B.Whon
for Lieut. Colonel,
Commanding 49th (W.R.) Divl. Tram.

Vol 36

CONFIDENTIAL

WAR DIARY

of

Lt.Colonel R.G.J.J.BERRY

Commanding 49th W.R.Divisional Train

From MARCH 1st 1918   to   MARCH 31st,1918.

(Volume 36)

Army Form C. 2118.

WAR DIARY
or
INTELLIGENCE SUMMARY.   29th DIVISIONAL TRAIN.
(Erase heading not required.)

Place	Date	Hour	Summary of Events and Information	Remarks and references to Appendices
1918 March	1		Major CAMERON was evacuated to No 59 General Hospital MOULLE R.M.A.	
"	2		Inspected all companies of the Train and found everything very satisfactory R.M.A.	
"	3		Lt SLINGSBY transferred from No 1 Coy. to No 3 Coy. as S.O.; 2nd Lt CLIFFORD was posted from No 3 Coy. to No 4 Coy. as Transport Subaltern and 2nd Lt MADDEN from No 4 Coy. to No 1 Coy. as a transport Subaltern R.M.A.	
"	4		Routine as usual R.M.A.	
"	5		Routine as usual R.M.A.	
"	6		Routine as usual R.M.A.	
"	7		Routine as usual R.M.A.	
"	8		No 4 Coy. moved from 28.G.22 c.8.7 to 28.G.30 c.1.9 R.M.A.	
"	9		Routine as usual R.M.A.	
"	10		Routine as usual R.M.A.	
"	11		Received notification that Lieut. Col. B HAIGH D.S.O. had been transferred to England on 26.2.18 and was struck off the strength of the Train as from that date. LIEUT. BAXTER proceeded to CAESTRE to draw reinforcements from the Details there and rejoined the same day R.M.A.	

Army Form C. 2118.

WAR DIARY
or
INTELLIGENCE SUMMARY.
(Erase heading not required.)

Instructions regarding War Diaries and Intelligence Summaries are contained in F. S. Regs., Part II. and the Staff Manual respectively. Title pages will be prepared in manuscript.

Place	Date	Hour	Summary of Events and Information	Remarks and references to Appendices
France	12		The weekly coal train arrived and 150 Tons of coal was cleared. The transport of the Train party received R.M.A.	
"	13		Routine as usual R.M.A.	
"	14		Routine as usual R.M.A.	
"	15		Routine as usual R.M.A.	
"	16		2nd Lt BAXTER returned from Palais in charge of the party of remounts R.M.A.	
"	17		Routine as usual R.M.A.	
"	18		Considerable enemy shelling in the vicinity of OUDERDOM Railhead and No 4 Coy's lines (G.3.0.C.1.9 Sheet 28) but no casualties reported or damage done. Whilst employed on R.E. work Dr OLFORD of No 3 Coy was wounded near CORK CAMP (Sheet 28.I.10.a.1.4) & was evacuated to C.C.S. R.M.A.	
"	19		Major CAMERON on evacuation from hospital reported and took over temporary command of the Train. There was considerable enemy shelling of affair to-day particularly round DICKIEBUSCH. There are 307879 Pte. FALKINGHAM of 243 Coy amputation & 3147111 Pte WRIGLEY was killed and Pte [illeg.] slightly wounded at DICKIEBUSCH Railhead. R.M.A.	
"	20		Considerable enemy shelling again all day. S/Sgt Jackerith was killed and Lieut. TURNER & two bodies wounded about 9 p.m. at 28.H.27.C.1.8. S/Sgt TURNER died the same night R.M.A.	

Army Form C. 2118.

WAR DIARY
or
INTELLIGENCE SUMMARY.
(Erase heading not required.)

Place	Date	Hour	Summary of Events and Information	Remarks and references to Appendices
Arach.	21		Owing to hostile shelling the 148 Bde Rgt. Wing Point was moved to H.19.b Central and the 146 Bde R.P. was moved to the No 2 Corps Hosiery M.O.	
"	22		No.1 Coy moved from 28.G.30.c.1.9. to 28.G.22.c.8.7. R.M.A.	
"	23		Routine as usual R.M.A.	
"	24		Routine as usual R.M.A. T.A/25128 Pte Oleford. A. died of wounds in No 7 Canadian General Hospital R.M.A.	
"	25		The ration strength of the Park Train was reduced by the N.Z. Div. Troops to the S.A.A. 3rd Bde. N.Z. Div on leaving the area R.M.A.	
"	26		The extending Bos of the N.Z. Division left the area, also reinforcement allotments made for MG Coy & others. Received notification that Lt. Oleford intended on the 11th inst had died in hospital R.M.A.	
"	27		LIEUT. COL. H.G.J. BERRY reported for duty and assumed command of the Train No.1 Coy moved from 28.G.22.C.8.7. to 28. H.1.a.6.6. A conference was held at 49 Division Q reference the reduction of Rat. Rolls. We were informed that should the Division move they would move on foot as had been in War Establishment. The van arranged to O.C. Coy S. & nine such labor. Lt Col. Bonny reported to Div. H.Q. R.M.A.	
"	28		Inspected No 1 Coy R.M.A.	
"	29		Inspected No 2,3 & 4 Coys. & found everything satisfactory R.M.A.	

Army Form C. 2118.

WAR DIARY
or
INTELLIGENCE SUMMARY.
(Erase heading not required.)

Place	Date	Hour	Summary of Events and Information	Remarks and references to Appendices
March	30		Routine as usual. P.M.A	
"	31		Interviewed O.C.'s & discussed the question of supplies in open warfare & selected new Camp, at 29.B. M.5 and at WESTOUTRE with a view to moving into that area. P.M.A	
			Visited Div². H.Q. and interviewed G.O.C.	
			Brigade Routine order No 4222 of 24/3 st. hand. Stated the following award:- Military Medal to T/4/251948 Dr. A. OXFORD A.S.C. for gallantry on 12th March 1916. Whilst taking a load of stone up to the forward area a shell burst, wounding Dr. OXFORD & one horse. He however bolted and although wounded this man stuck to his horses and pulled them up and handed them over to his officer, after which he had to be lifted from his seat. P.M.A	

B.P. Dexyrill Col
Comdg HQ⁵ W.R. Div Trn

CONFIDENTIAL
-----oOo-----

War Diary

of

Lt. Colonel R.G.I.J.Berry.

Commanding 49th W.R.Divisional Train

From April 1st to April 30th 1918.

(Volume 37.)

WAR DIARY
or
INTELLIGENCE SUMMARY.

Army Form C. 2118.

49th DIVISIONAL TRAIN.

Place	Date	Hour	Summary of Events and Information	Remarks and references to Appendices
1918. APRIL	1		Visited the Cavan recently vacated by the 37 L. Divis. and selected Refilling Points and Cards for H.Q. Train and the 4 Train Companies. Reconnoitred for the Train to move into the new area try until 12 noon on the 2nd inst. Information & orders to the time of the move & Refilling Points selected & issued and the 6th Division orders which were to continue. The 49th Divn. Train could not move until the 5th inst. R.M.A.	
"	2		Lieut 28. The following moves took place. Train H.B. from H.21.c.5.8. to M.5.c.3.8. No.1 Coy from Hall.3.9 to WESTOUTRE, No.2 Coy from 28.G.34.b.4.b to 28.M.5.c.3.8, No.3 Coy from 28.H.19.d.7.8 to M.11.a.39 M.A. Ne 4 Coy from 28.H.19.d.7.8 to M.11.a.39 M.A. R.M.A.	
"	3		The Refilling Points of the three Inf. Bdes were changed to the following locations 146 Inf. Bde. to 28.N.8.a.2.9. 147 Inf Bde. to 28.N.8.a.1.6, 148 Inf Bde to 28.H.22.d.8.2. The new Train B/of sent 28.M.6.a.3.9. The 3 Bde Companies in the afternoon took over an Infested the new camps of the 3 Bde Companies in the afternoon.	
"	4		The Railhead unchanged from OUDERDOM to LA CLYTTE. Interviewed Q in the morning. R.M.A.	
"	5		Wanted H.Q. Machine Gun B.T. wagon lines & inspected them, and not finding considerable room for improvement. Arranged for our S.S.M. to Sergeants to go to No.2 Coy daily for instruction under the S.S.M. No.1 Coy moved from 28.H.15.x.3.9 to 28.M.5.c.1.6. R.M.A.	
"	6		Routine as usual R.M.A.	
"	7		Routine as usual R.M.A.	

Army Form C. 2118.

WAR DIARY
or
INTELLIGENCE SUMMARY.
(Erase heading not required.)

Instructions regarding War Diaries and Intelligence Summaries are contained in F. S. Regs., Part II. and the Staff Manual respectively. Title pages will be prepared in manuscript.

Place	Date	Hour	Summary of Events and Information	Remarks and references to Appendices
April	8		The 1.2.6.5. Train was one belonging to the three disbanded battalions of the Division were sent as white trains to 27 A.6.a.6.2. in accordance with instructions received from A.Q. Div. B. Received orders that 147 Bde were to move to the WIPPENHOEK Area at the Q.Master R.M.O.	
"	9		Received orders from Div. H.Q. preparatory to the move of the Division. No 3 Coy moved to the WIPPENHOEK Area and the necessary orders were issued to the Bde. Cops. with regard to supplies & the despatch of the Baggage Wagons to units in rear of the zone. Acts. presentation of honours by the Army Commander T4/251001 Dr. HOOK. E. was presented with the Military Medal. Our officer commanded pump Train in accordance with Operation Order awarded him 6 other badges. The Train was ordered forward in accordance with Operation Order No 35. Attacked. These orders were subsequently modified then cancelled proof that 147 & 148 If Bdes receiving orders to entrain at midnight No 3 Coy received orders to entrain to 11.P.M. to move and march to METEREN. They moved with this supply wagons full R.M.O.	
"	10		Owing to 147 & 148 If Bds having orders to entrain at 9 a.m. No 4 Coy moved off at 8 A.M. to march to NEUVE EGLISE. They bivouacked stopped about 10.30 A.M. at St JANS CAPELLE and about 3 P.M. they received orders to proceed to DRANOUTRE and to stop there til three. No 2 Coy were ordered to march to GODEWAERSVELDE and started about 10.30 A.M. but were afterwards turned back about 1 P.M. and marched to B.camp of M.b. Q.M.O. 94. R.M.O.	

Army Form C. 2118.

WAR DIARY
or
INTELLIGENCE SUMMARY.
(Erase heading not required.)

Instructions regarding War Diaries and Intelligence Summaries are contained in F.S. Regs., Part II and the Staff Manual respectively. Title pages will be prepared in manuscript.

Place	Date	Hour	Summary of Events and Information	Remarks and references to Appendices
Ofuil	11		No 3 Coy moved from METEREN to 27.R.35.C.6.3.8. with a view to betyp nearer to the transport lines of the 147 Inf Bde. No 4 Coy moved from DRANOUTRE and is outside standing by today to go to local R.E. task were eventually sent to the same Coy as No 3 Coy at 27.R.35.C.3.8. The 147 Inf Bde Supply Wagons were taken into the Bde 1st line transport to STEAM MILL 27.X.24.C.13 and returned to their Coys lines at 2 A.M. on the 12th inst. Visited No 3 & 4 Coys about 10 P.M. and found everything satisfactory. R.M.A.	
"	12		The railhead for the H.Q. 6th Division (as Div Arty was moved from LA CLYTTE to HAZEBROUCK GARAGE. The Div Arty were attached to the 21st Division and drew from RENINGHELST Railhead. Visited No 3 and 4 Coys at SCHAEKSCHEN (27.R.35.C.3.8) in the morning. About 2 P.M. No 3 Coy got orders from Div Bde to move towards BERTHEN. They accordingly moved to 27.R.23.1.8.8. No 4 Coy also had orders to march to reach to 27.R.16.8.0.5 and camped there. The pack train did not arrive at HAZEBROUCK GARAGE until about 3:30 P.M. Supplies for the 147 Inf Bde were delivered at their Refilling Point in the evening and No 3 Coy delivered the rations as far as the H.Q. of 7th WEST RIDINGS were reported to have lost some of their rations when their Battalion Transport had to retire. The rations for the remainder of the Division were left on the lorries for delivery at the Refilling Points to-morrow morning. Visited No 3 & 4 Coys about 11 P.M.	

WAR DIARY
or
INTELLIGENCE SUMMARY.

Place	Date	Hour	Summary of Events and Information	Remarks and references to Appendices
April	13		and found everything satisfactory. R.M.A. 2nd Lt. F.E. Clifford was slightly wounded in the head but remained at duty R.M.A. No 2 Coy moved from 28.M.6.a.9.4. to 28.G.22.d.2.4. owing to hostile shelling at the former.	
	14		Camp R.M.A. Visited all coys. and found all satisfactory R/M/A. Railhead was moved to St OMER. No 3 Coy. moved from 27.R.23.b.8.8. to 27.R.6.c.2.8.	
	15		Visited all Coys. and found all satisfactory. R.M.A. Railhead was changed to GODEWAERSVELDE. Wagon lines were evacuated stock to No 6 Casualty Clearing Station. S.S.M. WENBURN if was posted from No 3 Coy to No 1 Coy. and S.S.M. MACDONALD from No 1 Coy. to No 3 Coy. The 149th Division Artillery is now under the fighting strength of the Division after having been attached to the 2yst Division. T.H.Q. moved from the east of WESTOUTRE to billets in that village about 9 P.M. 2nd Lt F.E. Clifford was slightly wounded in the head, but remained at duty	
	16		Inspected every Shelling the ground at LOCREHOFF FARM 28.M.24.A.2.4. was untenable R.M.A. T.H.Q. and all companies were standing to all day ready to move but no orders to move were received except that No 3 Coy which moved from 27.R.6.C.2.8. to 27.Q.6.C.3.8g R.M.A. spent	
	17		WESTOUTRE on being shelled in the morning for about 40 minutes about 9.45 A.M. While its shelling ceased T.H.Q. and moved arranged to ABEELE. There was considerable shelling of woods on Hunu but no casualties. Sent with the Train Owing to heavy shelling No 4 Coy moved from 27.R.14.a.0.5.	

WAR DIARY or INTELLIGENCE SUMMARY

Army Form C. 2118.

Place	Date	Hour	Summary of Events and Information	Remarks and references to Appendices
	April 18		Co 27 A.11.d.8.8. Before moving beyond in lorres killed by shell fire in Stein lines. No 1 Co Scout was also killed at 28.M.5.C.1.6 and then moved to 27.L.29.6.1.9. No 2 Co also moved in the afternoon from 28.G.22.d.2.4 to 27.L.29.C.8.6. Q.M.O. Billets were changed to ARNEKE. Conference both O.C. Coys and fifty officers.	
	19		Held at T.H.Q. in the afternoon R.M.O. Visited all Companies offered everything satisfactory R.M.A.	
	20		Arranged to draw 2000 hand rations as a reserve for KEMMEL defences. These were duly delivered R.M.A.	
	21		Billets were changed to GRUBBEN. Hqrs Div Artillery still drawing from ARNEKE.	
	22		No 3 Coy moved from 27 Q.6.C.3.8. to 27.L.18.C.4.5. R.M.A. No 2 Coy moved from 27 A.11.d.d.7. No 1 Co moved from 27 A.11.d.8.8. to 28 G.16.d.7.7. R.M.A. Rain several. R.M.A.	
	23			
	24		Reconnaissance of T.M. (39677) Dr E.D. licott A.t.T. No 2 Coy at T.M. (39677) Dr E.D. licott A.t.T. No 2 Coy bombarded, 1 shell hit his shower being killed R.M.A.	
	25		Clouds fell in No 3 Coys lines about 2:30 A.M. killing 1 other D. and 1 rider wounding 2 H.D. and 5 riders, of which 2 H.D. and 3 riders had afterwards to be shot, and 3 H.D. + 2 riders evacuated. The deficiencies so far primarily made up by borrowing from the other Companies of the Bre	

Army Form C. 2118.

WAR DIARY
or
INTELLIGENCE SUMMARY.
(Erase heading not required.)

Instructions regarding War Diaries and Intelligence Summaries are contained in F. S. Regs., Part II. and the Staff Manual respectively. Title pages will be prepared in manuscript.

Place	Date	Hour	Summary of Events and Information	Remarks and references to Appendices
	April 26		Train. T/4/249829 S/t DRIVER G. of No.2 Coy. was wounded by shell while taking A.D. from No.2 Coy's lines to No.3 Coy's lines. The A.D. was taken to the Reserve DRIVER was admitted to No.139 Field Ambulance. Visited all centres and made the necessary arrangements for No.2 and 4 Coys to move if necessary. R.M.A. No.1 Coy moved from 27 L.29.c.1.9. to 27 K.18.a.9.9. No.2 Coy moved from 28 G.16.d.7.7. to 27 K.17.d.9.8. No.3 Coy moved from 27 K.18.c.4.5. to 27 K.18.c.4.4. No.4 Coy moved from 28 G.16.d.7.7. to 27 K.12.c.b.4. R.M.A. No.1 Coy moved from 27 K.18.a.9.9. to 27 K.18.c.4.4. No.4 Coy moved from 27 K.12.c.b.4. to 27 K.17.d.9.8. R.M.A.	
" 27			I.H.Q. moved from ABEELE to 27 K.16.c.8.8. T/4/249855 L/Cpl. MALE A.G. of No.2 Coy was wounded and admitted to hospital. R.M.A.	
" 28			(H.D.) T/4/252547 Dr DAWSON G. of No.1 Coy was wounded by shell fire and L/Cpl. ———— also wounded. 2 H.D. belonging to No.4 Coy were also killed by shell fire. Received notification that Major W.S. CAMERON	
" 29			Lieut. W.J. PATTISON reported for duty from the Base Depôt HAVRE and was posted to No.1 Coy. R.M.A.	
" 30			A conference of all officers of the Train was held at I.H.Q. at 5 P.M. R.M.A.	

W.R. D——, Lt Col.
Comdg. W.R. D——Train

SECRET   Copy No 6   49th Div Train No.S.T.6/2.

49th DIVISIONAL TRAIN O.O.No.35.

(1)   The 49th Division (less R.A.) will be relieved in the Line by the 21st Division.

(2)   R.A. (less S.A.A. Section) will remain in this section until furthur orders.

(3)   The S.A.A. Section D.A.C. will accompany the Division.

(4)   Entraining Stations for the Division will be GODWAERSVELDE and ABEELE. Entrainment will commence on the 11th inst. Furthur instructions in regard to time of entrainment will be issued later.

         148th Bde will entrain at - GODWAERSVELDE
         147th "   "   "   "   - ABEELE
         146th "   "   "   "   - GODWAERSVELDE and ABEELE.
         S.A.A.Section.D.A.C. Half Section will entrain at each of the above stations.

(5)   RAILHEAD will be at LA CLYTE until the 11th inst.

(6)   Supplies will be loaded at Railhead to-morrow morning 10th inst into Supply Column at 8 a.m. and arrangements will be made by the S.S.O. for Re-filling in Brigade Areas.

(7)   Onrelief 147th Bde will proceed into billets WIPPENHOEK on the 9th inst, and 148th Bde. to WESTOUTRE on the 9th inst and 146th Bde. to GODWAERSVELDE on the 10th inst.
     Divisional H.Q. will move to HOOGRAAF on the 11th inst.

(8)   On arrival in new areas the Division will be re-grouped as under:-

GODWAERSVELDE AREA 146th Bde.Group	WESTOUTRE AREA 147th Bde Group	WESTOUTRE AREA 148th Bde Group.
146th Inf Bde 456th Field Coy R.E. "A" Coy,49 M.G.Bn 1st W.R.Field Ambce. 464,Coy,Div Train	147th Inf Bde 57th Field Coy R.E. 19th Lancs Fus: "B"Coy,49th M.G.Bn. 2nd W.R.Field Ambce. 465,Coy,Div.Train.	148th Inf Bde 458th Field Coy R.E. "C" Co.49 M.G.Bn. 3rd Fld Ambce 466,Coy,Div.Train S.A.A.Sect.D.A.C.

HOOGRAAF AREA
Div.H.Q. Group

Div H.Q.
H.Q.R.E.
Div Signal Coy.
H.Q. and "D" Co.49 M.G.Bn.
243 Emp Coy
H.Q.,Div Train.
1/1st Mob.Vet.Section.

(9)   Baggage Wagons not already sent out will join their units not later than 8a.m. to-morrow. Baggage and Supply wagons will entrain with their units.

(10)   Train Coys will move as follows :-

         No.1.Coy - Stand Fast
         No.2.Coy - On 10th inst
         No.3.Coy - On 9th inst
         No.4.Coy - On 11th inst

and will go into billets in their Bde Areas. Camps to be handed over by 11a.m. to incoming units.

(11) Area Stores now held will be handed over to Area Commandants Certificates for these together with any taken over and certficate as to cleanliness of billets will be forwarded in duplicate to this Office not later than 3 days after moves.

(12) ACKNOWLEDGE.

APRIL 9th.1918.

Capt & Adjt.,
49th (W.R.) Divisional Train.

```
Copy No.1. to 49th Div "Q"
 "   No.2. to No.1.Coy.
 "   No.3. to No.2.Coy.
 "   No.4. to No.3.Coy.
 "   No.5. to No.4.Coy.
 "   No.6. to Office.
 "   No.7. to   -do-
```

Vol 38

CONFIDENTIAL

WAR   DIARY

of

Lieut Colonel R.G.J.Berry

Commanding 49th (West Riding) Divisional Train

from   May 1st 1918   to May 31st 1918

(Volume 38)

WAR DIARY or INTELLIGENCE SUMMARY

Army Form C. 2118.

49TH DIVISIONAL TRAIN.

(Erase heading not required.)

Place	Date	Hour	Summary of Events and Information	Remarks and references to Appendices
1918 May	1		Visited Advanced Div. H.Q. and received instructions to the effect that this a Composite Brigade of the 30th Division was to be attached to this Division. The A.S.C. Coy. belonging to this Bde was to be attached to his Train R.M.A.	
"	2		No. 4 Coy. 30th Div. Train came under the orders of this train after refilling to-day and was responsible for feeding the 30th Composite Bde and all units attached to that Bde R.M.A.	
"	3		The following alterations in posting took place in the Train: Capt. J.R. SIMPSON from No.3 Coy. to No.1 Coy. to command. Capt. W. MOLONY from No.1 Coy. to No.3 Coy. to command. Lt. W.J. PATTISON from No. Coy. to No.2 Coy. as left half Officer. Lt. W.P. BARRINGER from No.2 Coy. to No.1 Coy. as Transport Subaltern. S.S./1756 a/S/Sgt. DOWNES E.P. from No.2 Coy. to No.4 Coy. S4/250876 Sgt. GRIERSON A. from No.4 Coy. to No.2 Coy. R.M.A.	
"	4		Routine as usual R.M.A.	
"	5		T.H.Q. moved from 27 K.10.d.7.2. to WATOU. No.2 Coy. moved from 27 K.17.d.9.8. to 27 F.25.d.4.5. No. 4 Coy. moved from 27 K.17.d.9.8. to F.25.d.4.5. P.M.A.	
"	6		T.H.Q. about this time entrained in WATOU. No. 3 Coy. moved from 27 K.18.c.4.4. to 27 E.30.Central. R.M.A.	
"	7		Routine as usual R.M.A.	

Army Form C. 2118.

WAR DIARY
or
INTELLIGENCE SUMMARY.
(Erase heading not required.)

Place	Date	Hour	Summary of Events and Information	Remarks and references to Appendices
May	8		Inspected the 1st Line Transport of the 116 Inf. Bde. in Staffhorn and found everything in a very satisfactory Condition. Received orders at 10.30 P.M. that all units were to be prepared to move at short notice and issued the necessary instructions to all Coys. of the Train R.M.A.	
"	9		Inspected the 1st Line Transport of the 117 Inf. Bde. and found everything in a very satisfactory Condition. Considering the work the Brigade has had to Received orders at 12.15 P.M. that the orders received from Div. H.Q. yesterday with regard to being prepared to move were cancelled. R.M.A.	
"	10		Inspected the 1st Line Transport of the 118 Inf. Bde. Found everything in a satisfactory condition. R.M.A.	
"	11		Routine as usual. R.M.A.	
"	12		Received orders that the 117 Inf. Bde. were to go to Moulle for musketry practice and made the necessary alteration in Supply arrangements. R.M.A.	
"	13		No 3 Coy. marched to the Staple area escorting stores on their way to Moulle. The Supply details being set straight to Moulle to take charge of supplies which were sent there by Lorry. Nos 2 and 4 Coys. drew half lines from railhead by H.T. Major R.T. Pemberton D.S.O. reported	

WAR DIARY
or
INTELLIGENCE SUMMARY

Army Form C. 2118.

Place	Date	Hour	Summary of Events and Information	Remarks and references to Appendices
May	14		For duty and has been on the strength of the Train. R.M.A. Vet an inspection of the Division by the Army Commander. Suffers a party of 3 officers and 40 OR. Landed under Capt. J.R.Simpson. No 3 Coy marched from STAPLE to MOULLE. Lt ARGLES proceed to CALAIS to collect replacements for the Division. No 4 Coy moved from 27 F.25.d.4.5 to 27 E.30 Central R.M.A.	
"	15		Routine as usual R.M.A.	
"	16		Routine as usual R.M.A.	
"	17		Lt ARGLES returned from CALAIS with the party of reservists R.M.A.	
"	18		No 4 Coy marched from 27 E.30 Central to STAPLE on their way to MOULLE. No 3 Coy marched from MOULLE to 27 E.30 Central R.M.A.	
"	19		No 4 Coy marched from STAPLE to MOULLE. Inspected the 1st line transport of the H.Q. & Machine Gun Battn. which I consider better than on the occasion of the last inspection, still leaves room for improvement R.M.A.	
"	20		Went to MOULLE to visit 4 Coy R.M.A.	
"	21		Held an inspection of Nos 1, 2 & 3 Coys. preparatory to their inspection by the G.O.C. on the 22nd and 23rd insts. R.M.A.	

WAR DIARY or INTELLIGENCE SUMMARY

Army Form C. 2118.

Place	Date	Hour	Summary of Events and Information	Remarks and references to Appendices
	1918 May 22		O.C. 4th Divn Train inspected the 1 Coy of the Train	(CME)
	23		" " " " " 2 & 3 Coys of the Train	
			Capt C.C. Reynolds to C.C.S. 1st Battn. assumed command of No 2 Coy from unknown. L/R the Anglesea took over duties as supply officer.	(CME)
	24		No 2 Coy moved from 27 F.25.C.6.4. to the STAPLE area. No 4 Coy moved from the ST MARTIN AU LAERT area to 27 F.25.C.6.4. Time of leaving at CAUDHEM railhead changed from 10.0 am to 7.0 am.	(CME)
	25		Major J.B. Foster proceeded to England on 14 days special leave, handing over the duties of S.S.O. to Major R.T. Pembertin D.S.O. No 42 Coy moved from STAPLE area to the ST MARTIN AU LAERT area with 146 Inf Bde.	(CME)
	26		Routine as usual.	(CME)
	27		O.C. Train inspected No 2 Coy in their new billets, & issued instructions for the relief of the Coy on the 30th inst. to 27 F.25.C.6.4.	(CME)
	28		No 4 Coy inspected by the C.O.C. Divn I.	(CME)
			The following Officers W.O. & N.C.O were mentioned in Sir D. Haigh's Dispatch dated April 7th (The Times 27/5/18) T/Maj J.B. Foster, T/Capt N.N. Boome, Lt (A/Capt) C.N. Legg.	

A6945 Wt W11242/M160 350,000 12/16 D.D.&L Forms/C./2118/14

WAR DIARY
or
INTELLIGENCE SUMMARY.

(Erase heading not required.)

Army Form C. 2118.

Place	Date	Hour	Summary of Events and Information	Remarks and references to Appendices
1918 May	28		Lt (T/Capt) C L Reynolds T4/249618 C.S.M. Blakley S4/249925 S.Sgt H N Fairbank. (CHL)	
	29		Routine as usual. (CHL)	
	30		do (CHL)	
	31		Notification received from HQ Divl Q that the Divn would take over from the 41st Divn. The Divl Artillery which at present in att'd to the 6th Divn will cover the 49th Divn. H.Q. 41st Divl Train were intimated reference move & the Bde Coy lines & refilling points were inspected. (CHL)	

R Bush Lt Col
Comdg W R Divn Train

CONFIDENTIAL

War Diary.

of

Lt Colonel R.G.J.J.Berry

Commanding 49th W.R.Divisional Train

from June 1st to June 30th 1918

(Volume 39)

WAR DIARY
INTELLIGENCE SUMMARY

HQ 4th (W.R.) Divisional Train A.S.C.

Army Form C. 2118.

Place	Date	Hour	Summary of Events and Information	Remarks and references to Appendices
1918 June	1		Capt. C.L. REYNOLDS returned to duty from 4 to 13 C.C.S. (OML)	
"	2		Routine as usual. No 1 Coy had 12 men sick - chief cause Influenza (OML)	
"	3		Dvl. Remount party under Lt. BARRINGER No 1 Coy proceed to CALAIS to draw remounts. No 3 Coy moved HQ from 27 E 30 Central to 27 E 12 b 12 POMPEY CAMP (OML)	
"	4		Train HQ moved from WATOU to CHATEAU LOUVIE 27 F 16 d 2.8. Supply Section No 1 Coy moved to 27 F 16 b 3.3. the Baggage section remained at 27 K 18 c 54 as the Coy was unable to move complete owing to sickness. No 2 Coy moved from 27 F 2 g 4.4.5 to 27 F 14 a 4.3 PIGEON CAMP. No 4 Coy moved from 27 F 25 d 44 to 27 F 14 c 6.8 PARDO CAMP. Refilling Points changed to the following. Div Troops 27 F 18 3 3. 146 Bde 27 F 14 a 4.3. 147 Bde E 12 b 3.3. 148 Bde E 12 d 0.9. 1st R.W. Fusiliers returned from No 2 Coy to Train HQ. No 1 Coy had 42 men sick made up as follows 14 in bed 12 excused duty 16 detailed for light duty.	
"	5		The Div. Coal Dump at 27 F 25 c 9.7 was taken over from the 41st Div. The estimated quantities were Coal 27 tons Coke 1 ton Charcoal 1½ tons. OML	
"	6		No 1 Coy still had 39 men sick, those sufficiently well to complete their move T.M.A. Routine as usual. Lt. BARRINGER returned from CALAIS in charge of Remount Party. OML	

WAR DIARY or INTELLIGENCE SUMMARY

Army Form C. 2118.

Place	Date	Hour	Summary of Events and Information	Remarks and references to Appendices
June	7		Routine as usual R.M.A.	
"	8		Routine as usual R.M.A.	
"	9		The reserve rations in the right sector of the Divisional front were inspected and checked by Lt the Supply Officer of the 118 Inf Bde. and found correct. R.M.A.	
"	10		The reserve rations in the left sector of the Divisional front were inspected and checked by the Supply Officer of the 117 Inf Bde. and found correct. R.M.A.	
"	11		Owing to trenches in this hub being greatly reduced No 1 Coy resorts to handle the area. Hd qrs office return and H.Q. of the Coy moving to 27 F.18.d.3.3. R.M.A.	
"	12		Routine as usual R.M.A.	
"	13		Routine as usual R.M.A.	
"	14		Maj Foster and Lt McKenna returned from leave having been granted extension by the V. Corps	
"	15		Maj Foster took over from Major PEMBERTON D.S.O. as S.S.O. of the Division. R.M.A.	
"	16		Routine as usual R.M.A.	
"	17		Cpl W. Malony was admitted to Hospital. The following postings were made in the Coy on being via R.T. PEMBERTON D.S.O. to No 1 Coy. to command Capt. J. Simpson. R.E. Cpl. J. Simpson to No 2 Coy to command vice Capt V. MALONY admitted to hospital. R.M.A.	

Army Form C. 2118.

WAR DIARY
or
INTELLIGENCE SUMMARY.
(Erase heading not required.)

Place	Date	Hour	Summary of Events and Information	Remarks and references to Appendices
1916 June	18			
"	19		2nd Lt. A.W. MADDEN posted to No. 17 Army Aux. H.T. Coy. was struck off the strength of the Train. Lt (A/Capt.) W.I. THOMPSON reported for duty from No. 17 Army Aux. H.T. Coy. and was taken on the strength of the Train (posted supy. to 2 Coy (CHR))	1
	20		T2/146+3 C.S.M. Hull was medically examined by the a.d.m.s up Divl. & found unfit to fulfill the duties of a Coy Sgt. Major in the Field (CHR)	
	21		T2/146+3 C.S.M. Hull was evacuated to the Base. T4/250978 C.S.M. Turnbull posted to No 2 Coy from No 3. 28th C.O.s—mem. & G 40 to Coy sick with P.U.O. (AME)	
	22		T4/249822 T/SS'm Woburn A.E. awarded the Meritorious Service Medal (Authority London Gazette Supplement June 17, 1918.) Lt P.T.T. Holdsworth admitted to 1/2 (W.R.) Fd.	
	23		Ambulanc (AME) Routine as usual (AME)	
	24		do. (AME)	
	25		do. (AME)	
	26		do. (AME)	
	27		do (AME)	
	28		The Quartermaster stores of the 146th & 145th Inf Bde. were visited. The method of drawing & ration at Q.m.'s stores was noted. The great disadvantage of not knowing was observed. 1st rations were called for from the 146th Bde. The 145th Bde had no complaints.	

Army Form C. 2118.

WAR DIARY
or
INTELLIGENCE SUMMARY.
(Erase heading not required.)

Instructions regarding War Diaries and Intelligence Summaries are contained in F. S. Regs., Part II. and the Staff Manual respectively. Title pages will be prepared in manuscript.

Place	Date	Hour	Summary of Events and Information	Remarks and references to Appendices
June B 1916	28		Intimation was received from O i/c A.S.C Records that T4/250871 Wheeler S/Sgt Smith J.H., T4/249524 Sgt Wilson W. both of No 3 Coy, & T4/249512 Cpl Bruce G.G. of No 2 Coy had been awarded the Meritorious Service Efficiency medal. (AMC)	
	29		Routine in camp	
	30		The 1st line transport of the 147 Inf Bde. came to B.S. preceeding Regt's new motors, the horses and also the vehicles, the horses were in very fair condition, a well groomed	

W. W. Berry
Lieut. Colonel,
Commanding 49th (W.R.) Divl. Train.

Vol 40

CONFIDENTIAL

WAR   DIARY

of

Lt Colonel R.G.J.J.Berry

Commanding 49th W.R.Divisional Train

from JULY 1st to 31st 1918

(Volume 40.)

Army Form C. 2118.

WAR DIARY
or
INTELLIGENCE SUMMARY.
(Erase heading not required.)

Instructions regarding War Diaries and Intelligence Summaries are contained in F.S. Regs., Part II. and the Staff Manual respectively. Title pages will be prepared in manuscript.

Place	Date	Hour	Summary of Events and Information	Remarks and references to Appendices
1918 July	1st		11th Army Fld Artillery Brigade were transferred from the HQ Divl Group to the XIV Corps for training. — SKO. 3rd Divl R.E. transferred from the HQ Divl Group to the 4th Divl jurisdiction. (CML)	
	2nd		Routine in camp. (CML)	
	3rd		14th Inf Bde Refilling Point at 27.E.12.d.0.9 was vacated for the American Coy due July 4. The 1st Inf Bde Refilling Point was moved to 27.F.7.d.7.4. (CML)	
	4th		117 & 118 Regtl Ammunition Army joined the Divn for training. The Regtl Supply Coys were placed under the supervision of the OC Train. B Ellis refilling points were fixed at 27.F.1 & a.0.8. (CML)	
	5th		No 3 Coy Echls were to a Corps Refilling Point at 27.F.7.d.7.4 as it was not required by the American Coy. (CML)	
	6th		A "stand to parade of 704 Coy was ordered. 7th Coy turned out in marching order in 20 mins (CML)	
	7th		Lt WP Barringer proceeded to CALAIS in charge of the Divl Party to draw Remounts. 209 Field Coy R.E. were transferred to the 34th Divn jurisdiction. G.O.C. HQ Divn inspected No 2 Coy. (CML)	

Army Form C. 2118.

WAR DIARY
or
INTELLIGENCE SUMMARY.
(Erase heading not required.)

Place	Date	Hour	Summary of Events and Information	Remarks and references to Appendices
July	8		Routine as usual (R.M.A)	
"	9		Routine as usual (R.M.A) ½ Section to barracks of Nos.1 and 3 Coys. were ordered. No 1 Coy. turned out in 35 mins. No 3 Coy in 24½ mins (R.M.A)	
"	10		Routine as usual (R.M.A)	
"	11		Routine as usual (R.M.A)	
"	12		LT. P.T.J. HOLDSWORTH returned from hospital (R.M.A)	
"	13		CAPT. W. MOLONY returned from hospital and took over command of No.4 Coy. vice LT.P.T.J. HOLDSWORTH. LT.P.T.J. HOLDSWORTH was posted to No.1 Coy. R.M.A.	
"	14		Routine as usual (R.M.A.)	
"	15		LT.P.T.J. HOLDSWORTH was posted to No 2 Coy. to be temporarily in command vice Capt. C.H.REYNOLDS who proceeded on leave to England (R.M.A)	
"	16		The Refilling Point for the 116 Inf. Bde. was moved from 27F.10.d.4.3 to 27F.13.b.9.8 (R.M.A) A meeting of Coy. Commanders was held at T.H.Q. at 9 P.M. (R.M.A)	
"	17		Routine as usual R.M.A.	
"	18			
"	19		Received notification that Capt. H.H.BARNE attached Central Purchase Board was struck off the strength of the Train as from the 11th inst. on being posted to England, and also Lt. F.E.CLIFFORD who was held unable to establishment was to be taken on the strength of the Train. Train horses were stuffed by enemy aircraft in bivouac No 2 Coy. during about 11.15 P.M. causing the following casualties 2nd Lt. E.J.P. ROGER killed, T4/249911 Dr. DYSON N.B wounded, T4/241645 Dr. ORTON.H. wounded T4/259186 Dr. Robinson.C. wounded. There were also 6 H.D. horses wounded 4 of which were only slightly wounded R.M.A.	

WAR DIARY
or
INTELLIGENCE SUMMARY.
(Erase heading not required.)

Army Form C. 2118.

Place	Date	Hour	Summary of Events and Information	Remarks and references to Appendices
1918 July	20		Received notification that T/4/249911 Dr DYSON J.B., T/4/247645 Dr ORTON H. and T/4/250986 Dr ROBINSON C. had been evacuated to C.C.S. R.M.A. 2nd Lt. Rogers McCorquodale of Training party. Lt. Rogers was detailed at MENDINGHEM Cluster of 8pm. No. 3 in Row E	
"	21		Routine as usual. R.M.A. Lt. Rogers in charge of the party to collect remounts. R.M.A.	plot 10
"	22		2nd Lt. A.W. Rowe proceeded to CALAIS in charge of the party to collect remounts. R.M.A.	
"	23		Routine as usual. R.M.A.	
"	24		According to arrangements made with the A.D.M.S. 30 men of the train were inoculated with T.A.B. 30 men shed on duty until the whole have been inoculated. R.M.A.	
"	25			
"	26		Received 2nd Lt. A.W. Rowe returned from CALAIS in charge of the party in remounts R.M.A. Inspected the 1st line transport of the 148 H.F. Bde with the A.A. + 2 H.G. and found all in a satisfactory condition with the exception of one or two pairs of horses which I gave in low condition have arrangements for these to be attached to No 2 Coy of the Train for a period. New Coy efficiency clever will train most of the Coy (R.M.A.)	
"	27			
"	28		Routine as usual. R.M.A.	
"	29		Lt. P. WORRALL reported for duty with the Train from the B.H.T. Dept HAVRE and was posted to No 2 Coy. vice 2nd Lt. E.J.P. ROGER Killed in action. R.M.A.	
"	30		Routine as usual	
"	31		Visited Army and interviewed D.D.S.&T. with reference to holding a three days reserve ration with the H.T. Coy. R.M.A. Arew allotment throughout the month 50 trainings. 2 Special engagements During month Mr. Pearce instructed American Supply Co in reap. of construction of sewer. Earth Hygiene & horse observance has been created. Weather has been generally wet & unsettled throughout.	

E. in C. A.H.Q. W.R. Dun Train |

(CONFIDENTIAL)

WAR DIARY

of

Lieut Colonel R.G.J.Berry

Commanding 49th (West Riding) Divisional Train

from AUGUST 1st to AUGUST 31st, 1918

(Volume 41.)

WAR DIARY or INTELLIGENCE SUMMARY

Army Form C. 2118.

H.Q. (W.R.) DIVISIONAL TRAIN

Place	Date	Hour	Summary of Events and Information	Remarks and references to Appendices
1918 Aug.	1		S.G.S. wagons went placed at the disposal of the C.E. II Corps who bring at OAKHANGER DUMP at 6.30 A.M. Supplies drawn at Railhead included 63½ fresh meat and 75½ Bread.	
"	2		Weather very wet. "A" + "B" tracks were closed in consequence. 8 wagons were detailed for C.E. Corps who bring at the same time and places as before. 11 men were sent down to the Army rest camp. Deficiencies in the train area as follows:- Dr.s 7, Riders 4, H.Drs. 7. Supplies at Railhead 2nd meal 63½, Bread 76½ (R.M.A)	8.02 ration of vegetables was drawn (RMA)
"	3		2 wagons were detailed for C.E. II Corps as before. 2 N.C.Os and 8 men proceeded to MENDINGHEM Band returned to the O.C. The band's detailed for the Choral Parade tomorrow. There was several heavy storms of rain making the horse lines very wet indeed. Supplies at Railhead 65½ fresh, Bread 76½. 7 drafts of vegetables (R.M.A)	
"	4		2 wagons detailed for C.E. II Corps. ~~Supplies at Railhead~~ meat 60½ fresh, Bread 76½. An Army Church Parade was held at TURDEGHEM on the 4th Anniversary of the declaration of war against Germany. A party of 2 N.C.Os. + 8 men represented the train. R.M.A. Capt. R. FROST A.M.C. reported for duty with the Train from C.C.S.	
"	5		8 wagons detailed for C.E. II Corps Command. Two men were sent to a farm at 19.V.30.d.21 to mow down the hay bought to supplement the forage ration for the horses in the Train.	
"	6		On the occasion of the visit of His Majesty the King, 1 officer + 15 O.Rs. paraded between the Train with the detachment from the Division forming the Guard of Honour. Lt. Col. R.G.L. BERRY was among the officers who were presented to the King at la Lovie Chateau. 8 wagons were detailed for work with C.E. II Corps. 65½ fresh meat was railed + 75½ Bread (R.M.A)	
"	7		8 wagons were detailed to work for C.E. III Corps arrived. H.Q. Div. Reception Camp. and 1/6 L.D. Cy. R.E. combined. Strength 93 men were added to our Trains Strength. 25 Category "B" drivers reported from the Base to take the place of Category "A" drivers to be sent to Base for transfer to the Infantry. The new Divisional leave allotment came out giving 36 ordinary leaves for men + 2 for officers in the Train between Aug 9 and Sept 8. 67½ Bread 63½ meat railed (R.M.A)	
"	8		With a view to the reclassification of category of the men in the train the following particulars were ascertained: 70% of the men serving with the Train came out in April 1915. ~~Between~~ 65% of the Train have never been	

WAR DIARY
or
INTELLIGENCE SUMMARY.
(Erase heading not required.)

Army Form C. 2118.

Place	Date	Hour	Summary of Events and Information	Remarks and references to Appendices
	Aug. 9		Classified in a category. 165 ORs of the rest received at railhead as detailed of 9/8/16. The remainder are apt for work as a greatdeal of the men are in+a mediocre Point. We considered doubtful whilst unclassified. (S.M.) The Wounded, the was delivered to railhead on to-day. Also to Cook it. Percentage of freshmen at railhead 64% of Brad 73. 8 wagons were detailed for work for C.E. II Corps. (R.M.O.) 8 wagons detailed for C.E. II Corps. 25 Category "A" drivers left for the Base in place of the Category "B" drivers received on the 7th inst. On the exchange of the Bases in the lines the N.S. of Bde have been brought into those of No.4 Coy's lines & those of Army Pref. Bde sent up to the Bdes No.3 Coy. Cdn. S.Sgt. Robinson was returned to the Base on return from Base of S.Sgt. Crombie on account of his refusal to accept the rank of P.S.C. in R.M.T. Irish mer at Railhead 572; Brad 738. Deficiencies in Train B=58. H.D.7 (R.M.I)	
"	10		8 wagons detailed for C.E. II Corps as usual. Train met at Railhead 586; Irish 736. (Kh.I.)	
"	11		At a ceremonial Church parade held at TURDEGHEN H.Q. today the King was present. All arrangements were made by Second Army & the following were present from the train :- Lieut. Col. R.G. J. J. BERRY with the Divisional Staff and 2 N.C.O.s and 8 men from each of the detachments from the Division. Orders were issued that 1st Traynor was to be posted to the Train from the 149th Bre. M.T.Coy and 2nd Lt. Simpson of No.46 Train was to be posted to the M.T.Coy as S.O. The necessary arrangements for their transference were made. Capt. W.J. THOMPSON was posted from No.1 Coy to No.4 Coy as S.O. Irish 63 b; Bred 75 b at railhead. (R.M.I.)	
"	12		Authority having been obtained for the classification by category of the men in the Train hitherto unclassified before sending them to the Base No.1 Coy. 7 OR personnel of T.H.Q. were medically examined with the exception of 8 men were all classified "A". 8 wagons were detailed for C.E. II Corps as usual. 676 men at Irish. 75 B Broad at Railhead. (R.M.I.)	
"	13		8 wagons as usual for C.E. II Corps. Irish first 60 B, Bred 72 B at Railhead. The personnel of No.2 Coy were medically examined and all classified "A" with the exception of 72 B at Railhead. 2 of Field Coy R.E. were taken on the ration strength of HQ Div. Train. (R.M.I.)	

WAR DIARY
or
INTELLIGENCE SUMMARY.
(Erase heading not required.)

Army Form C. 2118.

Place	Date	Hour	Summary of Events and Information	Remarks and references to Appendices
August	14		2nd Lt. BAXTER proceeded to CALAIS in charge of the party to collect reinforcements. CAPT. C.L. REYNOLDS returned from leave to England having been granted 10 days' extension. Fresh meat 60%, Bread 60% at railhead. Onions for C.E.II. Unfortunately 6 wagons for C.E.II. Cops arrived. The remainder of No.1 Coy were medically examined.	(T.O.M.M.)
"	15		2 wagons allotted for C.E.II Corps arrival, these are sufficient. No.5, 3 and 4 Coys. As the baggage wagons with No.1 Coy were all set into the units. Fresh meat at railhead 60%, Bread 75%. Deficiencies in the Train supplies. Bnig.a. H.D.Q.R.M.M. being to several baggage wagons being employed in the moving of infantry into dry bivouacs were detailed for C.E.II. Coy.'s instead of the usual 8. Fresh meat at Railhead 60%, Bread 75%. 2nd Lt. BAXTER returned from CALAIS in charge of the Coy. with reinforcements. 2nd Lt. A.N. ROWE was posted to the Base Supply Depot BOULOGNE.	The removal of No.3 Coy was indefinitely intended.
"	16			
"	17			
"	18		Train struck off the strength of the Train R.M.A. H.Q. Orders were received from Division that as Divisional cavalry were to rest and O.O. No.2 H.Q. attached, was issued. Brig. the newly supply getting to the places for refilling for the railing points. O.M.T's then in the Train should Be at the indication of their Batteries were indicated by the A.Q.M.G. and the following divisions were classified B: from No.1 Coy. 8. No.2 Coy. 4. No.3 Coy. 5. No.4 Coy. 3. No.5 Coy. 5. att. 11/5 (N.R.) Fild Coy. 2. att. 1/2 w.R. Fild a.m. 7. att. 15 m.m. Fild a.c. 3. making a total of 32. Percentage of bread attn railhead 70%. Fresh meat at 35%. R.M.A.	
"	19		No. wagons were detailed for C.E.II. Corps owing to the little same. Lt HOLDSWORTH having retired from Clone was posted to No.I. Coy from duty. Baxter Holdsworth Batlass. T.H.O. handcart marched with the handcart of D.H.A. to HERZEELE. R.M.A. Rations at railhead were hard brought near taken and stored at H.E.M.T. Coy. lines to be held as a reserve ration. R.M.A. No.2 Coy. march to HERZEELE. Bivouacking hard in flat day being just to the S. of the village. Fresh meat 53% Bread 80%.	
"	20			
"	21		No.2 Coy. marched to LEDERZEELE with the 11/5 W. Rdg. Transport Coy. T.H.Q. moved from CHATEAU LOVIE to BERTHEM 4 kilometres N.W. of NORDAUSQUES on the CALAIS road. Fresh meat 80% Bread 60%.	(T.O.M.M.)
"	22		No.2 Coy. marched to RECQUES. No.3 Coy. marched to WORMHOUDT "C" area. No.4 Coy. marched to HERZEELE too Coy at 27. D.2.C.4.7. Bread 75% Fresh meat 66% at Railhead. Lt. McKENNA was evacuated to No.10 C.C.S. The vellum on the 21st & 22nd with how any hot bit Collowes all stood the task very well.	(T.O.M.M.)

Place	Date	Hour	Summary of Events and Information	Remarks and references to Appendices
Aug	23		No 2 Coy moved to YEUSE. Railhead was changed from GRUBHEM to BONNINGUES for the 146 and 147 Inf Bde Coys. The 148 Inf Bde of the 33rd Division detained at LICQUES also drew from the same Railhead at BONNINGUES being attached to this Division. The 149 Div Arty and its 148 Inf Bde continued to draw from GRUBHEM being attached to the 1st Div. Division supplying Truck loaded Railhead 77b Bread 958, Groceries in the Trains & follows: 1st Div D.3. Wal Dr.1, H.D.5, I.D.2 (X mls) Am Supply drew from railhead by H.T. the Divisional H.Q. units being attached to the 148 Inf Bde. Refreshments Cont. Bread at railhead 77b Bread 962 No 1 Coy moved from PROVEN to Du RUBROUCK area. R.M.A. Fresh meat at railhead 77b Bread 958 R.M.A.	
"	24			
"	25		Received a warning order that the Division was to move. Transport to move to day the remainder by Rail next train	
"	26		Inclusively in the 27th. The necessary arrangements were made for the delivery of the landration in days of the M.T. Coy, and for lorries to deliver supplies from railhead direct to units except for Group at Group of B.E.146, H.M.Inf. Bdes. These were drawn by H.T. & 3rd... when to HELFAUT since the transport shifted there night. T.H.Q. transport and No. 2 & 3 Coys moved to HELFAUT getting orders to move at 3.30 P.M. Remainder due conditions slowed the extreme undesirability of holding a days reserve ration with the M.T. Coy. Rations were drawn at railhead at 2 P.M. by the M.T. Coy. for move from 27th. Owing to the stillitts of Regts the consecrate difficulty of getting in the respective figures for the Transport and Train held the delay at railhead uncommonly considerable and it was 7 P.M. before the wagons of No. 2 Coy. left railhead with the rations for 2 days for the Transports in lorry of the 146 Inf Bde Group. They then had to march to HELFAUT and did not arrive until 2.30 A.M. on the 27th inst. By the drawing of 2 days rations from the last train for the transport group, the train group was consequently left short. This shortage was made up by their receiving some 8 a days land ration. No 4 Coy moved from HERZEELE to Du RENESCURE area being billeted in a farm at CHARMARAIS. No 1 Coy moved from RUBROUCK to RENESCURE. Fresh meat at railhead 74b Bread 948 R.M.L. The wagons of No 2 Coy drew supplies from GRUBHE M railhead this morning and therefore did 36 miles in the day. (X mls)	

Army Form C. 2118.

WAR DIARY
or
INTELLIGENCE SUMMARY.
(Erase heading not required.)

Instructions regarding War Diaries and Intelligence Summaries are contained in F.S. Regs., Part II. and the Staff Manual respectively. Title pages will be prepared in manuscript.

Place	Date	Hour	Summary of Events and Information	Remarks and references to Appendices
August	27		No 1 Coy. moved from RENESCURE to NEDONCHELLES will bivouac there until on arrival, a whole of the Div Artillery moved by road. No 2 and 3 Coys. moved to Divisional starting at 12 noon and arriving at 7 P.M. (M.T.) Trains met at railhead 602 Bread 752 (pm). T.H.Q. moved to ROQUECOURT 2½ kilometres E. of GT. POL. nr railhead, being at BONNINGUES for the last time. Railhead for the Divisional Artillery moved WARDRIQUES. The 1st IInf Bde 23rd Div. left the leading trains of their Div. until 2 of Bde. being supplied from BONNINGUES.	
"	28		No 1 Coy supplied at NEDONCHELLES and moved to GAUCHIN delivering on arrival there. No 2 Coy refilled at AMES at 8 A.M. and a refill at GOSNAY and arrived at ST POL-SUR at 5.30 P.M. their billets being at ROCOURT ST LAURENT. The supply wagons delivered and arrived at billets 1.30 P.M. No 3 Coy refilled and delivered the increased rations being been billets being at CROIX. No 4 Coy also refilled after delivering to units returned to Div Coy lines Railhead at PETIT HOUVIN. Railhead at railhead 752 Bread 602 Bird.	
"	29		Railhead now changed from BONNINGUES to ST POL. Visited all Coys. & found all the horses looking well with very few galls or attributable to after the trek. Railhead at Railhead 502 Bread 73½ (pm)	
"	30		Bread met at railhead 602 Bread 752 Deficiencies in the Train as follows:- 10 Officers Wheeler Drs. 9 Drs. 21 D. 7 H.D. with 2 riders & mules (pm)	
"	31		Received orders at 9.30 A.M. of bread to meet at 2 landanche. The reconnoitring parties were sent to the Companies. Orders have received to be in for the Division to move to the AUBIGNY area. All the horses were left. 1st Train arrived at railhead 602 Bread 752 & the remainder by train all 10.00 am no. left. 11st Train went at railhead 602 Bread 752 the 27 Bde. moved up, only sent the coy of artillery arrived in support of the Fire in support of the train & a reconnaissance of our front the future of French & B. all mechanical was jettison of B.D.A.S. that the gun went my front.	

SECRET   49th (W.R.) Div: Train.G.T.14/2.

49th (W.R.) DIVISIONAL TRAIN O.O. 40

(1)   The 49th (British) Division (Less Artillery) will be relieved on the night 20th/21st August by the 34th (British) Division (Less Artillery).

(2)   The 49th Divisional Artillery will be relieved by the 34th Divisional Artillery on the nights 21st/22nd and 22nd/23rd August. On relief the 49th (British) Divisional Artillery will be withdrawn to the HANDRUM AREA.

(3)   On relief by 34th (British) Division, 49th (British) Division (Less Artillery and 148th Infantry Brigade) will move to the BECQUES AREA.
      148th Infantry Brigade Group will move to MERISUR AREA.

(4)   Transport will move by march route, except vehicles detailed in entraining instructions to go by train.
      Intervals on the march will be as laid down in 49th Division O.O.268 dated, 1st JUNE 1918.
      Except where restricted, marches will take place between 4 a.m. and 8 a.m. and 4 p.m. and 8 p.m. (or later if necessary)

(5)   For the move, Brigade Groups will be as follows:-

146th Infr Bde.	147th Infr Bde.	148th Infr Bde.
456th Fld Co.R.E.	576th Fld Co.R.E.	458th Fld Co.R.E.
"A" Coy.49th M.G.	"C" Coy.49th M.G.	19th Bn.Lancs Fus:rs
"B" -do-	"D" -do-	466 Coy, A.S.C.
464 Coy, A.S.C.	465 Coy, A.S.C.	1/2nd W.R.Fld:Ambce
1/3rd W.R.Fld Ambce	1/1st W.R.Fld Ambce	

(6)   On completion of Move, 49th Bn.M.G. Bn., will be concentrated in the BECQUES AREA.

(7)   On the 23rd inst. RAILHEAD for 49th (W.R.) Division (Less 49th Divisional Artillery and 148th Infantry Brigade Groups) will change to BERGUEHEM. 49th Divisional Artillery and 148th Infantry Brigade Groups will continue to draw from CAUBRUN from the 14th Divisional Pack. Numbers 1, and 4, Companies will be attached to the 14th Divisional Train.

(8)   Companies will move under Orders of their Brigades. No.2.Company moving to MERISUR on the 20th instant, and will be billeted by their respective Staff Captains.

(9)   Baggage Wagons of 147th, and 148th Infantry Brigades will be sent to Units the day before they move.

(10) Attention is called to 49th Divisional Administrative Instructions Nos.10,13, & 14. Companies hold the following tents on Divisional charge. No.1.Company,10; No.2.Company.7; No.3.Company,10; No.4.Company 6;. Companies will take these tents to the new Area.
      The Chaff Cutters, and Oat Crushers, in possession of Companies, are Divisional property, and will be carried to the new Area.

(11) Certificates for Stores handed and taken over will be forwarded to this Office, not later than 3 days after relief (in Duplicate) together with certificate as to cleanliness of billets.

12. During the Move Officers Commanding Coys will keep in close touch with their Brigades through their Supply Officers.

(13) The Coal Dump personnel will march under orders issued by the S.S.O.

(14) Train H.Q. will close at CHATEAU LOVIE at 10.a.m. 21st inst and will re-open in the New Area at 2.p.m.

(15) Transport and Supply arrangements are contained in attached Tables and issued herewith.
The Areas named in attached tables shews the location of the Groups at Midnight.
Special attention is drawn to the Supply Grouping which will necessitate changes of wagons between Coys.
Baggage and Supply wagons of Div H.Qrs Group will march with Mule Transport.
The H.Qrs Supply wagon of the H.S.Bn will march with Mule Transport.

(16) ACKNOWLEDGE

Capt. & Adjt.,
49th (W.R.) Divl. Train.

8/18.

```
Copy No.1.  to Div H.Q.
"    No.2.  "  No.1. Coy.
"    No.3.  "  No.2. Coy.
"    No.4.  "  No.3. Coy.
"    No.5.  "  No.4. Coy.
"    No.6.  "  S.O. Div Troops
"    No.7.  "  S.O. 146th Bde
"    No.8.  "  S.O. 147th  "
"    No.9.  "  S.O. 148th  "
"    No.10. "  49th Div M.T.Co.
"    No.11. "  O.C. Train
"    No.12. "  S.S.O.
"    Nos 13 & 14. War Diary
"    No.15. File.
```

S E C R E T.   49th Div.Train S.S.14/2/1.

49th DIVISIONAL TRAIN O.O. 41.

(1) The last sentence of para 7 of Operation Order No.40 is CANCELLED. Nos.1 and 4 Coys will NOW be attached to the 14th Divisional Train for discipline and accomodation.
   Major Pemberton DSO, will be in command of the detachment formed by these 2 Coys. Supply Officers of Divnl. Troops and 146th Brigade will submit their figures for Railhead through S.S.O. 14th Division.

(2) No.4 Coy will be billeted in the HERBUVAL Area, actual accomodation to be made by Staff Captain 146th Brigade.
   On completion of delivery of Supplies to Units of the Bde in the HERBUVAL Area on the 22nd inst. No.4 Coy will move into their new camp.

                                             R.M. Anglesett.
                                          for Capt. & Adjt.
AUGUST 19th 1918   49th (W.R.) Divisional Train

```
Copy No.1 to Div. H.Q.
   No.2 "  No.1 Coy.
   No.3 "    " 2 Coy.
   No.4 "    " 3 Coy.
   No.5 "    " 4 Coy.
   No.6 "  D.C. Divl.Troops
   No.7 "  S.C. 146th Bde.
   No.8 "  S.C. 147th Bde.
   No.9 "  S.C. 148th Bde.
   No.10" 49th Div.M.T. Coy.
   No.11" O.C.Trains
   No.12" S.S.O.
   Nos.13&14 War Diary
   No.15 " File.
```

RAILHEAD - 19th   MIDNIGHT - 19/20   CONSUMPTION 20th

Div. Arty.	146th Bde.	147th Bde.	148th Bde.
H.Q. R.A.	H.Q. 146th Bde.	H.Q. 147th Bde.	H.Q. 148th Bde.
245 Bde.	146th T.M.B.	147th T.M.B.	148th T.M.B.
246 Bde.	5th W. Yorks.	4th D. of W.	4th Y. & L.
D.A.C.	6th "	6th "	5th "
A.V. T.M.B.	7th "	7th "	4th K.O.Y.L.I.
1 Coy. Train.	2 Coy. Train	3 Coy. Train	4 Coy. Train.
H.Q. Divn.	1st Fd. Ambce.	2nd Fd. Ambce	3rd Fd. Ambce.
A.M.S.	456 Fd. Coy. R.E.	57 Fd. Coy. R.E.	458 Fd. Coy. R.E.
C.R.E.		R.V. Section	
H.Q. Train			
Signal Coy.			
Ordnance			
Belgian Missn.			
49th M.G.C.			
19th Lancs. F.			
Salvage Coy.			

RAILHEAD - 20th   MIDNIGHT - 20/21   CONSUMPTION 21st.

Div. Arty JOURKE'S AREA	Div. H.Q. AOVIE	Div. H.Q. Troops LEDERZEELE	146th Bde. AIRE-S-E
H.Q. R.A.	H.Q. Div.	H.Q. Div.	H.Q. 146th Bde.
245 Bde.	A.M.S.	A.M.S.	146th T.M.B.
246 Bde.	C.R.E.	C.R.E.	5th W. Yorks.
D.A.C.	Train H.Q.	Train H.Q.	6th "
A.V. T.M.B.	Signals.	Signals.	7th "
1 Coy. Train.	Ordnance	R.V. Section.	2 Coy. Train.
	Belgian Missn.	H.Q. M.G.C.	456 Fd. Coy. R.E.
	Salvage Coy.		3rd Fd. Ambce.
	R.V. Section		A & B Coys. M.G.C.
	M.G.C. H.Q.		
—:—:—:—:—	—:—:—:—:—	—:—:—:—:—	—:—:—:—:—
	Delivered by	Delivered by	deliver
	No.1 Coy. Train	M.T. to	M.T. to R.R. MARKELE
		LEDERZEELE	SQUARE. M.T. deliver
			to units.

147th Bde. ARMY BUCKET	148th Bde. RESERVE
H.Q. 147th Bde.	H.Q. 148th Bde.
147th T.M.B.	148th T.M.B.
4th D. of W.	4th Y. & L.
6th "	5th "
7th "	4th K.O.Y.L.I.
3 Coy. Train.	4 Coy. Train.
57 Fd. Coy. R.E.	458 Fd. Coy. R.E.
1st Fd. Ambce.	2nd Fd. Ambce.
C&D Coys. M.G.C.	19th Lancs. Fus.

RAILHEAD - 21st	MIDNIGHT - 21/22	CONSUMPTION 22nd.	
Div. Arty. Forward Area	Div. H.Q. RECQUES	146th Bde. HERZEELE	146th Bde. Transport. LEDERZEELE
H.Q. R.A. 245 Bde. 246 Bde. D.A.C. X.Y. T.M.B. 1 Coy.Train.	H.Q. Div. M.M.P. C.R.E. Train H.Q. Signals. Ordnance. Belgian Missn. Salvage Coy. M.V.Section. 49th M.G.C.H.Q.	H.Q. 146th Bde. 146th T.M.B. 5th W.Yorks. 6th .. 7th .. 456 Fd.Coy.R.E. 3rd Fd.Ambnce. A&B Coys.M.G.C.	H.Q. 146th Bde. 5th W.Yorks. 6th .. 7th .. 2 Coy. Train. 456 Fd.Coy.R.E. 3rd Fd.Ambnce. A&B Coys.M.G.C.
-:-:-:-:-	-:-:-:-:-	-:-:-:-:-	-:-:-:-:-
	M.T. deliver to R.P. at RECQUES. Collected by H.T. on arrival.	Refill HERZEELE SQUARE. Delivered by supply wagons which after delvy. proceed to LEDERZEELE.	Rations delivered by M.T. to HERZEELE & carried to LEDERZEELE by supply wagons.
	147th Bde. DIRTY BUCKET H.Q. 147th Bde. 147th T.M.B. 4th D.of.W. 6th .. 7th .. 3 Coy.Train. 57 Fd.Coy.R.E. 1st Fd.Ambnce. C&D Coy.M.G.C.	148th Bde. PROVEN H.Q. 148th Bde. 148th T.M.B. 4th Y.&L. 5th .. 4th K.O.Y.L.I. 4 Coy.Train. 458 Fd.Coy.R.E. 2nd Fd.Ambnce. 19th Lancs.Fus.	

RAILHEAD - 22nd.	MIDNIGHT - 22/23	CONSUMPTION 23rd.	
Div. Arty. HENDEKOT AREA	Div. H.Q. RECQUES	146th Bde. RECQUES	147th Bde. DIRTY BUCKET
H.Q. R.A. 245 Bde. 246 Bde. D.A.C. X.Y. T.M.B. 1 Coy. Train.	H.Q. Div. M.M.P. C.R.E. Train H.Q. Signals. Ordnance. Belgian Missn. Salvage Coy. M.V.Section. H.Q. M.G.C.	H.Q. 146th Bde. 146th T.M.B. 5th W.Yorks. 6th .. 7th .. 2. Coy.Train. 456 Fd.Coy.R.E. 3rd Fd.Ambnce. A&B Coys.M.G.C.	H.Q. 147th Bde. 147th T.M.B. 4th D.of.W. 6th .. 7th .. 3 Coy.Train. 57 Fd.Coy.R.E. 1st Fd.Ambnce. C&D Coys.M.G.C.
-:-:-:-:-	-:-:-:-:-	-:-:-:-:-	-:-:-:-:-
	To R.P. by M.T. Units draw from R.P. by H.T.	To R.P. by M.T. Supply wagons deliver to units.	Supply wagons del- iver & proceed to WORMHOUDT (C)
	147th Bde. Trans. WORMHOUDT (C) H.Q. 147th Bde. 4th D.of.W. 6th .. 7th .. 3 Coy.Train. 57 Fd.Coy.R.E. 1st Fd.Ambnce. C&D Coy.M.G.C. Rations carried by supply wagons.	148th Bde. HERZEELE H.Q. 148th Bde. 148th T.M.B. 4th Y.&L. 5th .. 4th K.O.Y.L.I. 4 Coy.Train. 458 Fd.Coy.R.E. 2nd Fd.Ambnce. 19th Lancs.Fus. H.T. deliver at HERZEELE.	

RAILHEAD - 23rd		MIDNIGHT 23/24	CONSUMPTION 24th	
Div. Arty. HANDEKOT AREA	Div. H.Q. RECQUES	146th Bde. TOURNEHEM	147th Bde. RECQUES	
H.Q. R.A. 245 Bde. 246 Bde. D.A.C. X.Y. T.M.B. 1 Coy. Train.	H.Q. Div. M.M.P. C.R.E. Train H.Q. Signals. Ordnance. Belgian Missn. Salvage Coy. M.V.Section. H.Q.M.G.C.	H.Q. 146th Bde. 146th T.M.B. 5th W.Yorks. 6th .. 7th .. 2 Coy.Train. 456 Fd.Coy.R.E. 3rd Fd.Ambnce. A&B Coys.M.G.C.	H.Q. 147th Bde. 147th T.M.B. 4th D.of.W. 6th .. 7th .. 3 Coy.Train. 57 Fd.Coy.R.E. 1st Fd. Ambnce. C&D Coys.M.G.C.	
-:-:-:-:-	-:-:-:-:-	-:-:-:-:-	-:-:-:-:-	
To 14th Div. drawn by H.T. from Railhead.	Drawn from Rail head by H.T.	Drawn from Rail head & delivered by H.T.	Drawn & delivered to Q.M.Stores by M.T.	

147th Bde. Trans. LEDERZEELE	148th Bde. HERZEELE
H.Q. 147th Bde. 4th D.of.W. 6th .. 7th .. 3 Coy.Train. 57 Fd.Coy.R.E. 1st Fd. Ambnce. C&D Coys.M.G.C.	H.Q. 148th Bde. 148th T.M.B. 4th Y.&.L. 5th .. 4th K.O.Y.L.I. 4 Coy.Train. 458 Fd.Coy.R.E. 2nd Fd.Ambnce. 19th Lancs.Fus.
-:-:-:-:-	-:-:-:-:-
To LEDERZEELE AREA by M.T.	To 14th Divn. Drawn from Rail head by H.T. & delvd.to units.

RAILHEAD - 24th		MIDNIGHT - 24/25	CONSUMPTION 25th.	
Div. Arty. HANDEKOT AREA	Div. H.Q. RECQUES	146th Bde. TOURNEHEM	147th Bde. RECQUES	148th Bde. HERZEELE
Same as 23rd.	Same as 23rd	Same as 23rd	Same as 23rd but transport absorbed.	Same as 23rd.
-:-:-:-:-	-:-:-:-:-	-:-:-:-:-	-:-:-:-:-:-	-:-:-:-:-
Drawn by H.T.	Drawn by H.T. from Railhead.		Drawn by M.T. & delivered by supply wagons.	Drawn by H.T. from Railhead.

RAILHEAD 25th	MIDNIGHT - 25/26	CONSUMPTION 26th.
A L L	D R A W N	B Y H.T.

CONFIDENTIAL
--------oOo--------

WAR DIARY
of

Lt.Colonel R.G.J.J.Berry

Commanding 49th W.R.Divisional Train.

from Sept 1st,1918. to Sept 30th,1918.

(Volume 42.).

Army Form C. 2118.

WAR DIARY
or
INTELLIGENCE SUMMARY.   49th DIVISIONAL TRAIN
(Erase heading not required.)

Place	Date	Hour	Summary of Events and Information	Remarks and references to Appendices
1918 Sept.	1		The Division moved to an area N. of AUBIGNY. Train Hd Qrs. moved to MINGOVAL, No.1 Coy. moved to CAPELLE FERMONT, No.2 Coy. to LE PENDU, No.3 Coy. to CAMBLAIN L'ABBÉ, No.4 Coy. to ESTRÉE GAUCHÉE. The Brigade Companies marched under the orders of their respective Brigade Commanders. No.1 Coy. marched under the orders of the C.R.A. The march was made in the afternoon & evening, no transport being allowed E. of a line running S. from GAUCHIN LEGAL until after 7 P.M. Lt. P.T.J. HOLDSWORTH was sent in accordance with instructions received from XXII Corps to report to XXII Corps M.T. Coy. at FREVIN CAPELLE for supply duties, taking with him his batman and 1 clerk from No.2 Coy. Aubrity, 1st Army S.o.T. 626 dated 25.8.18. Percentage of fresh meat at railhead 75%. Bread 73% (R.M.A.)	
"	2		Orders were received at 12 noon that the 148 Inf. Bde. group were to proceed to an area E.S.E. of ARRAS during the night 2nd-3rd. No.4 Coy. moved from ESTRÉE GAUCHE to a camp N. of MAREUIL arriving there about 9.45 P.M. Railhead was moved from AUBIGNY to St.POL to AUBIGNY. Fresh meat at railhead nil, the whole lack being a hard ration which was taken by the M.T. Coy. & kept by them as a reserve ration R.M.A.	
"	3		Railhead was moved from AUBIGNY to Mt. ST. ELOY. Fresh meat at railhead 63% bread 79%.	

WAR DIARY
or
INTELLIGENCE SUMMARY.
(Erase heading not required.)

Army Form C. 2118.

Place	Date	Hour	Summary of Events and Information	Remarks and references to Appendices
	Sept. 4		By order of DDST. 1st Army the flat rate of gallons of hay at railhead was to be varied as follows: H.D. 11½lbs, L.D. 8½ lbs, Col's 7½ lbs (R.M.O). Supplies were drawn from railhead by Horse Transport with the exception of those for the 148 Inf. Bde Group, which were drawn by lorry. 6 lorries were also allotted to the Horse Transport, 2 being allowed for the 147 Inf. Bde Group which included Divisional H.Q. 2nd and H. allowed to the Divisional Troops Supply Train. H.Q. moved with D.H.Q. 2nd Lt. C.W. HOWIE reported for duty from the 26th Divn. Train and was posted to No.1 Coy. from MINGOVAL to CHATEAU DE LA HAIE. Bulk meat at railhead 598 bread 752 (R.M.A)	
"	5		No 4 Coy moved from their Cant. N. of MAROEUIL to ESTRÉE GAUCHIE. The weather during last and afternoon and the lorries were considerably affected by it. Fresh meat at railhead 626 bread 766 R.M.A.	
"	6		The H.Q. D.S. and Nos 1 & 2 Sections of the 49th D.A.C. moved to camps near ARRAS their rations being delivered by lorry. Arrangements were made for No 4 Coy Horses to have a rest for 3 days. Supplies were drawn from railhead by lorry and from refilling point by pack transport. Deficiencies in the train were as follows: Capt 1, Dr 13, H.D. 7, L.D. 2. A meeting of officers of the train was held at T.H.Q. at which the various alterations and modifications in the supply system in the case of a rapid advance or of a retirement were fully discussed, including	

WAR DIARY or INTELLIGENCE SUMMARY

Army Form C. 2118.

Place	Date	Hour	Summary of Events and Information	Remarks and references to Appendices
	Sept. 7		The scheme for the delivery of Ordnance Supplies at the refilling point and bein transport leave to units by the Supply wagons. Train went at railhead 626 bread 782 R.M.A. Ordnance received from XXII Corps for one officer with his batman and one clerk to report for duty to the Central Purchase Board FRUGES. Authority (A.M.C. 6236 (AB.2) dated 3-9-18) HOLDSWORTH from duty with the XXII Corps M.T. Coy. for this duty. Pending a reply no further action was taken. Train went at railhead 626 bread 77 R.M.A. *Capt. W. MOLONY proceeded to leave to U.K. 2nd/Lt C.W. HOWIE was invalided from No Coy. to No 4 Coy as S.O.*	
	8		A reply having been received from XXII Corps 2nd Lt. F.E. CLIFFORD was detailed to report to the XXII Corps M.T. Coy for duty to take over from LT. P.T.J. HOLDSWORTH. Train went at railhead 626 bread 77 R.M.A.	
	9		LT. P.T.J. HOLDSWORTH reported to the Central Purchase Board at FRUGES for duty. LT.M.J. McKENNA returned from hospital and reported for duty with No 4 Coy. Train went at railhead 636 bread 77 R.M.A.	[FRUGES &c collect remounts for the Division] M.M.
	10			
	11		LT. COL. R.G.I.J. BERRY proceeded on leave to U.K. and MAJOR R.T. PEMBERTON D.S.O. took honorary command of the Train. CAPT. J. SIMPSON also proceeded a leave to U.K. and 2nd LT. J.C. BAXTER took temporary command of No 3 Coy. Received orders that the 49 Div was to relieve	

WAR DIARY
or
INTELLIGENCE SUMMARY.
(Erase heading not required.)

Army Form C. 2118.

Place	Date	Hour	Summary of Events and Information	Remarks and references to Appendices
	Sept. 12		the 51st Division in the line. The necessary arrangements were therefore made with a view to the move. All Category "B" men of the train who had been classified as such by the A.D.M.S. H.Q Div. were inspected by the D.D.M.S. Inspection of Drafts at St Catherines N.W. of ARRAS. Train went at railhead 62f, bread 77f, R.M.A.	
	13		No 2 Coy moved from LE PENDU to 51 Dt F.13.a.3.7. No 4 Coy moved from ESTREE CAUCHEE to 51 Dt F.13.a.3.8. New refilling points were selected as follows:- H.Q Div. Troops 51 Dt G.1.d.5.5. 146 Bde Bn at 51 Dt F.13.a.4.3. 147 Inf. Bde at 51 Dt F.13.b.6.6. 148 Inf. Bde at F.13.a.4.1. Train arrived at railhead 62f, bread 78f, R.M.A. Lt Worrall who had been in charge of the body of reinforcements from	
	14		No 1 Coy moved from CAPELLE FERMONT to 51 Dt G.1.b.4.8. No 3 Coy moved from CAMBLAIN L'ABBÉ to 51 Dt F.13 c.4.8. Train arrived at railhead 63f, bread 77f, R.M.A.	
	15		Train went at railhead 62f, bread 77f, R.M.A. T.H.A. moved from CHATEAU DELA HAIE to BRAY. Train went at railhead 61f, bread 77f. 10 reinforcements arrived from Base H.T. Depot. These were all Category B men but will on exception of found to be un likely to be made ordinary train	
	16		The hand ration to the motor in charge of the M.T. Coy was delivered by them at refilling points in the afternoon and the wagons were refilled and stood loaded on the Coy, lines during the night. Train went at railhead 60f, bread 73f. Information was received that CAPT TRAYNOR	

Army Form C. 2118.

WAR DIARY
or
INTELLIGENCE SUMMARY.
(Erase heading not required.)

Instructions regarding War Diaries and Intelligence Summaries are contained in F. S. Regs., Part II. and the Staff Manual respectively. Title pages will be prepared in manuscript.

Place	Date	Hour	Summary of Events and Information	Remarks and references to Appendices
			Another tent to No 33 C.C.S. Orders given from Base to D.K. load was to be evacuated to the Base. Capt. BROADHURST A.V.C. was transferred from No 3 Coy to No 1 Coy R.M.A.	
Se/t	17			
"	18		Two days bread ration was issued to units. Fresh meat at railhead 608 bread 75 by M.A.	
"	19		Fresh meat at railhead 608 bread 748 R.M.A. A warning order was received from Division that the 29th Div. was to be relieved in the line by the 51st Div. on the night of the 22-23rd inst. The necessary previous arrangements were made to branches & affected having the sending of traffic refugees to units. Fresh meat at railhead 608 bread 748 R.M.A.	
"	20		Fresh meat at railhead 618 bread 748 R.M.A. Deficiencies in the Train as follows: 3521 Gnr SMITH 2nd Bn H.D. 1 R.M.A.	
"	21		Fresh meat at railhead 662 bread 762. New areas having been allotted by Division, the necessary arrangements were made for the accommodation of the Companies in the new area. The necessary orders were issued. See O.O. No 43 attached. R.A.	
"	22		Fresh meat at railhead 662 bread 652. Orders were received that the accommodation at Y cook E.TRUN.dict the commencement of the train were to move in the 23rd inst. would not be available until the 24 inst. Nos 2 & 3 Coys were therefore ordered to move to BRAY and on the 23rd and No 4 Coy to remain in their present cantonment till the 24 Sept inst. R.M.A. for the night.	

WAR DIARY
or
INTELLIGENCE SUMMARY.

Army Form C. 2118.

Place	Date	Hour	Summary of Events and Information	Remarks and references to Appendices
Sept.	23		Fresh meat at railhead 68 lb. bread 76 lb. Nos. 2 & 3 Coys moved to BRAY Camp. R.M.A.	
"	24		Nos. 1, 2, 3 T.H. Coys all moved to Y Camp. 57C/L 2.C.O.b. Fresh meat at railhead 66 lb bread 77 lb.	
"	25		Fresh meat at railhead 66 lb bread 76 lb. Orders were received at 10 P.M. that the supply arrangements of units were to be held ready to proceed to unit at a moments notice. Arrangements were therefore made for supplies to be drawn from railhead by lorry with the exception of those for 148 Inf Bde. & R.H. Brigade & ismobilated in Y camp. Representatives visited Corps of Highest & the supply wagons were then available for railhead R.M.A.	
"	26		Fresh meat at railhead 66 lb bread 76 lb. On returning from leave to U.K. Lt Col. R.G.H. BERRY resumed command of the train. R.M.A.	
"	27		Major R.T. PEMBERTON D.S.O. assumed Command of No 1 Coy. Fresh meat at railhead 66 lb bread 75 lb R.M.A. Officers in the train as follows: C.A.M.S. 2, Coll Inomans 1, Pte Clerks 1, L.Cpl 1, Sgts 23, R. 2, H.D.S. R.M.A.	
"	28		Fresh meat at railhead 66 lb bread 66 lb. R.M.A.	
"	29		Ration drawn were 50% Bread, 66% Fresh meat.	
"	30		No 3 Coy moved to E of ARRAS Sht 51b. S.10. G.30.b.15. The accommodation is poor, the men living in tents & damaged dugouts. Area is freely shelled at times.	

WAR DIARY
or
INTELLIGENCE SUMMARY.

(Erase heading not required.)

Army Form C. 2118.

Place	Date	Hour	Summary of Events and Information	Remarks and references to Appendices
1915				
	Sept 8	30 (cont)	Cayman difficult the reinforcements are available. 9 hrs 66% Burned 76%. E 2/L T mallinson proceeded in charge of the Bn's Remount Party to FRUGES, one Charger in to his care for the Bn. (ends)	

A.H. Knight Col.
B/mdt 119th R Div. ??

AMENDMENT TO 49th (W.R.) Divisional Train O.O. No.42.

Commencing 13th instant, Bde Companies will draw from Railhead by Horse Transport.

   Addressed all concerned.

               Capt & Adjt.,
12th. Sept, 1918.   49th (W.R.) Divisional Train.

ANNEX A.   49th Div. Train A.E.15/2/1

                    49th DIVISIONAL TRAIN O.O. No.42.
                    -o-o-o-o-o-o-o-o-o-o-o-o-o-o-o-

(1)   The 49th Division will relieve the 51st Division in the line
       between the 13th and 14th insts, move to be completed by 10 a.m.
       14th inst.

(2)   Companies of the 49th Divisional Train will relieve Companies
       of the 51st Divisional Train as follows:-

       No.1 Coy. 49th Div. Train will relieve No.1 Coy. 51st Div. Train on
       the 13th inst at MAYENLLY CAMP Sheet 51b O.1.b.1.4.

       No.2 Coy. 49th Div. Train will relieve No.4 Coy. 51st Div. Train
       on the 13th inst at BROUVRES.

       No.3 Coy. 49th Div. Train will relieve No.3 Coy. 51st Div. Train
       on the 13th inst at BROUVRES.

       No.4 Coy. 49th Div. Train will relieve No.2 51st Div. Train on
       the 13th inst at BROUVRES.

       Each Company will send an Officer or Warrant Officer to take
       over the Camps from the 51st Divisional Train on the above
       mentioned dates.   In all cases the Camps will be free by 12 noon.

(3)   Supply arrangements are as follows:-   RAILHEAD - St. MARS.-
       Times of drawing - as at present:-

       12th inst. -   Supplies for 49th Div.Troops, 146th & 148th Infantry
                      Brigades will be drawn from Railhead by M.T. 147th
                      Infantry Brigade by M.T.   Supply wagons deliver
                      rations for 49th Div.Troops,146th & 148th Infantry
                      Brigades to units.   First line transport draw from
                      Refilling Point for 147th Brigade.

       13th inst. -   M.T. will draw from Railhead for 49th Divl. Troops,
                      147th & 148th Infantry Brigades, 146th Infantry Brigade
                      will draw by M.T.

       14th inst. -   M.T. will draw from Railhead for Divl. Troops and
                      147th Infantry Brigade, 146th & 148th Infantry Bdes.
                      will draw by M.T.

       15th inst
       & onwards -   M.T. draw from Railhead for 49th Divl. Troops. Inf.
                      Bdes. by M.T.

       From the 13th inst. onwards Train will deliver supplies from
       Refilling Point to B.H.Stores.   The two lorries at present detailed
       to draw supplies from Railhead for Divl. H.T. Group will continue to
       carry out this duty.
       Refilling Point for 49th Divl. Troops on the 13th inst. will be
       situated at 51b/O.1.d.3.5.   Refilling Points for Brigade Coys. will
       be situate between Railhead and BROUVRES - exact location will be given
       later.

       The above supply arrangements will necessitate Baggage Lorries
       being returned to Coys. as soon as possible.   Os.C. Coys. will make
       necessary arrangements with their Staff Captains.

(4)   Coke and firewood may be drawn from 51st Divisional Fuel Dump at
       BROUVRES O.7.b.1.3. until such time as the 49th Division take over this
       Dump.

- 2 -

(5) Solidified Alcohol will be issued as follows :-

    3½ tins per day to 146th Inf. Brigade.
    1½ tins per day to either 147th or 148th Inf. Brigades, whichever Brigade is in the Line.
    ½ tins per day to the 49th Bn. M.G.C.

(6) Certificates for stores handed and taken over will be forwarded to this office not later than three days after relief, together with certificate as to cleanliness of billets.

(7) Train Headquarters will close at CHATEAU de la HAIE at 10 a.m. on the 14th inst. and open at BRAY at the same hour.

(8) ADDRESSEES (Train Coys. and Supply Officers).

September 11th, 1918.   49th (West Riding) Divisional Train.   Capt. & Adjt.,

    Copy No.1 to H.Q. 49th Division.
    " No. 2 to No. 1 Company.
    " No.3 to No. 2 Company.
    " No.4 to No. 3 Company.
    " No.5 to No. 4 Company.
    " No.6 to O.C. 49th Divl. Troops.
    " No.7 to H.Q. 146th Inf. Brigade.
    " No.8 to H.Q. 147th Inf. Brigade.
    " No.9 to H.Q. 148th Inf. Brigade.
    " No.10 to 49th Divl. M.G. Coy.
    " No.11 to A.D.C.
    " No.12 to O.C. Train.
    " No.13 to War Diary.
    " No.14
    " No.15   File.

SECRET   49th Div Train A.T.16/2.

49th DIVISIONAL TRAIN O.O. No. 43

(1) The 49th Division will be relieved in the line by the 51st (H) Division on the 22nd, 23rd, and 24th insts, relief to be completed by 10.a.m. 24th inst.

(2) Companies of the Train will move to "Y" Camp, MERIS area.= 51D. A.2.c.0.6. on the 23rd inst.

Huts are allotted as follows:-

"A" BLOCK   No.2.Coy. - 4.mens huts and 1.Officers' hut
             No.3.Coy. - 2.   "

"B" BLOCK   No.4.Coy. - 4.mens huts
             No.3.Coy. - 2.   "   and 1.Officers' hut

"C" BLOCK   No.1.Coy. - 6.mens huts and 1.Officers' hut.
             No.4.Coy. - 1.Officers' hut.
No.1.Coy's Officers' hut is detached, but close to, "C" block.

Tents in possession of Companies will be taken.

A. N.C. or S.C.O. from each Coy will report to the Adjutant at "Y" Camp by 9.a.m. on the 23rd inst when horse lines and wagon parks will be allotted.

(3) Locations of Refilling Points are as follows:-

    Divnl Troops   - 51.Q.. A.1.d.6.3.
    146th Inf Bde   -   "   " A.2.B.2.2.
    147th   "   -   "   " A.2.d.8.7.
    148th   "   -   "   " A.1.B.2.3.

Companies will refill in the New Area on the 23rd instant.

the SUNK DUMP will remain in its present location.

Supplies for 147th and 148th Infantry Bdes for consumption 24th inst will be delivered on the 23rd inst. Supplies for consumption 25th inst for 146th Inf Bde will be delivered on the 24th inst.
It will seem that on the 22nd inst Nos 3 & 4 Coys draw from Railhead but do NOT deliver. On the 23rd inst No.2.Coy draw from Railhead but do NOT deliver.
M.T. will draw from Railhead as follows:-

    23rd inst - for 147 and 148 Inf Bdes and Div Troops
    24th "   - " 146,147 and 148 Inf Bdes and Div Troops
    25th "   - " 146 Inf Bde and Div Troops
    26th " and onwards Supplies will be drawn by Horse Transport
for Bde Coys. Lorries will continue to draw for Divnl Troops.
Rations will continue to be delivered to Q.M. Stores from Refilling Point by Train wagons.

(4) Baggage wagons will report to Units as follows:-

    147th Inf Bde - on the morning of the 22nd inst
    148th "   " -   ditto
    146th "   " - on the morning of the 23rd inst

(5) Train Headquarters will remain at MEAL.

(6) AMBULANCES (Train Coys and H.Qs only)

                                              Cecil H Rogg
21.9.18.   Capt. & Adjt.
                                              49th Divnl Train.

DISTRIBUTION OF:

Copy No. 1.	to	A.A., 49th Division.
" " 2.	to	No.1.Company.
" " 3.	to	No.2.Company.
" " 4.	to	No.3.Company.
" " 5.	to	No.4.Company
" " 6.	to	G.O., 49th Divl; Troops.
" " 7.	to	G.O., 146th Infantry Brigade.
" " 8.	to	G.O., 147th Infantry Brigade.
" " 9.	to	G.O., 148th Infantry Brigade.
" " 10.	to	49th Divl; M.T.Company.
" " 11.	to	D.A.Q.
" " 12.	to	O.O., Train.
" " 13.		War Diary
" " 14.	to	File.

15 }
16 }

War Diary
of
49th. (WR) Divisional Train

October, 1918

Vol 43

(6392) Wt. W6192/P875 1,500,000 4/18 McA & W Ltd (E 2815) Forms W3091/4.   Army Form W.3091.

Cover for Documents.

Nature of Enclosures.

Notes, or Letters written.

WAR DIARY or INTELLIGENCE SUMMARY

Army Form C. 2118.

Place	Date	Hour	Summary of Events and Information	Remarks and references to Appendices
1915 October	1.		The Transport of the 146 Inf. Bde were inspected, the horses were in good condition with the exception of two remounts of the 1/4 KOYLI which were poor. The harness was in very fair condition with the exception of a few breechings & girths which lacked dubbin. The saddlers were employed in a standard pack the exact make is laid down in G.R.O. 1,992 being copied from militia. Modifications were made from the D.A.D.S.&T. 1st Army that Cart [?] ammunition out of [?] the pack & Bn. T. [?] would no longer be required to draw from the Great Corps Supply Officers. (OHL)	
	2.		The Div.S. Remount Party returned from FRUGES. One in charge for the Gun wheelers was sent, & was inspected & Rigueur was inspected. Return normal. (OHL) Routine normal. (OHL)	
	3.			
	4.		A practice attack was made by the 146 Inf Bde. The packmules were employed. The fitting for the stokes mortar gun was inspected; found made of string when the gun is placed in buckets on top of the pack saddle. The slings were too great. The buckle holding the pack in [?] of wire was roughly arranged, the Bgde or Offrs guide the pack animal. The plate is secured to [?]. The harness deficient of the following 2 HT S/cle 2 Cpl Harness 1 Pl Harness 1 Cple 2 4 Dro 3 Riders SHD	

Army Form C. 2118.

WAR DIARY
or
INTELLIGENCE SUMMARY.
(Erase heading not required.)

Instructions regarding War Diaries and Intelligence Summaries are contained in F. S. Regs., Part II and the Staff Manual respectively. Title pages will be prepared in manuscript.

Place	Date	Hour	Summary of Events and Information	Remarks and references to Appendices
1918				
Oct	4 C.O.D.		T/4/246313 Sgt Scadden C. & T4/249592 Sgt Creey G [—] appointed a/Cy C.Q.M.So as from 23.9.18	Comm
	5		Lt Davinger & 10 O.R. proceeded to FRUGES for remounts. These are 2 Chargers for the C.O. to HQ. 1 for 2 Coy, 1 NCO for No 1 Coy.	
			A meeting of officers was held at H.Q. Train at Q.73. Spinal complaints on the principle of dressing to horses & the precautionary measures laid down in QRO S119 was discussed. It was decided to clip the horses of the Train all over with the exception of the principles of the legs. Companies were compared with the importance of this being a necessary in billets & dug outs recently by the enemy. The question of Cops working with 4 officers per No 1 Coy & only 3 officers per B&c Coy instead of 5 officers for [—] Coy & 4 officers for B&c Coy was fully discussed, & it was found that although reduction took place companies would be able to manage. It would be necessary to ensure that the W.O. Class I be fully trained in supply duties. // 1 L Cpl, 2 O.R. reported from 56 Div. Train for duty. 19 reinforcements arrived from the B.M.T. Depot of which 7 [—] have no experience of horses, on reaching T/376657 Dr [—] H.P. had his discharge certified [—] was needed to [—] did a month in H.A.S.E. but we all [—] the line (OML)	
	6		The [—] present [—] of [—] a new [—] being unsatisfactory, a new dropt, for which the [—] were carried on the new side & [—] also the last log, & the input plate arrived on the offside was actually submitted to Div "found satisfactory. (CH.I) [—] to the XXII Confrmin"	

A9945 Wt. W1142/M1160 350,000 12/16 D.D. & L. Forms/C./2118/14

WAR DIARY
INTELLIGENCE SUMMARY
(Erase heading not required.)

Army Form C. 2118.

Place	Date	Hour	Summary of Events and Information	Remarks and references to Appendices
Oct.	7		No 3 Coy moved to from "Y" Camp to 51b.V.21.L-cent No 2 Coy moved from "Y" Camp to 51b.U.12.d.5.4. Trench mortar railhead 7/10/28. head 12/10/28. R.M.A.	
"	8		No 1 Coy moved from "Y" Camp to 51b.O.25.b.8.6. No 4 Coy from "Y" Camp to 51b.P.35.c.0.3. Pack at railhead 8 O.25. head 13.O.25. R.M.A.	
"	9		T.H.Q. moved from BRAY to 51b.O.25.b.8.4. No 2 Coy moved from 51b.U.12.d.5.4 to 51b.W.27.d.4.9. No 3 Coy moved from 51b.V.21.L.C.t.to 51b.W.22.C.4.4. No 4 Coy moved from 51b.P.35.C.0.3 to 51b. W.21.d.4.6. These moves were all carried out owing to orders being received that the 40th Div were to relieve the 2nd Canadian Division in the line. Fuel pack at railhead 8 O.25. head 13 O.25. R.M.A. Railhead moved to ARRAS 51.M.A.	
"	10		T.H.Q. moved from 51b.O.25.b.8.4 to SAINS-LEZ-MARQUION. No 1 Coy received orders to move from 51b.O.25.b.8.6 to BARALLE later arriving there were ordered on to St. OLLE. No 2 Coy moved from 51b.W.27.d.4.6 57/A.S.20 C.5.9. No 3 Coy moved from 51b.W.22.C.4.4 to 51b.X.18.C.2.2. No 4 Coy moved from 51b.W.21.d.4.6 to 51b.A.6.C. Cent R.M.A. The Div. moved to the line on night of 10th - 11th. Railhead was cleared to CROISILLES. Solidified alcohol received 10the Bn. they which were in the line R.M.A.	
"	11			
"	12		T.H.Q. moved from SAINS-LEZ-MARQUION to TILLOY FARM 51a.S.21.C.4.7. The supply wagons of the Bns. 147 I.F. Bde. the delivering rations were taken on by the Bns to their near billets as they were moving forward. Day's would to whom battn. Coy. lorries that night stayed at Railhead at a place arranged	

WAR DIARY
or
INTELLIGENCE SUMMARY

Army Form C. 2118.

Place	Date	Hour	Summary of Events and Information	Remarks and references to Appendices
Oct.	13		by 2nd Lt. CLEGG who is in charge of Dn. returned to stn. Corp. Reve. stores. of all the No 1 Coy. moved from STOLLE to ESCADOEUVRES. R.M.A.	
			No 2 Coy. moved from 57A.S.20.c.5.9 & 57A.T.27.a.2.0 No 3 Coy. from 51B.X.18.C.2.2 & 57A.T.26.c.2.2. No 4 Coy. moved to 57A.T.B.1.6.8.8. 6 Brigade lorries were ordered to take up trolley material to the line. They came under a heavy enemy barrage and 4 of the men drivers were ordered to abandon their lorries. This they did losing it was killed & one slightly wounded. The lorries were afterwards recovered at nightfall but no damage. T/370650 Dr UNSWORTH Pnr was wounded by shellfire at T.H.Q. at TILLOY FARM. and was evacuated by the Field Amb. to C.C.S. Railhead moved to CANTIMPRE. R.M.A.	
	14		Capt. W.S. TRAYNOR returned to the train from leave & was posted to No 3 Coy. Sub attached to No 2 Coy. for duty as Supply Officer. R.M.A.	
	15		Received notification that Lt. Col. R.G.J. BERRY was T.D. posted to the Supply Directorate and that Lt. Col. D. HAMILTON was posted to the train to relieve him. R.M.A.	
	16		Considerable difficulty was experienced during this period owing to the returning of refugees, prisoners of war and stragglers and wounded men at the 7d. ambulances and in order to ensure that these calls for rations should be always	

WAR DIARY
or
INTELLIGENCE SUMMARY.

Army Form C. 2118.

(Erase heading not required.)

Place	Date	Hour	Summary of Events and Information	Remarks and references to Appendices
			from pdr. so that it was arranged that each Supply officer should hold a reserve of about 100 rations on his refilling pt. This arrangement proved very satisfactory as owing to the railhead being so recently established the usual reserves of rations there were not available P.M.O.	
Oct.	17		Routine as usual. R.M.O.	
"	18		Lt.Col. D. HAMILTON departed from the Base H.T. Depôt and assumed command of the Train. The Division came out of the line but as transport billets were not for back none of the Train Coys had to move. R.M.O.	Authority:- RMG. GHQ. No A.S.C. 203 SS. 11.10.18.
"	19		Deficiencies in the Train as follows: Dr's 5, Fore. GL 1, Sergts 2, Supply GL 1, Supply Details, H.D. 8, R. 3. R.M.O.	
"	20		Lt.Col. R. G. J. BERRY proceeded to refer to the Supply Directorate in accordance with the above quoted authority. R.M.O.	
"	21		Owing to the demand for lorries the supplies for the 148 Inf Bde were drawn from Railhead H.T. of No 2 Coy. the units drawing from refilling points with their lorries as usual. R.M.O.	
"	22		No 3 Coy. moved from 57A T3 b.c.2.2 to 57A N.16.d.5.9. No 4 Coy moved from 57b.B1.6.6.8 to 57b. A.5.a.q.2. No 4 Coy again drew Supplies from Railhead by H.T. R.M.O.	

WAR DIARY
or
INTELLIGENCE SUMMARY.

Army Form C. 2118.

Place	Date	Hour	Summary of Events and Information	Remarks and references to Appendices
Det.	23		T.H.Q. moved from TILLOY FARM to ESCAUDOEUVRES. No 1 Coy moved from ESCAUDOEUVRES to IWUY N.35.a.cent. No 2 Coy moved from 57A T.7.a.2.0 to IWUY T.b.c.0.5. R.M.A.	
"	24		2nd Lt BAXTER proceeded to STUART CAMP near ARRAS in charge of a party to draw reinforcements. R.M.A.	
"	25		2nd Lt BAXTER returned with the party of reinforcements to TILLOY FARM. T.H.Q. moved from ESCAUDOEUVRES to IWUY. 2nd Lt MALLINSON was attached to No. 4 Coy for duty from No 2 Coy. Instructions were received that Lt. PATTISON was to be struck off the strength of the Train he having been evacuated sick to England. he holed the 1st line transport of the 147 Inf Bde he found everything in a very satisfactory condition. R.M.A.	
"	26		2nd Lt BAXTER was posted from No 3 Coy to No 1 Coy. No 4 Coy moved from 57 I. A 5.a.q.2 to LIEU ST AMAND. Warning orders were received that the Division was to be prepared to move at 6 hours notice. R.M.A.	
"	27		No 2 Coy moved from IWUY to DOUCHY. No 3 Coy moved from 57A N.1.b.d.5.q.6 NEUVILLE. Deficiencies in the Train as follows:- Opt H.T. 2, Iron G.S.1, Supply details 2, Bys 5, R4, H.D.6, with 2 Officers surplus owing to the alterations in establishment. R.M.A.	
"	28		No 1 Coy moved from IWUY to HASPRES. No 3 Coy moved from NEUVILLE to 57A. O.b.a.s.2 R.M.A.	

Army Form C. 2118.

WAR DIARY
or
INTELLIGENCE SUMMARY.
(Erase heading not required.)

Instructions regarding War Diaries and Intelligence Summaries are contained in F. S. Regs., Part II. and the Staff Manual respectively. Title pages will be prepared in manuscript.

Place	Date	Hour	Summary of Events and Information	Remarks and references to Appendices
Oct.	29		THANCOURT from IVUY to AVESNES-LE-SEC R.M.O.	
"	30		No. 4 Coy. moved from LIEU St AMAND to DOUCHY R.M.O	
"	31		Coy. bits leaving derailed. Hi jack train did not arrive at railhead until 06.00 hrs on Nov. 1st R.M.O.	
			Under 127/France/2726 (S.D.2) dated 16.9.18 & G.R.O. 3795. The establishment of a subaltern Brigade Coy was reduced from 2 to 1 per Coy — The duties of the second subaltern to be carried out by the Coy W.O. Class I. The establishment of officers on a Div. Train was thus reduced from 22 to 19.	

J. Hamilton
Lt-Col.
Comndg. 49th (W.R.) Divn. Train A.S.C.

SECRET   49th Divl:Train.S.T.18/2.

49th DIVISIONAL TRAIN O.O.44.

1. XXII Corps is relieving Canadian Corps in the Line.

2. 49th Division will relieve the 2nd Canadian Division on the Front BLECOURT (inclusive) to S.27.d between 6th and 11th October in accordance with accompanying table.

3. Infantry Reliefs to be completed by 1000 on 11th October, at which hour Command of the Sector held by 2nd Canadian Division (less such portion taken over by 2nd Canadian Division from 11th Division) will pass to G.O.C., 49th Division.

4. Groups for the purposes of moves to Canadian Corps E Area will be as follows :-

DIVISIONAL HEADQUARTERS GROUP.	146th Infantry Brigade Group.
49th Bn.M.G.C. and "C" Coy.	146th Inf: Brigade.
19th Bn.Loyal Fusrs.(Pnrs)	"D" Coy, M.G.Bn. $
	456th Field Co.R.E.
147th Infantry Brigade Group.	**148th Infantry Brigade Group.**
147th Inf: Brigade	148th Inf: Brigade.
"B" Coy,M.G.Bn.	"A" Coy,M.G.Bn.
457th Field Co.R.E.	458th Field Co.R.E.

$ Marches from MRMM to ARRAS to join 146th Inf: Brigade Group on 7th October under arrangements to be made between D.M.G.O. and G.O.C. 146th Inf: Brigade.
      Divl H.Qrs. Group will march with 148th Infantry Brigade.

5. Field Ambulances will move as follows :-

     1/1st Field Ambce. - will remain at MINGOVAL.
     1/2nd " " - will move to E Area on the 10th inst.
     1/3rd " " - will move to ARRAS on the 10th inst taking over from the 1/2nd Fld Ambce.
     Supply Arrangements for Field Ambces will be notified later.

6. The Signal Coy. will move on the 6th/7th inst to "E" Area.

7. When moving to "E" Area Brigade Coys will be billeted east of HENDECOURT under arrangements to be made by Os.C.Companies. They will remain there two days (including day of arrival). On the 3rd day they will move to billets in the vicinity of those at present occupied by the 2nd Canadian Divisional Train.
     Throughout the move Os.C.Companies will arrange their own Refilling Points notifying their location to this Office.

8. The following restrictions with regard to the moves will be adhered to:-

     (a) Brigades will move at night. Brigade Coys will move in the early morning the day following.
     (b) Transport will arrange to avoid main roads as far as possible, when a main road is used transport will keep to the tracks following alongside the main road where such tracks exist.
     (c) Transport will proceed via GOMMECOURT - CHERISY - HENDECOURT thence as convenient by roads NORTH of XXXXX QUEANT

9. Baggage wagons will be sent out on the morning prior to move of units.

-2-

(10) Special attention is called to First Army Circular No.G.S. 1367/9 d/- 9.9.18. "PRECAUTIONARY MEANS TO BE TAKEN ON OCCUPYING BILLETS VACATED BY THE ENEMY", to 49th Division Administrative Instructions No.Q./1775/12 d/- 23.9.18. "IN THE CASE OF ENEMY WITHDRAWAL", and G.R.O. 5119 "PREVENTION OF CONTAGIOUS DISEASES TO HORSES".

(11) Certificates for stores handed over and taken over will be forwarded to this office not later than three days after relief, together with certificate as to cleanliness of billets.

(12) Advanced H.Q. XXII Corps opens in V.27.c (N.E. of QUEANT) at 10.00. 10th October. Rear Echelon remains at ECOIVRES until accomodation is provided in V.27.c.
52nd Squadron R.A.F. is remaining with XXII Corps.

(13) 49th Division H.Q. will open at 57C/E.4.a.6.1. at 10.00 11th October.

(14) Moves of Train Headquarters and No.1 Company will be notified later.

(15) ACKNOWLEDGE. (Train Coys and S.Os. only)

Cecil H Berry
Capt & Adjt.
49th (W.R.) Divisional Train

OCTOBER 6th. 1918

```
Copy No. 1 to H.Q. 49th Division
  "    "   2  " No.1 Company
  "    "   3  " No.2    "
  "    "   4  " No.3    "
  "    "   5  " No.4    "
  "    "   6  " S.O. 49th Div. Troops
  "    "   7  " S.O. 146th Inf. Brigade
  "    "   8  " S.O. 147th Inf. Brigade
  "    "   9  " S.O. 148th Inf. Brigade
  "    "  10  " 49th Div. M.T. Coy.
  "    "  11  " S.O.        do.
  "    "  12  " S.S.O.
  "    "  13  " O.C. Train
  "    "  14 )
  "    "  15 )  " WAR DIARY
```

March Table to accompany 49th Divisional Train O.O. No.44.

Date October	Serial Number	UNIT	FROM	TO	Bus or Road	REMARKS
6th/7th	1.	147th Bde. Group.	BLANGY-FAMPOUX Area.	Canadian Corps "E" Area.	Bus.	Canadian Corps "E" Area runs as follows 5lb/W1.d.0.0.--W1.d.0.0.--P26.b.0.0.--U17.a.5.4.--U18.c.0.0.--V15.d.0.0.--V23.c.0.0.--W26.d.1.9.
7th	1.A.	No.3.Coy.49th Div:Trn.	--do--	Hendecourt-les-Cagnicourt. Area.	Road.	
7th/8th	3.	146th Brigade.	ARRAS	"E" Area, Canadian Corps.	Bus.	
8th	3.A.	No.2.Coy.49th Div:Trn.	ERUN	Hendecourt-les-Cagnicourt. Area. Reserve Area	Road.	
8th/9th	2.	147th Bde.	"E" Area Canadian Corps.	2nd Canadian Div.	Road.	Relieving 4th Canadian Inf: Bde.
8th/9th	6	148th Bde. Group.	ERUN AREA	"E" Area Canadian Corps.	Bus.	
9th	2.A.	No.3.Coy.49th Div:Trn.	Hendecourt-les-Cagnicourt Area.	Reserve Area	Road.	Billetting in Area of 2nd Canadian Divisional Train.
9th	6.A.	No.4.Coy.49th Div:Trn.	ERUN AREA	Hendecourt-les-Cagnicourt Area.	Road.	Taking over vacated by No.2.Coy. 49th Divl. Train.
9t./10th	4.	147th Brigade.	Reserve Area 2nd Canadian Div.	Line (Left)	Road.	Relieving 6th Canadian Inf: Bde.
9th/10th	5.	146th Brigade.	"E" Area Canadian Corps.	Reserve Area 2nd Canadian Div.	Road.	Replacing 147th Canadian Inf: Bde.
10th	5.A.	No.2.Coy.49th Div.Trn.	Hendecourt-les-Cagnicourt.	Reserve Area.	Road.	Billetting in Area of 2nd Can: Div: Trn.
10th/11th	7	1/2nd Field Ambce. 1/3rd " 146th Brigade.	ARRAS ERUN Reserve Area	New Area. ARRAS		Taking over from 1/2nd Field Ambce.
10th/11th	8	148th Brigade.	2nd Canadian Div.	Line (Right) Reserve Area 2nd Canadian Div.	Road.	Relieving 5th Canadian Inf: Bde.
11th	8.A.	No.4.Coy.49th Div.Trn.	Hendecourt-les-Cagnicourt.	Reserve Area.	Road.	Billetting in Area of 2nd Can:Div:Trn.

CONFIDENTIAL.

WAR DIARY

of

Lieut-Colonel D.Hamilton T.D.
Commanding, 49th (W.R.) Divisional Train.

From November 1st, to November 30th. 1918.

(Volume 44)

WAR DIARY
or
INTELLIGENCE SUMMARY.

(Erase heading not required.)

Army Form C. 2118.

Place	Date	Hour	Summary of Events and Information	Remarks and references to Appendices
November	1		Routine as usual. (OML)	
	2		do (OML)	
	3		do (OML)	
	4		147 Inf Bde moved from DOUCHY area to AUBY area. No 3 Coy of the train moved to CUINEY. This march necessitated a trek of 23 miles, after which supplies were delivered from AUBY refilling point to Quartermasters' dumps, the outfit wagons remained with units overnight. Capt Broadhurst AVC attached rejoined the train from hospital. Notification was received that T/4/252275 Driver W B Smith had been awarded the "Medaille d'Honneur avec glaive en bronze" (OML)	
	5		Train HQ moved from AVESNES LE SAC to LE FOREST. Nos A Coys moved from DOUCHY to CUINEY. The Coy had a 24 mile march. Supplies were refilled in the new area vij Inf Bde Group at EVIN, 147 Bde Group at LE FOREST. Wagons remained with units overnight. No 1 Coy which was left behind in XXII Corps moved from HASPRES to S1A,E,27 Φ 2.2. Capt Hooton proceeded from No1 CC3 to 10 Ξ General Hospital ROUEN (OML)	
	6		Railhead changed from LAFONTAINE to DOUAI. The 63rd Divl Arty Group were added to the 49th Divl Park. No 1 Coy 63rd Divn is situated at COURCELLES. Instructions were received that the train will attack an officer & 3 supply details to VIII Corps MT Coy to assist in delivery.	

WAR DIARY
or
INTELLIGENCE SUMMARY.
(Erase heading not required.)

Army Form C. 2118.

Place	Date	Hour	Summary of Events and Information	Remarks and references to Appendices
1918 Nov.	6 (Cont)		attached troops. Instructions were issued to 2Lt F.S. Clifford at present att⁴ to VIII Corps troops to report to VIII Corps M.T. Coy. Unnecessary personnel was detailed. (CHL)	
	7		The 132 Coys of the Train commenced drawing from railhead by Horse Transport. No 1 Coy 63 Div Train continuing drawing by M.T. Coys continue to deliver to units Q Motive. 132 Coys. of the points were moved to GUINEY. The Mayor & Municipal Council of VALENCIENNES having expressed their desire to thank the British Army for the liberation of their town a grand parade was held, the Div⁴ sent a detachment to the parade, a party of our officers (Capt C Reynolds + 7 OR returned from S1A E27. to No 1 Coy at present in the forward area were visited. The Coy moved from S1A E27.1-22 to SEBOURG. The supplies which ought to have arrived Coy were not issued until after 7.0 p.m. The Supply wing of the Coy are not returning to the Coy E22.6.2.6 before 7.0 p.m. ATR wiring to the fine front Forward every day. Railhead for DT⁰ to BAUCHAIN. 575410 Pte S. Button T. 243 Div⁴ Emp⁰ Coy att⁴ to No 1 Coy	
	8		of the Train died on the night 7/8 whilst on guard. (CHL) No 1 Coy used from 45/T/16 + 3 + 6 ROMBIES.	
	9		The purchase to date of the 148 F/BR were unfa⁴, concerning the advance the Adv. motor condition the line get more very satisfactory with the arrival of the horses good (CHL)	
	10		The Supply Train during early yesterday arrived at DOUAI railhead at 6.0 a.m. The Transport	

WAR DIARY
or
INTELLIGENCE SUMMARY.
(Erase heading not required.)

Army Form C. 2118.

Place	Date	Hour	Summary of Events and Information	Remarks and references to Appendices
1918 Thur	10 (Cont'd)		of the 1/2(WR) & 1/3(WR) Field Ambs was inspected & found to be in a satisfactory condition. Several minor deficiencies were found to be required (QM2). No1 Coy moved from ROMBIES to ELOUGES.	
"	11		The first line transport of the 146 Inf Bde was inspected. The horses were good, & the harness was well geared. (QM2.)	
"	12		Routine as usual. (QM2.) No1 Coy moved from ELOUGES to FRAMIERES	
"	13		No1 Coy was visited in the forward area. This Coy moved to from FRAMIERES to ELOUGES. The Coy have been very hard worked owing to the retreat of the Germans, & the irregularity of supply trains.	
"	14		Routine as usual (RMA)	
"	15		Deficiencies in the Train as follows: Brs 3, W.O.s I, 1; A.D. 10. Saddler Officers 2. RMA	
"	16		Routine as usual RMA	
"	17		Routine as usual RMA	
"	18		The 1st line transport of all units on the strength of the 3 Inf Bde of not attached to HQ from refilling point. This procedure has been ordered by HQ 3 inf to be followed in order to give the Train drivers a long relaxation. RMA	
"	19		The tilletts etc of the 3 Brigade Coys of the Train at CUINCY were inspected by the A.A & M.G RMA. In accordance with instructions received the Ford motor cars belonging to	

A6943   Wt. W11422/M1160 350,000 12/16 D. D. & L. Forms/C,2118/14

WAR DIARY
or
INTELLIGENCE SUMMARY.
(Erase heading not required.)

Army Form C. 2118.

Place	Date	Hour	Summary of Events and Information	Remarks and references to Appendices
~~Aub~~	20		The Train was sent to Army at AUBERCHICOURT for transfer to 2 Divisional Train Army	
			troops, as the Germans advanced to the RHINE. No orders could therefore be sent to	
			No 1 Coy, R.A.S.C.	
Nov.	20		Routine as usual. R.M.A.	
"	21		Inspected No 3 Coy, and found everything very satisfactory. R.M.A.	
"	22		Inspected the transport of the (Nov. R.) 2d. Ambulance. There were on parade 3	
			Horse Ambulances, 3 L.G.S. wagons, 2 other carts, 3 J.S. Wagons, 1 Forge cart, 16	
			H.D., 4 L.D., 8 mules, and 8 Riders. The whole parade was very satisfactory. R.M.A.	
"	23		Deficiencies in the Train as follows: D.R. 7. W.D. Class I 1, W.D. ? , H.D. 10, mules	
			staff sgts. 1 and 2 officers short. R.M.A.	
"	24		Routine as usual. R.M.A.	
"	25		Received information that the HQ Div. Arty. were to rejoin the Division and were to be	
			billeted in the RACHES area. Visited No 1 Coy at ELOUGES and called on D.D. of S.+T. 1st	
			Army at VALENCIENNES. R.M.A.	
"	26		Inspected a contention of 16 teams and 9 pairs of forewards and harness of the HQ	
			H.S. Bn. at AUBY. R.M.A.	

WAR DIARY
or
INTELLIGENCE SUMMARY.

(Erase heading not required.)

Army Form C. 2118.

Place	Date	Hour	Summary of Events and Information	Remarks and references to Appendices
Nov.	27		Inspected the Billets, cookhouses &c of Nos 3 and 4 Coys, and found every thing satisfactory. R.M.A.	
"	28		No.1 Coy. moved from ELOUGES to ONNAING area. R.M.A.	
"	29		No.1 Coy. moved from ONNAING area to ABSCON. The HQ Div. Arty. & the 311 A.F.A. Bde. were added to the lock of the HQ Div for consumption &c. R.M.A.	
"	30		No.1 Coy. moved from ABSCON to WAZIERS. Sent in a W.17.d.9.11 ration Indent. Deficiencies in the Train &were delivered to them by H.T. from railhead. as follows S.S.q S.Sgths, Cpls.H.T.1, W.O.Class.1, H.D.10. There are 2 officers and 1 HCA. surplus. R.M.A.	

F Hamilton
Commdg. 49th (W.R.) Div. Train A.S.C.

SECRET   49th (W.R.) Divl. Train S.T.19/2

49th (W.R.) DIVISIONAL TRAIN O.O.45.
---000---

1. The 49th (W.R.) Division will move into the VIII Corps Area into Army Reserve on the 4th and 5th instants, being relieved in the line by the 63rd Division.

2. The Grouping for the Move will be as follows :-

   Moving on 4th November - 147th Infantry Brigade Group.   *REFILL IN NEW AREA. 4TH INST.*

   147th Infantry Brigade   57th Field Co.R.E.
   1/2nd W.R.Field Amboe.   No.3.Coy 49th Divl: Train.

   Moving on the 5th November - 146th Infantry Brigade Group   *Refill in new area 5th Inst.*

   146th Infantry Brigade   49th Bn.M.G.C.
   456th Field Co.R.E.   19th Bn. Lancs Fusrs.
   1/1st W.R.Field Amboe.   No.2.Coy, 49th Divl: Train.

                148th Infantry Brigade Group.   *Refill in new area 5th Inst.*

   148th Infantry Brigade   458th Field Co.R.E.
   1/3rd W.R.Field Amboe.   No.4.Coy, 49th Divl: Train.
   Divisional Hd.Qrs.

3. Headquarters in the New Area are as follows :-

   VIII Corps - ORCHIES (10 Miles N.E. of DOUAI.)
   49th (W.R.) Division - BLANCHE MAISON (4 Miles N.by E. of DOUAI)
   146th Infantry Brigade - EVIN
   147th Infantry Brigade - AUBY
   148th Infantry Brigade - LE FOREST.

4. After Refill on the 4th instant.

   1/2nd W.R. Field Amboe wagon will join its Unit and march with it, rejoining No.3.Coy, in the New Area.

   1/3rd W.R. Field Amboe wagon after delivering will join No.4.Coy.

   The Supply Wagons of the 19th Bn. Lancs Fusrs, will report to O.C., No.2.Coy, in time for Refill 4th instant. The necessary adjustments have been made by 49th Div: M.T.Coy.

   The wagons of Divl: Hd.Qrs. Group will remain with *THEIR UNIT,* drawing from No.4.Coy, commencing 5th instant.

   The necessary adjustments of Supply Officer's A.Fs. W3316 have been made in this Office for Railhead 4th instant.

5. Any Baggage Wagons not sent out to Units will be sent out on the 4th inst.

6. For the present the Divisional Artillery will remain in XXII Corps. Separate Operation Order will be issued for the move of No.1.Coy.

7. Further details will be notified later.

8. ACKNOWLEDGE.

                                              Capt & Adjt.
3.11.1918.   49th (W.R.) Divisional Train.

-2-

Copy No.1.to A.Q.,49th Division.
" No.2.to No.1.Coy.
" No.3.to No.2.Coy.
" No.4.to No.3.Coy.
" No.5.to No.4.Coy.
" No.6.to C.O., Div Troops.
" No.7.to C.O.,146th Infantry Brigade.
" No.8.to C.O.,147th Infantry Brigade.
" No.9.to C.O.,148th Infantry Brigade.
" No.10.to 49th Div M.G.Coy.
" No.11.to C.O., 49th Div M.T.Coy.
" No.12.to D.A.D.,
" No.13.to O.C., Train.
" No.14.) War Diary.
" No.15.)

<u>49th (W.R.) Divl: Train No. S.R.918.</u>

Headquarters,

    49th (W.R.) Division "A"

    Herewith my War Diary for the month of DECEMBER.
Kindly acknowledge receipt.

                                 D. Hamilton

31.12.1918.   Lieut-Colonel
                          Commanding, 49th (W.R.) Divisional Train

CONFIDENTIAL.

WAR DIARY
of
Lieut-Colonel D.Hamilton T.D.,
Commanding, 49th (W.R.) Divisional Train.

From Dec.1ST 1918.   To Dec. 31ST 1918.

(VOLUME 45)

Army Form C. 2118.

WAR DIARY
or
INTELLIGENCE SUMMARY.
(Erase heading not required.)

49TH DIVISIONAL TRAIN

Instructions regarding War Diaries and Intelligence Summaries are contained in F. S. Regs., Part II. and the Staff Manual respectively. Title pages will be prepared in manuscript.

Place	Date	Hour	Summary of Events and Information	Remarks and references to Appendices
Dec.	1		No pack train arrived to day it having been detained on route	
"	2		The pack train which should have arrived yesterday arrived at 10.30 p.m. To day pack train arrvng. before at 09.00 p.m.	
"	3		By orders of VIII Corps no horses were available for drawing Supplies from railhead. 16 horses only being allowed to ship for drawing from RSD, in other such emergency. By arrangement with Divnl. Supv. S. Troops 12 G.S. wagons with drivers and conductor attached to No 1 Coy. from the 49 D.A.C. to assist in drawing Supplies from railhead. The 1st Training Coy. consisting of 368 men and 23 horses were attached to the 447 Inf. Bde.grpt. for rations.	
			On non-railhead to-day P.M. Routine as usual. (O.H.L)	
"	4		Train H.Q. moved from LE FORREST to 25 Rue de Paris, DOUAI (O.H.L)	
"	5			
"	6		A meeting of representatives of Corps was held at Train HQ to discuss its quiet prevention. It was found possible to run a train from but only leaving to play Association matches as reported owing to the fact that the train were both drawing & delivering the necessary run to play & not to forward. It was decided to run Train Sports Cross Country run & also for the Div. Bay Tournament (OHL)	

WAR DIARY or INTELLIGENCE SUMMARY

Army Form C. 2118.

Place	Date	Hour	Summary of Events and Information	Remarks and references to Appendices
1918 Dec	6 (Cont)		the Train on detached the following: 5 Drivers, 1 Farrier Sgt, 1 Saddler S. Sgt, 1 M.T. Cpl, 1 W.O. Class I.	
			M.D. Supplies 2 Officers 1 L. Cpl. (CMR)	
	7		Routine in course (CMR)	
	8		Instruction was received that the 262 Army Troop Coy R.E. would draw rations from the H.Q. Div. Train Commencing railhead today (CMR)	
	9		23,000 lbs of hay received at railhead were found to be unfit for consumption. A board was called from the 12th unit. (CMR)	
	10		Routine as usual (CMR)	
	11		A State committee was held at Train HQ when arrangements were made for the Xmas Sports which were to take place in Alexandria. (CMR)	
	12		Routine as usual	
	13		A meeting of O.C. Coys was held at Train HQ to discuss the coming Brigade Parade. (CMR)	
	14		A preliminary drill was had together for the Brigade Parade (CMR)	
	15		Routine as usual (CMR)	
	16		The train was on parade at the inspection of the Div. T. by L. Gen. Robley Commd'g 2 xx11 Corps. Under instructions received by VIII Corps 311 Road Construction Coy & detachment of 170 Labour Coy	

WAR DIARY
or
INTELLIGENCE SUMMARY.
(Erase heading not required.)

Army Form C. 2118.

Instructions regarding War Diaries and Intelligence Summaries are contained in F. S. Regs., Part II. and the Staff Manual respectively. Title pages will be prepared in manuscript.

Place	Date	Hour	Summary of Events and Information	Remarks and references to Appendices
1915 Dec	16 Cont		Both Battns at DOUAI await orders to the 49 Divn for return	
	17		The following message received from the G.O.C. Divn "O.C. Train. Many congratulations to all your Corps on their steadiness of fighting movements & admirable performance today." (data 16/12/15)	
			Under instructions rec'd from Corps 5th Canadian A.T. Coy attd to the Divn for rations & supplies as usual (ORC)	
	18			
	19		The supply train did not arrive till the evening, as arrangements were made to draw on the e.g. unit (ARC)	
	20		No 1 & 2 Coys ammn and details to provide to megander up to & including the 24th inst - for R.E. work - 146 & 148 Bde Refilling Points moved from QUINCY to BLANCHE MAISON (CHL)	
	21		The Train although at Railhead was unable to carry up to the fact that the wagons fell into a mess order. 1st Canadian Tramway Coy transferred to Corps on 31 folks Railless (ORC)	
	22		253 Tunnelling Coy R.E. added to Divn Group for findng (CHL)	
	23		Owing to an accident on the railway the pack train did not arrive in time to be. Cleared today (CHL)	

WAR DIARY or INTELLIGENCE SUMMARY

Army Form C. 2118.

Place	Date	Hour	Summary of Events and Information	Remarks and references to Appendices
Dee.	24		The lorry & pack train now cleaned as usual to-day & this latter arriving in Ford time this morning. OMA	
	25		Eight additional lorries obtained to assist in the clearing of the pack train as it was Xmas Day. No refilling took place as ample refills had been made the day before. OMA	
"	26		Routine as usual. OMA	
"	27		Deficiencies in the train as follows: Bn 3° 17, Divn Qr. I, Divn Sr. I, Senior I, W.O. Class I, Qr. H.T. I. There were also I Officer Surplus & large G.S. H.T. Surplus. OMA	
"	28		Routine as usual. OMA	
"	29		The billets & other accommodation of the 3 Bde Coys. at CUNCY were inspected by the G.O.C. HQ Division and everything being found in a very satisfactory condition. OMA	
"	30		Routine as usual. OMA	
"	31		The billets etc. of No I Coy were inspected by the G.O.C. HQ Division and everything found in a satisfactory condition. In fact a large dump of forage at BEAUVRAGES which had been left by the enemy which we found to consist	

Army Form C. 2118.

WAR DIARY
or
INTELLIGENCE SUMMARY.
(Erase heading not required.)

Instructions regarding War Diaries and Intelligence Summaries are contained in F. S. Regs., Part II. and the Staff Manual respectively. Title pages will be prepared in manuscript.

Place	Date	Hour	Summary of Events and Information	Remarks and references to Appendices
			Almost entirely of Wheat and rye straw in bales having very little hay. The hay was in stock & was not therefore suitable for unit's a distant unit (RMA)	

L. Hamilton. Lt-Col.
Commandg. 49th (W.R.) Divl. Train A.S.C.

WD46

CONFIDENTIAL.

WAR DIARY
of

Lieut-Colonel D. HAMILTON T.D.

Commanding, 49th (W.R.) Divisional Train.

VOLUME 46.

JANUARY
~~October~~, 1st/1919 to ~~October~~ January 31st/1919.

Army Form C. 2118.

WAR DIARY
or
INTELLIGENCE SUMMARY.   49th (W.R.) DIVISIONAL TRAIN
(Erase heading not required.)

Place	Date	Hour	Summary of Events and Information	Remarks and references to Appendices
1919 January	1		Routine as usual (CM)	
"	2		Lt R.M. Ogden reports at Coutiches to attend a conference of Educational Officers	
"	3		Capt. Q.M. Mills, L.T.P.B.S. & Infantry T/4/24930 Yeo S. Sgt. W Perkins mentioned in dispatch. Capt Q.M Mills awarded the O.B.E. CM	
"	4		No supply train arrived at railhead Supply train for 3rd arrived at about 19.00. A very Lt. train received from R.S.O.'s reserve, sugar, milk, cheese were short. No meat, potato, bran etc.	
"	5		The following units added to Dock Groups Company: Companies 7th "K" A.A. Battery, 5/5A.T.C. y R.8 H Cat. Group Park & alt.? 31 M.A.C.	
"	6		The Supply Train due on the 4th inst. arrived in the early morning, more duly cleared RMA	
"	7		The L/M/H. Train due on the 5th & 6th inst. both arrived to-day unreclained. With the days ration drawn from R.S.O.'s Store. Therefore the supply situation again is remedied with the exception of hay and about a half ration of oats for one day - ie, of the two train being deficient of these commodities. RMA	
"	8		The supply train due on the 7th inst. arrived this morning with 2 days hay sufficient oats to make up deficiencies. RMA	

WAR DIARY or INTELLIGENCE SUMMARY

Army Form C. 2118.

Place	Date	Hour	Summary of Events and Information	Remarks and references to Appendices
Jan.	9		Routine as usual. RMA	
	10		Officers in the Train as follows:- Lt Col B, Hon Capt 1, 2nd Lts X31, Pte Clerks 1, Capt M Gasser 1, Pte Gunner 1, W.O. Class I 1, Capt A.T. 1, & 1 officer surplus. Deficient H.D.B RMA	
"	11		Owing to a breakdown on the line the Supply train did not arrive till night. Drivers therefore arranged to clean stations tomorrow. Received notification that Lt. HOLDSWORTH attached to the Central Purchase Board had been sent to England before the line struck off the strength of the Train. RMA	
"	12		A large fuel dump at ARLEUX evacuated by the enemy was taken over containing Coal 1500 tons and wood 250 tons. Three Supply Trains arrived this morning 2 of which were cleared, the remaining one going to the R.S.O. to make up the days ration drawn from its store on the 4th inst. RMA	
"	13		Received notification that a horse collecting station was to be formed at WASNON-VILLE for the collection of horses within the Corps for distand consignments were made for the rationing of this count on & after the 15th inst. RMA	
"	14		Owing to the 17 Batt. West Yorks Regt going to LILLE on the 16th inst arrangements were made for them to draw 2 days rations from railhead on the 15th for Consumption 17th & 18 inst. & the latter of which days they are to return from LILLE RMA	

WAR DIARY
INTELLIGENCE SUMMARY

Army Form C. 2118.

Place	Date	Hour	Summary of Events and Information	Remarks and references to Appendices
Jun. 15			Routine as usual (RMA)	
" 16			Routine as usual (RMA)	
" 17			Deficiencies in the Train as follows: Sgts 11, Gun.Cpl.1, Clerk Cpl.1, Gunner Cpl.1, Gunner Pte.1, W.O.Class1, Cpl. H.T.6, HDs. 6 RMA	
" 18			Routine as usual. RMA	
" 19			The pack train did not arrive until about 18.00 hrs. Trains from abroad were therefore postponed until tomorrow. A coal train carrying about 1500 tons of coal arrived about 1600 hrs. Arrangements were made for extra coal pickers. Sent to-morrow. RMA	
" 20			Yesterdays pack train was cleaned +16 days train abandoned in the morning and cleared at the afternoon. in the section of about 150 tons of coal in the 8 Trains which coals got cleared simultaneously with the coal train. RMA	
" 21			The cleaning of the coal train was almost completed. RMA	
" 22			The coal train was cleaned + also the accumulated pool + deficient trains with the ration of stock. In accordance with instructions received from D.A. of S. + T. 1st army reserve ration were drawn for all attached units to be held in reserve in case of hrs. precaution coming into force RMA	
" 23			16 days reserve rations were drawn for Sin. Troops to be held by No.1 Coy of the Train. RMA	

Army Form C. 2118.

WAR DIARY
or
INTELLIGENCE SUMMARY.
(Erase heading not required.)

Place	Date	Hour	Summary of Events and Information	Remarks and references to Appendices
	Jan. 24		One day's reserve rations were drawn by No 3 Coy. for the 147 Inf. Bde. R.M.A.	
	25		No pack train arrived to-day. (RMA) Lt-Col. HAMILTON To proceeded to England on leave and hour F.B. FOSTER took temporary Command of the Train. RMA	
	26		Yesterday's pack train was cleared in the morning & reserve rations for 146 & 147 Inf. Bdes were drawn by Nos 2 & 4 Coys. respectively. In the afternoon another pack train arrived which was cleared by 17.00 hrs. R.M.A.	
	27		Routine as usual. (RMA)	
	28		An allotment for demobilisation of 15 per/ per/week was received from D.D.A.S.T. 2nd Army. This allotment to include all R.A.S.C. personnel with this Division and also those units attached to the Train as well as those of other units in the Armoured Divisional Area. Instructions were received for Lt. WORRALL to be detailed for demobilisation and also instructions that Capt. R.L. REYNOLDS is now on leave to U.K. is to be demobilised forthwith. RMA	
	29		Routine as usual. (CMC)	
	30		No Supply Train received at railhead. (CMC)	
	31		Supply train arriving at hours late. No yes 3-2 gals per died to C. No. 6 Convalescent Horse Cp. truck. Capt. J.R. Simpson assumed command of the Train. (CMC)	

Signed _____ Capt. for _____ Lt-Col.
Commdg. 49th (W.R.) Divl. Train A.S.C.

Vol #1

CONFIDENTIAL.

WAR DIARY
of
Lieut-Colonel D.Hamilton T.D.,
Commanding, 49th (W.R.) Divisional Train.

From Feb.1st 1919.   To Feb.28th 1919.

(VOLUME 47.)

Army Form C. 2118.

WAR DIARY
or
INTELLIGENCE SUMMARY.
(Erase heading not required.)

L9 (W.R.) Divisional TRAIN.

Instructions regarding War Diaries and Intelligence Summaries are contained in F.S. Regs., Part II. and the Staff Manual respectively. Title pages will be prepared in manuscript.

Place	Date	Hour	Summary of Events and Information	Remarks and references to Appendices
Lahore	Feby	1	146 & 148 Bde Res Groups were amalgamated (OML)	
		2	No orderly train arrived at railhead, yesterday; however cars in Battalion were warned that units wouldered one day's consumption. The arrangement was in effect, parts were delivered to Q.M. stores. One days issue returns to country trade of bread meat & bread are to be taken in Rs. Rs. There were drawn for Div. Troops & 3rd A.T.C. (CML)	
		3	Units yesterday on Kings Birthday were warned. A bird was ordered from R.S.O. Leisure joined the Lahore's a consumption. A 9.22 p Capt mill 94 a 95 Rent. R.C. was med with DPB7 of Army, who made to and leave office of double duty — DDBr 7 1st Army no visit, as officers and was afts flows it was arranged the that were to report at 10 ths H.G. & 15 mate. (CML)	
		4	Routine in camp - (CML)	
		5	Capt S Christie OBE, el T/L R.E. Beale proceeded to Walthalia — Capt Mudly was placed in command from 1st Coy 1st Barnards 2 Coy 1st Coyle 3 Coy, L McKenna 4 Coy	
		6	Routine in camp (CML)	
		7	Instruct noted that 1st Cornwalls in part of solution of [illegible] was and with R flanger (OML)	

Army Form C. 2118.

WAR DIARY
or
INTELLIGENCE SUMMARY.
(Erase heading not required.)

Instructions regarding War Diaries and Intelligence Summaries are contained in F.S. Regs., Part II. and the Staff Manual respectively. Title pages will be prepared in manuscript.

Place	Date	Hour	Summary of Events and Information	Remarks and references to Appendices
1919 July	9		2/Lt Gowie proceeded to Egypt and for investigation (OHL)	
	10		Routine as usual (OHL)	
	11		D.S.R.T. was visited. The Burma Mtd Coy reported sick, the being only 10 men left, the rest which were to be despatched on the 10th did not leave until	
			The attempt to demobilisation of the train on 5 HT per week including 10% parlofeen, 2 supply detail including per week (OHL)	
	12		HORSES reported for duty from 3rd Dn Train. Posted to No 2 Coy as Supply Officer OHL	
	13		Routine as usual. 190 tons Eshra hill Cleared handed over to mans Aleccon.	
	14		One Cat and 2 started yesterday returning. D of service in the Train are a follows : 7 Officers 1 WO Class I 23 dinners 3 and two 2 Whalers 7 supply details 3 HD; 1 Off Supplies making a total of 7 Officers, 142 O.R. 3 H.D OML	
	15		Routine as usual (OHL)	
	16		26 HD Company left Basra.	
	17		The despatchment came into force at 10.01. Wooden Coffins in - Several, about 50% had. The time for and shells on midst. 2nd Aug. Got tents to be dismissed 98 3/9th were given to no. of them as were 12 JOR's 10 ... 2nd S.C. the Commanded a 39/5 received on the ... Supplies again. Hospitality 10755 ...	
			43 OLD 46 other 36 2/Lt G.E. Helner to depend from Basra (?nd)	
	18		Routine as usual OHL	
	19		do OHL	

Army Form C. 2118.

WAR DIARY
or
INTELLIGENCE SUMMARY.
(Erase heading not required.)

Instructions regarding War Diaries and Intelligence Summaries are contained in F. S. Regs. Part II. and the Staff Manual respectively. Title pages will be prepared in manuscript.

Place	Date	Hour	Summary of Events and Information	Remarks and references to Appendices
1915 Feby	20		Routine as usual. (RMcL)	
	21		There are deficit of the following of Officers 7 WO Class I 2. D.25. Whlrs 3 Saddlers 3. Suppy	
			Detailed Opr. 2. HD 61. LD 3. 10 days supply from base not arrived (RMcL).	
	22		Feeding Strength 1 Dw r att: 10118 mm 4304B 4416 LD 43 Col. Supply Drawn for 22"/23" classed as Day (RMcL)	
	23		Routine as usual. RMcL	
	24			
	25		A Board was appointed by Sir to select chargers suitable for Infantry Officers in the A. of O. 2 chargers were selected for the riders in the Train Regt	
	26		The Rhl & Y.Ch. Regt returned returned detached for the Rhine Army being transferred to the 32nd Division, taking with them 4 Trainsmasmen's Ration. RMcL	
	27		Routine as usual. RMcL	
	28		Routine as usual. RMcL	

Manchester
H. Ackerford
Lt-Col.
Commdg. 49th (W.R.) Divl. Train A.S.C.

H.Q.
49th Division "A"

Herewith my War Diary for the month of March 1919 please.

1/4/19

D. Hamilton
Lt.-Col.
Commdg. 49th (W.R.) Divl. Train, A.S.C.

Army Form C. 2118.

WAR DIARY
or
INTELLIGENCE SUMMARY.
(Erase heading not required.)

49 DIVISIONAL TRAIN.

Instructions regarding War Diaries and Intelligence Summaries are contained in F. S. Regs. Part II. and the Staff Manual respectively. Title pages will be prepared in manuscript.

Place	Date	Hour	Summary of Events and Information	Remarks and references to Appendices
DOUAI	March 1		Routine as usual. RMG	
"	2		The 1/5 West York Regt. left the Division for the RHINE ARMY, taking with them their supply and baggage wagons complete with horses. Owing to the 146 Inf. Bde. moving into DOUAI on the 3rd inst. a rearrangement of the Refilling Points was made. The 147 & 148 Inf. Bde. Refilling Points were amalgamated at CUINCY and the 146 Inf. Bde's R.P. was changed to No 2 Coys lines in DOUAI. The necessary adjustment of the reserve rations lots on R.P.s was also made. Train Transport commenced delivering Coal to Inf. Battalions & Inf. Bdes H.Q. RMG	
"	3		The 149 & Bn H.Q.C. was transferred from the 147 Inf. Bde. Supply detail/146 Inf. Bde. owing to their moving into DOUAI on that date. The taking of fuel from railhead 6 day. RMG	
"	4		Routine as usual. RMG	
"	5		Allotment of Demobilisation was increased to 15 for week ending 8th inst. Information was received that on the 245 & 246 Bdes R.F.A. leaving the Division Army will take the Train wagons as C.T.S. with them. RMG	
"	6		Instructions were received from Division as to the number of Horse teams & also the number of NCOs. to be sent with the Train wagons accompanying the Artillery. RMG	
"	7		Horses H.D. Classified X were transferred from the Bde Coys to No 1 Coy in order to make up the necessary 56 X H.D. horses to accompany the 2 R.F.A. Bdes RMG	
"	8		Routine as usual. RMG	

WAR DIARY
or
INTELLIGENCE SUMMARY.
(Erase heading not required).

Army Form C. 2118.

Place	Date	Hour	Summary of Events and Information	Remarks and references to Appendices
March	9		Routine as usual. R.H.A.	
"	10		An allotment of 8 O.Rs. was received for demobilisation from First Army. These went to all Supply Personnel. R.H.D.	
"	11		An allotment of 45 O.Rs. (A.T.) for demobilisation was received from First Army. A warning order for the move of the 2 R.F.A. Bdes. was received to the effect that they would probably leave on the 19th inst. R.H.A.	
	12			
	13		Routine as usual. C.H.	
	14			
	15			
	16			
	17		63 O. Rank proceeded for Demobilisation. T.4/250904 Sgt. J.E. Keighley awarded the Médaille Barbatre in Grade 2nd Class – J Rouvenaire. (C.H.)	
	18		Routine as usual (C.H.) — 44 Hours end to enable Reception Camp Staff only I done in the Town on those to travel to their Homes in England. (C.H.)	
	19		Routine as usual (C.H.)	
	20		6 Supply & details proceeded for demobilisation (C.H.)	
	21		130 O.Rs. proceeded for demobilisation. All boys moved to new billets behind Casere de Camp Donai. nos 1 & 4 boys from WAZIERES. No. 2 & 4 boys from Rue de la Madeline, Donai and no 3 & 6 boys from Quincy. J.H.	

Army Form C. 2118.

WAR DIARY
or
INTELLIGENCE SUMMARY.
(Erase heading not required.)

Place	Date	Hour	Summary of Events and Information	Remarks and references to Appendices
Rouen	22	—	Major R.J. Pemberton, D.S.O. proceeded to the Rhine to join Instructions received that he should report to O/C and Rail Trns ILL	
	23	—	Routine as usual	
	24	—	Instructions from D.D. of S. 1st Army that one days fresh rations are to be held in reserve for Rhine for Pack train as being arranged afterwards S.I.J	
	25		Routine as usual	
	26		T/Major R.G. Rowbottom reported for duty was posted as O.C. t/w/1 Coy of the Train (CML)	
	27		Capt J.R. Smithson seconded to A.2 CCS Rouen (CML)	
	28		J.O.B. Downes inspected Coys lines and billets. (ILL)	
	29		Routine as usual	
	30		3.O.R left for demobilisation	
	31		Lt. R. in Angles & Lt T. Hallinan left the Train for the Rhine, the former as supernumary R.S.O. & the latter to report to O C A S C 1st Cavalry Div.	

D. Hampton Lt-Col.
Commdg. 49th (W.R.) Divl. Train A.S.C.

H.Q.
49th Div. "A"

Herewith my War Diary for the month of April 1919, please.

[signature]
Capt.
for Lt-Col.
Commdg. 49th (W.R.) Divl. Train, A.S.C.

30/4/19.

Army Form C. 2118.

49 D Train

WAR DIARY
or
INTELLIGENCE SUMMARY.
(Erase heading not required.)

Instructions regarding War Diaries and Intelligence Summaries are contained in F.S. Regs. Part II. and the Staff Manual respectively. Title pages will be prepared in manuscript.

Place	Date	Hour	Summary of Events and Information	Remarks and references to Appendices
Douai	1919 Apl 1/2	—	Routine as usual CMH	
	3	—	All attached units transferred to RSO Douai for supplies etc	
	4	—	Routine as usual	
	5			
	6		Reed H.Q. & batts station for duty from 1st Cav. Divn. Train	
	7		Routine as usual	
	8		Capt W. Molony & Major F.B. Foster, Major Pemberland L/S	
	9		War from Agricl area, Capt G.H. LEGG proceeded to Divn Sub-Area on detailed duty	
	10		Routine as usual	
	11		Party of 132 m.y. & 10 m + 28E 311 AFA Proceed to Rhine	
	12		Men of no mayle	
	13		D.A.D.O.S. sent instruction to check stores and arrange nestry with him wil	
	14		Demobilisation allotments rec'd today 192 form AF divisions	
	15		Routine as usual	
	16		Instructions received re attg/1098 and method of dealing	
	17		Took me 2 tons Equipment going how	
	17½		with boy Equipment	
	18		Routine as usual	
	19		Checking of boy Equipment completed	
	20		Routine as usual	
	21		"	
	22		10 OR left from 1/4 T D of Ws, 13 from 1/4 T 2 + 9 from 1/5 West Yorks	

Army Form C. 2118.

WAR DIARY
or
INTELLIGENCE SUMMARY.
(Erase heading not required.)

Place	Date	Hour	Summary of Events and Information	Remarks and references to Appendices
DOUAI	23.		Routine as usual	
	24.		Recd. 2/Lt. R. Hooken ordered to report to Base Supply Depot Rouen.	
	25.		All available hands employed on moving 3H AFA vehicles to Rouen Station. 2/Lt. Hooken left for Rouen.	
	26. 27. 28		Signed below of AF G/1098 returned from DADOS. Routine as usual (with Supply details proceeded to Base Supply Depot, 4 ORs.) Balance.	
	29		8 ORs (returnable personnel) proceeded to 1st Army (HT) Reception Camp for reposting. 8 ORs (ento tas offn 1st June 1915) proceeded to 20th Army Aux. Horse Dep. for reposting. Remainder accounting for week ending 23rd May, 10 ORs ordered to proceed to Calais station comp. on 1st	
	30th		10 ORs ordered to proceed to Calais station comp. on 1st May	

49 Div Train
Army Form C. 2118.
PA&C
Vol 50

WAR DIARY
or
INTELLIGENCE SUMMARY.
(Erase heading not required.)

Place	Date 1919	Hour	Summary of Events and Information	Remarks and references to Appendices
DOUAI	1st May		10 OR's proceeded to Concentration Camp Lamain for dispersal. R. to Thisma granted authority to proceed after dispersal for demobilisation. ALL	
	2nd "		20 H. Air Ranks proceeded from 1/4th F.O.V. L.I. to P.O.W. Bargun. One day what rations given to officer. ALL	
	3rd "		Supply & Baggage Wagons sent out to 1/5th K.O.Y.L.I. 1/4th West Riding Rgt & 1/4th F.O.V.L.I. to proceed to England. 6th West Riding all bodies of that Battalion Vehicle equipment, Harness etc sent ALL	
	4th "		Move of Battalion Cadres temporarily cancelled. ALL	
	5th "		Routine as usual. ALL	
	6th "		Notified by R.S.O. that Park Train would only arrive alternate days, commencing 8th inst. Arranged to draw from Railhead on alternate days. ALL	
	7th "		Baggage and Supply Wagons, Vehicle Equipment & Harness sent out to Wakefield as notified from Div. Headquarters. Consolidated allotment for week ending 10th instant. Arranged with Div. Hqrs. to issue 5 days rations to units on alternate days, commencing 9th. ALL	15 HT PERSONNEL

Army Form C. 2118.

SHEET
No. II

WAR DIARY
or
INTELLIGENCE SUMMARY.
(Erase heading not required.)

Instructions regarding War Diaries and Intelligence Summaries are contained in F. S. Regs., Part II. and the Staff Manual respectively. Title pages will be prepared in manuscript.

Place	Date	Hour	Summary of Events and Information	Remarks and references to Appendices
DOUAI	May 1919			
	8		15 O.R.s proceeded to Embarkation Camp for demobilisation.	nil
	9		Lt Barnes ordered to proceed to 13th Divl. Train. DOUAI CADRE WIRE.	nil
	10		Most of Lt Barnes equipment by A.D.S.&T. Not ARRIVED. Porter out that only order offers arrange with TRAIN.	nil
	11, 12, 13		ROUTINE AS USUAL.	nil
	14		Allotment (Naval.) for week-ending 17th.	nil
	15		Reporting of Lt Barnes to be carried out (A.D.S.&T. Instructions). Lt. W.P. Barnes proceeded to 13th Divl. TRAIN. 13 H.T. DRIVERS.	nil
	16		Entire Army host in front Barnes informed by War Office 49 Divl MT Coy left for BASE. Pending out transfer for supply & all duties	nil
	17		Rate no orders	nil
	18		Notification from A.D.S.&T. that boat train 250 tons dispatched and asking no to arrange with VIII Corps troops & S.S.O. 13 Divn. to take as much as possible from nil.	nil
	19		Boat train arrived (240 tons) arranged with VIII Corps MT Coy that it would clear the train of other Personnel Transport	Title

Army Form C. 2118.

WAR DIARY
or
INTELLIGENCE SUMMARY.
(Erase heading not required.)

Place	Date	Hour	Summary of Events and Information	Remarks and references to Appendices
Donai	MAY 1919			
	20.		12 H.T Drivers furnished to Demonstration Coys for depot unit now at Cadre Strength.	
	21.		List of Officers attached to Cadre received from A.D.S.& T. Lt. Col. D. HAMILTON, T.D., Capt. W.S. TRAYNOR, Lieut. F.E. CRIPPS.	
	22.		Allotment for Parel. of Suppy. Details received — One Issuer.	
	23.		Had for finally cleared. Great difficulty in getting labour from DONAI SUB-AREA.	
	24.		Cadre R.A.S.C. Personnel attached to FIELD AMBULANCES reduced by One W.O, One Sgt, & two rank & file. Allotments for DEMOB.	
	25. 26. 27.		Suppy & Baggage wagons being sent out to DIV. UNITS. Horses. Offt Suppt personnel being sent out. The remainder	
	28.		DESTINATION of Cadre of all Coys of Train received : GEORGETOWN.	
	29.		Instructions by Divl HQrs to return remaining Motor Lorries to VIII CORPS M.T. Coys for dispatches	
	30.		A.D.S.& T. DIVL AREA advised by TRAIN by PHONE that 75% reduction Cadre does not yet affect R.A.S.C. inasmuch as	
	31.		Kit and date of entrainment of Cadres received	